DATE DUE

GAYLORD			PRINTED IN U.S.A

Mary Gordon

Twayne's United States Authors Series

Frank Day, Editor

Clemson University

TUSAS 671

MARY GORDON

The photograph of Mary Gordon is reprinted by permission of Joyce Ravid. All rights reserved
© *Joyce Ravid.*

Mary Gordon

Alma Bennett

Clemson University

Twayne Publishers
An Imprint of Simon & Schuster Macmillan
New York

Prentice Hall International
London Mexico City New Delhi Singapore Sydney Toronto

Twayne's United States Authors Series No. 671

Mary Gordon
Alma Bennett

Twayne Publishers
An Imprint of Simon & Schuster Macmillan
1633 Broadway
New York, New York 10019

Library of Congress Cataloging-in-Publication Data
Bennett, Alma.
    Mary Gordon / Alma Bennett.
        p. cm. — (Twayne's United States authors series: TUSAS 671)
    Includes bibliographical references and index.
    ISBN 0-8057-4024-4 (cloth)
        1. Gordon, Mary, 1949– —Criticism and interpretation. 2. Women and literature—United States—History—20th century. I. Title. II. Series.
PS3557.0669Z55 1996
813'.54—dc20   96-12774
                                                          CIP

The paper used in this publication meets the minimum requirements of American National Standard for Information Sciences—Permanence of Paper for Printed Library Materials. ANSI Z39.48-1984.∞ ™

10 9 8 7 6 5 4 3 2 1 (hc)

Printed in the United States of America

In memory of Robert W. Corrigan
"lo mio maestro e 'l mio autore"

Contents

Preface   ix
Acknowledgments   xi
Chronology   xiii

Chapter One
"Getting Here From There": About the Author   1

Chapter Two
Offices of the Dead and Living: *Final Payments*   16

Chapter Three
"radical closeness": *The Company of Women*   42

Chapter Four
the art of dangerous limits: *Men and Angels*   68

Chapter Five
a serious person's stories: *Temporary Shelter* and Others   89

Chapter Six
"Respice, Adspice, Prospice": *The Other Side*   108

Chapter Seven
"a great deal I wanted to say": Gordon as Essayist-Critic   128

Chapter Eight
"neither night nor morning":
The Rest of Life: Three Novellas   148

Chapter Nine
"a local habitation and a name": *The Shadow Man*   165

Notes and References   183
Selected Bibliography   197
Index   215

Preface

Gordon is a writer who has never played it safe. From her first novel, *Final Payments* (1978), to her memoir-biography, *The Shadow Man* (1996), and in dozens of publications in between, she has been purposefully experimental, even provocative, in her choices of subjects, language, genres, structures, and narrative personae. Still, in comparison with her flashier or more radical writer contemporaries, hers is an experimentation that can be missed if we read only one or two of her works. But to read all of her works, in order, is to discover the challenges she sets for herself in each of her novels, novellas, short stories, and essays; as she once described her work as a writer, "nothing is enough." Thus, a major goal of my book, the first full-length book on Gordon, is to discuss her experiments and maturation chronologically through the first twenty years of her career.

From the start, Gordon could afford to take risks because as critics recognized in her first major work, *Final Payments,* her craft and prose were already virtuosic. Any study of her experimentation thus requires a parallel study of the evolution of that virtuosity, as well as her even more fundamental preoccupation with language itself. With this and my readers in mind, I provide what I hope will be a helpful, if not generous, number of excerpts from her works to demonstrate something of the agile range of her language and tactics.

Gordon's language and craft also make us aware that they can, and often do, serve other purposes. One of these purposes is to address moral, relational, or societal dilemmas by means of, in Gordon's words, "dailiness" as well as "closed (and enclosed) systems" within, for example, intense relationships, nationalities, and such institutions as the Catholic Church. A more overriding purpose, first made explicit in Gordon's third novel, *Men and Angels,* seems to be her desire, as novelist Margaret Drabble has described it, to use "mutually exclusive ways of being and seeing" to reach "for a sense of wholeness, . . . for a way of connecting the different passages of existence."

In this attempt, Gordon's habitual manipulation of autobiographical material within both fiction and nonfiction genres may prove to be one of her most radical innovations, an innovation that suggests the coining of a term such as *trans-genre*. Clearly, an unusual blurring of traditional genre boundaries is operative in Gordon's writing, and I examine several examples of that penchant.

The first chapter of my book begins with another set of confusions: critics' attempts to label Gordon as a writer. After cataloging highly diverse labels, I move to the most persistent tag, "Catholic writer," which has followed Gordon since her first two novels and which she emphatically rejects and replaces simply with "woman writer." I establish a context for our society's confusions about religious art and works with religious subjects, a context much more fully developed at the end of the third chapter on *The Company of Women,* where I discuss Gordon's first two novels within the tradition of religious fiction.

I then approach Gordon's life and career, what she once described as her "getting here from there"—in other words, from a working-class, Irish-Catholic neighborhood in Valley Stream (Long Island) to her becoming not only the Millicent C. McIntosh Professor of Writing at Barnard College in Manhattan but also "one of America's most gifted writers," "one of our most passionate and perceptive novelists," an essayist with "an extraordinary critical intelligence."

The next seven chapters focus, respectively, on Gordon's novels *Final Payments* (1978), *The Company of Women* (1980), and *Men and Angels* (1983); her collection of short stories, *Temporary Shelter* (1987) and other uncollected stories; the novel *The Other Side* (1989); the collection of essays, *Good Boys and Dead Girls and Other Essays* (1991) as well as uncollected essays and articles; and *The Rest of Life: Three Novellas* (1993).

The ninth and final chapter addresses Gordon's 1996 memoir-biography, *The Shadow Man.* With this publication, Gordon has, in fact, given a circular shape to my book: an introduction and conclusion of auto/biography and judgment. Certainly, the memoir-biography seems to represent, as Gordon herself recognizes, some sort of pivotal moment in her career, one in which many of Gordon's fictional and nonfictional interests fuse in unusual ways. Scholars and critics who study Gordon's subsequent works will have the opportunity to judge if and to what degree the memoir-biography marks a change in her preoccupations. Whatever the case, *The Shadow Man* is a remarkable point of closure, one in which Gordon's life and family and her parents' lives and families come together under the scrutiny of her mature critical, aesthetic, moral, and emotional judgment. Still, Gordon's multigenred obsession with language and its profound implications in people's lives forms the core of her first two decades of writing—a center, I wager, that will hold.

Acknowledgments

I first want to thank Frank Day for introducing me to Mary Gordon's works and for lending his expert guidance to my book. A Faculty Development Grant from Clemson University funded my 1994 and 1995 interviews in New York with Gordon, and a later grant from the South Carolina Humanities Council helped to sponsor Gordon's visit to and lecture at Clemson University. Scholars Tim Redman and Zsuzsanna Ozsvath of the University of Texas at Dallas generously shared their respective scholarship on Ezra Pound and anti-Semitism with both Gordon and me. I also am grateful to Ashley Hawkins and Tammy Harvey for excellent assistance and to the Cooper Library staff at Clemson University for help with countless details and interlibrary loans. The encouragement of my parents, Caroline and A. G. Bennett; my university colleagues; and my friends, especially Linda Smith and Jessi Ogburn, energized my project from start to finish. Finally, I want to thank Mary Gordon for her openness and candor and for her generosity in sharing manuscripts, memorabilia, bibliographies, and most important, time and conversations—gestures that enlivened the book in important ways.

Excerpts from the following are reprinted by permission of Random House, Inc. and Sterling Lord Literistic, Inc.: *Final Payments.* Copyright © 1978 by Mary Gordon. *The Company of Women.* Copyright © 1981 by Mary Gordon. *Men and Angels.* Copyright © 1985 by Mary Gordon. *Temporary Shelter.* Copyright © 1987 by Mary Gordon. *The Shadow Man.* Copyright © 1996 by Mary Gordon. "The Common Life" from *W. H. Auden: Collected Poems.* Copyright © 1963 by W. H. Auden.

Excerpts from the following are reprinted by permission of Viking Penguin: *The Other Side.* Copyright © 1989 by Mary Gordon. *Good Boys and Dead Girls and Other Essays.* Copyright © 1991 by Mary Gordon. *The Rest of Life: Three Novellas.* Copyright © 1993 by Mary Gordon.

Excerpts from the following are reprinted by permission of Sterling Lord Literistic, Inc.: Previously unpublished work (unfinished biography, 1959). Copyright © 1996 by Mary Gordon. "Getting Here From There: a Writer's Reflections on a Religious Past." Copyright © 1988 by Mary Gordon. Published in *Spiritual Quests: The Art and Craft of Religious*

Writing. New York: Houghton Mifflin, Co., 1988. "The Angel of Malignity." Copyright © 1995 by Mary Gordon. Published in *New York Times Book Review*, 6 April 1995. "Separation." Copyright © 1990 by Mary Gordon. Published in *Antaeus*, nos. 64–65 (Autumn 1990).

Excerpts from the following are reprinted by permission of Clemson University: "Conversations with Mary Gordon" [interview by Alma Bennett]. Copyright © 1995 Clemson University. Published in *South Carolina Review*, vol. 28, no. 1 (Fall 1995).

Excerpts from the following are reprinted by permission of *Grand Street* magazine: "At the Kirks'." Copyright © 1990 by Mary Gordon. Published in *Grand Street* IX, no. 2 (Winter 1990), edited by Ben Sonnenberg.

Excerpts from Mary Gordon's *Introduction to Zelda Fitzgerald: The Collected Writings*, ed. Matthew J. Bruccoli, Copyright © 1991 by the Trustees under agreement dated 7/3/75 created by Francis Scott Fitzgerald Smith. Used by permission of Scribner, a division of Simon & Schuster.

Chronology

1949   Mary Catherine Gordon born 8 December in Far Rockaway, New York, to David (writer and publisher) and Anna Gagliano (legal secretary) Gordon. Grows up in Valley Stream (Long Island), New York.

1955   Begins school. Attends parochial schools: Holy Name of Mary School (grammar school through eighth grade), Valley Stream, and Mary Louis Academy (high school), Jamaica Estates, N.Y.

1956   Death of father, David Gordon, at Bellevue Hospital, New York City. Anna and Mary move to maternal grandmother's home, also in Valley Stream.

1967   Receives scholarship to Barnard College of Columbia University.

1971   Completes BA degree in English, Barnard. Spends summer in Europe. Enrolls in graduate writing program at Syracuse University.

1973   First publication, "To a Cow" (poem), in *American Review.* Completes MA degree in English and Creative Writing, Syracuse University. Thesis: "Living With the Body," a collection of poetry. Enrolls in PhD program in English at Syracuse University. Begins dissertation on Virginia Woolf.

1974   Marries James Brain, a British-born anthropologist and professor, State University of New York, New Paltz. Begins four years as teacher of English at Dutchess Community College, Poughkeepsie.

1975   First fiction publication, "Now I Am Married" (short story), in *Virginia Quarterly Review.*

1976   "Now I Am Married" receives Balch Award.

1977   Separates from James Brain. Moves to New Paltz, New York.

1978   *Final Payments* (first novel). Novel is named one of the outstanding books of 1978 by the *New York Times Book Review,* is nominated for the National Book Critics Circle Award.

1979   Receives the 1979 Janet Heidinger Kafka Prize for best novel written by an American woman. Divorces James Brain. Marries

Arthur Cash, Professor of English at the State University of New York, New Paltz, and biographer of Laurence Sterne. Begins teaching as Visiting Professor, 1979–80, Department of English, Amherst College, Amherst, Massachusetts.

1980   Birth of first child, Anna Gordon Cash. *The Company of Women* (novel). Novel receives 1981 Janet Heidinger Kafka Prize.

1983   Birth of second child, David Dess Gordon Cash. "The Only Son of the Doctor" included in *Prize Stories 1983: O. Henry Awards*.

1984   Honorary doctorate, Belmont Abbey College, Belmont, North Carolina.

1985   *Men and Angels* (novel). Receives a Literary Lion of the New York Public Library Award.

1987   *Temporary Shelter* (short-stories collection).

1988   Adjunct Professor, teaching fiction, at Barnard College. Honorary doctorate, Assumption College, Worcester, Massachusetts.

1989   *The Other Side* (novel). Honorary doctorate, State University of New York, New Paltz.

1990   Appointed Millicent C. McIntosh Professor of Writing at Barnard College. Also appointed Adjunct Professor, Graduate School of the Arts, Columbia University. Receives Barnard Woman of Achievement Award.

1991   *Good Boys and Dead Girls and Other Essays* (essay collection). "Separation" included in *Best Short Stories of 1991*.

1992   Receives a Lila Wallace-Reader's Digest Writers' Award.

1993   *The Rest of Life: Three Novellas.* Awarded a Guggenheim Fellowship. "Abortion: How Do We Really Choose?" included in *Best Essays by American Women*. "The Important Houses" included in *Best American Short Stories 1993*.

1994   Honorary doctorate, Saint Xavier University, Chicago.

1996   *The Shadow Man* (nonfiction memoir-biography).

Chapter One

"Getting Here From There": About the Author

"I wondered what one did with the past . . . my past is the most interesting thing about me."—from *Final Payments* (1978)

The question posed by the protagonist of Mary Gordon's highly acclaimed first novel has run like a subtext through her work. Almost two decades later, her memoir-biography *The Shadow Man* (1996) offers not only a definitive answer to the question. For Gordon, the completion of this nonfiction project also represents a "pivotal" moment in her career as novelist, essayist, and short-story writer: "my instinct is that it's an important book. I think it brings a lot of preoccupations together. 'Traces them' is the word—'tracks them.'"[1]

To track them from the start of her career is to discover, first of all, Gordon's reaching for, as Margaret Drabble describes it, "a sense of wholeness, for the possibility of inclusion rather than exclusion, for a way of connecting the differing passages of existence."[2] A second discovery is the continuing evolution of Gordon's thematic and genre preoccupations. Her four novels, three novellas, collections of essays and short stories, the memoir-biography, and several dozen uncollected publications variously have addressed: Catholicism, immigrants, other writers and writing, art, film, ethics, feminism, and in particular, women, men, and children within enclosed circles of love, enmity, and loss. Whatever her interest, certain hallmarks of Gordon's writing have remained constant: a mastery of language, a moral seriousness, logical acuity, candor, and intensity. Nevertheless, each shift in her preoccupations has caused critics to revise earlier labeling of her work. Thus, to track Gordon's work across two decades is also to follow a trail of critics' labels.

Attempts to label Gordon remain slippery business. In addition to being cited regularly as one of her generation's finest writers, she has been called a Catholic writer, a feminist writer, "her generation's preeminent novelist of Roman Catholic mores and manners," "a kind of collective contemporary American Mother," a neo-realism novelist, "Tolstoy in

1

Queens," and a master novelist of both the Irish-Catholic immigrant subculture and the family saga genre. Even in 1980 Gordon was recognized as a moral novelist "on the verge of moving into the company of such writers as William Golding, Bernard Malamud, Walker Percy and Samuel Beckett."[3] A decade later and under the rubric of essayist-novelist, she was placed within the ranks of George Eliot, William Thackeray, Nathaniel Hawthorne, Henry James, Mary McCarthy, Salman Rushdie, and V. S. Naipaul.[4]

Gordon herself resists labels, especially that of "Catholic writer," a labeling William Zinsser has described teasingly as "her penalty for writing the hugely popular and hugely Catholic *Final Payments*."[5] Gordon insists that she is not a Catholic writer, but rather a writer who, particularly in her earlier novels, was interested in "how Catholicism provides both high esthetic standards and a closed (and enclosed) social system that are invaluable tools for a novelist" ("Getting Here," 14). Despite such explanations, the Catholic labeling has continued, as has her weariness with it. For example, in a 1993 interview she suggested, "When they start calling John Updike a 'white, male Protestant writer,' they can call me a 'Catholic writer.'"[6] Yet Gordon has always been comfortable with being called a feminist writer, a label she affirmed as early as 1981: "Sure. What is terribly important to me, deeply important—and this is where I feel a sense of vocation—is to write about issues that are central to women's lives, to write about them beautifully and in high style."[7] Fourteen years later, when asked to describe herself as a writer, Gordon commented quietly, "I think it's kind of like what Sartre says about being a Jew: that you're a Jew if somebody calls you one. And so a lot of the time you have a label if people give it to you often enough. . . . in all honesty, I have to call myself a 'woman writer.' I won't call myself 'a Catholic writer.' That's too limiting. I just won't do it because it makes me sound like this Graham Greene, Evelyn Waugh, Flannery O'Connor . . . I feel no affinity. I don't feel that was how I was formed. But I do think I was formed as a writer by my femaleness" (Bennett interview, 33).

But labels aside, how does one account for the superb craft of her work, the erudite, ever-curious voice, and the moral seriousness, all of which were evident from the start of her career? The aim of the following brief exploration of Gordon's life is to trace how a little girl from Valley Stream, Long Island, became—as critics have described her— "one of our most passionate and perceptive novelists," one with "an extraordinary critical intelligence." It is an exploration that she has augmented in the auto/biographical *The Shadow Man* (1996), which is

addressed in my final chapter. Thus, with the fortuitous timing of her
first nonfiction book, Gordon herself has created the shape of my study:
a full circle that begins and ends with Mary Gordon, her parents, and
appraisals, both of and by Gordon.

Early Years in Valley Stream

Mary Catherine Gordon was born on 8 December 1949 in a hospital in
Far Rockaway and grew up in Valley Stream, a working-class, Irish-
Catholic suburb on Long Island, New York. She was the only child of
David and Anna Gagliano Gordon; as Gordon explained in 1985, "I was
born when my mother was 41 and he 50; she, a polio victim, gave birth
in an aura of miracle. So there were no more."[8] Gordon discovered in
1994 that her father was actually 55 when she was born. While this and
many other facts about her father have turned out to be his self-fabrications, no such uncertainty surrounds her mother.

Anna Gordon, a legal secretary with the same firm for fifty-five years
until she retired in 1983, was the family's breadwinner, just as her father
had predicted when she married David, an unemployed writer. Their
marriage, like that of Anna's parents, was cross-cultural; she was one of
nine children born to peasant-stock immigrants: a Sicilian father who
came to America with his family and became a jeweler, and an Irish
mother who arrived alone at Ellis Island in 1897 when she was seventeen. Their crippled daughter Anna, like the rest of her siblings, was
expected to work; she excelled at business school and after graduation in
1928 immediately assumed the mortgage payments for her mother and
father's home and also began putting her brothers through college and
her sisters through nursing school. Anna built her young adulthood
around work and women friends who shared her serious religious life. In
the mid-1940s, she was introduced to David Gordon by a priest who
later officiated at their October 1947 wedding. What had brought the
couple together was their shared religious commitment. That, their
humor, and their daughter gradually became their only intimate bonds.

From young Mary's vantage point, her parents represented disparate
worlds. On the one hand was the pragmatic, peasant-stock parochialism
of her mother and her mother's large family. From her witty, bright,
tough-minded mother, Gordon learned a certain intellectual precision, a
preoccupation with what she has called "dailiness," and the ability to
remember jokes, stories, and conversations. The world and influences of
her father were altogether different.

David Gordon, a Lithuanian Jew, had moved to New York from Ohio during the Depression. In 1937, he became an archconservative convert to Catholicism, a decision prompted in part by his sympathy with Franco in Spain. However, as his daughter pieced together during the summer and fall of 1994, he also brought with him a complex and highly fabricated identity. What David told Anna—and subsequently Mary—was that he was a Lithuanian Jew, born in Lorain, Ohio, in 1899, the only child of a store- or saloon-keeper father and a concert violinist mother, who broke with him completely when he converted to Catholicism. What he did not tell them was that he was born in Vilna, Lithuania, in 1894, that he had three sisters, and that he spoke only Yiddish until the age of six, when he and his family arrived in Baltimore. Nor had his family declared him dead after his conversion; he actually kept in close contact until his death with one sister, whose room was filled with pictures of Mary. Nor did he tell Anna that he had been married previously to an Ohio woman with a son. Moreover, the highly intelligent David, who spoke and/or read some eight languages, also said that he had gone to the University of Pennsylvania and then to Harvard for a year, but dropped out, after which he spent some time during the twenties in Paris and in England, where the *Hibbert Journal* in Oxford published his essay comparing Anglican priests and American Protestant pastors.

As Mary Gordon discovered during her research in Ohio and New York, her father, in fact, had dropped out of high school in the tenth grade and, at the age of sixteen, started working for the Baltimore and Ohio Railroad. He neither attended college nor ever had a passport; thus, he never went to Europe. The article on priests and pastors evidently was written in New York during the twenties, probably at the same time of his only financially successful publishing venture, a girlie magazine *Hot Dog*. Where and how he learned so many languages and so much literature remain mysteries. As Mary Gordon has mused, "How did he teach himself? He just must have been one of those kids who sat in the library. He must have been extraordinarily gifted, which is another real sadness" (Bennett interview, 8).

There is no question, however, about her father's having been a person of endless publishing schemes that habitually folded after a few issues. In a pattern that would mark New York City as his daughter's "real" home, David Gordon often took young Mary into Manhattan, where they shared his visits to potential backers for his publishing schemes, lunches in the theater district, and films at Radio City Music Hall. Describing those magical trips, Mary Gordon also recalls their living in the top floor of a two-family house in Valley Stream and her "waiting for my father to be recognized as the man he was, the man he and I (but not my mother) knew him to be. My mother thought he was a failure. Unlike her father, her brothers, he could not make a living. She could" ("My Father's," 184). In 1956, David Gordon's death at the age of sixty-two left the forty-eight-year-old Anna to do just that for herself and their seven-year-old daughter. While working on research for a book on Paul Claudel, he had a massive heart attack at the New York Public Library on 42nd Street. Without getting to see Mary again—whom he once told he loved more than God—he died a month later at Bellevue Hospital.

David Gordon's death left Mary with a remarkable but problematic legacy. She had been the adored child of this man who, in the midst of their working-class neighborhood, taught her to read at the age of three, taught her the Latin of the Mass at the age of five and French at the age of six, who said a Hebrew blessing over her head each night, gave her French coloring books, taught her to despise female domesticity, and ripped Beethoven's picture out of the encyclopedia to hang near her toy box. And surpassing descriptions of the fanciful bedtime stories that, for instance, William Faulkner shared with his young daughter, the games and bedtime stories David Gordon and his young daughter devised were prescient models—in their selections of plots, characters, and episodes of ordinary adult life—for Mary Gordon's future career as a fiction writer.

With all this and her father gone, the seven-year-old Gordon retreated into a private world of unmediated grief and "otherness." This was exacerbated by her mother and her mother's family reminding Mary, sometimes kiddingly, but more often pejoratively, that she was "her father's daughter." Early on, she understood that this meant not only that she resembled him physically and verbally, but also that she was a too-bookish outsider and a Jew. Moreover, his death left her to spend her youth and adulthood struggling to untangle their mutual adoration from what she only gradually learned about his self-inventions and from what she discovered in his radically conservative and, even more disturbing, overtly anti-Semitic writings. Typical of these disturbing publications is "Roosevelt the Antichrist," an article filled with pronouncements against the "conspiracy of international bankers" (to which Mary Gordon adds "read Jews"). An equally vitriolic example is his essay that endorses Paul Claudel (the conservative and intensely Catholic French dramatist, poet, and diplomat) and attacks Joyce, Yeats, and Swinburne for "merely beautiful" works that make a religion of art; David Gordon insists that "the Religion of Art is a *religion*. It pretends to supplant Christianity as the solution for the deepest problems of life and for the fear of death. Like its predecessors, . . . the high priests of the Religion of Art have been Jews" ("My Father's," 250–52).

In Gordon's descriptions of and quotations from her father, one is reminded, for example, of Ezra Pound's complex familial life, his anti-Semitic vitriol, endless publishing enterprises, verbal posturing, anger, charm, humor, and kindness, including that love and intellectual mentoring directed toward his own daughter Mary. This and other such examples have never comforted Mary Gordon. Her refusal to excuse or sentimentalize her father's mind-set—which she insists must be considered either mad or evil—attests both to the firm foundation of his unqualified love for her and to her mother's strong, unsentimental, and candid approach to life. That Gordon has shared publicly her horror and puzzlement in essays and in *The Shadow Man* also reflects her recognition of the problematic legacies many others face. Nevertheless, what has survived is an abiding sense of love; as Gordon has described her father, "In the world ruled over by the senses, he is the first, the most real hero. In the province of the heart, he rules. Unstained and shining: the first man loved" ("My Father's," 252).

The Rest of Childhood

The night of David Gordon's heart attack, Mary was taken to her grandmother's home, three blocks from their apartment. Mary was not allowed to return to the apartment or retrieve her belongings, which were disposed of, without explanation, by relatives. One object that was not lost remains her most prized possession: a copy of Robert Louis Stevenson's *A Child's Garden of Verses,* in which her father inscribed, in seven languages, "To my daughter, Mary Catherine, with love from her father. I love you."[9]

At the time of her father's death, she was a second-grader at the Holy Name of Mary School in Valley Stream, New York. From then until the obedient, industrious Gordon graduated from high school, little changed about the environment of her crowded, poorly equipped parochial schools with their undereducated teaching nuns, only one exception of whom was a brilliant but mad, high school literature teacher, prone to sudden rages. However, the scope of Mary Gordon's life had changed drastically. Unlike her early years when she accompanied her father into Manhattan, the rest of Gordon's childhood and adolescence was circumscribed by her widowed grandmother's Old World-style matriarchy and somber home, family, neighborhood, and Irish-Catholic parish. Gordon remembers having known only two Jewish shopkeepers and a couple of Protestant librarians. And only once did her mother take her into Manhattan, where they saw *Gigi* at Radio City Music Hall.

Nevertheless, young Gordon found a way to combine her father's and mother's influences. As an eight-year-old, she began turning out religious treatises on prayer and the Trinity as well as her first poems. Two years later, in a lined Manhattan Special notebook, she began a biography of her father with the sentence, "My father had one of the greatest minds I have ever known."[10] The project trailed off on page twenty-eight, but its careful format and ambition document the seriousness of her early decision to be a writer (actually, a writing nun) when she grew up. Years later, while describing this phase of her childhood, Gordon observed, "I thought I'd write poetry in my habit and lead a very disciplined life. A very cool life" (Schreiber interview, 26). In hindsight, she also has recognized that her father had not been directing her toward this; he, instead, had probably wanted her to be a scholar and his pal ("My Father's," 252). Still, as a child within her community and her mother's large family, she had understood clearly that no professional success could match the honor given to one of their own who became a nun or a priest. Equally clear was her family's ambivalence about her and her mother's living in the grandmother's home, an ambivalence that resulted in young Mary's being expected to nurse her grandmother during the year before her death in 1962. As Gordon recalled in 1995, "When I think about it now . . . and I would think about it when my daughter was twelve . . . the kind of things I was asked to do at twelve was just unbelievable. I was changing colostomies, I was using suction machines when my grandmother was choking. Everyone just thought, 'Well, she's there.' It was awful . . . awful." For this and many other reasons, her grandmother's home holds few fond memories for Gordon; she has laughingly admitted, "I would just torch it if I could" (Bennett interview, 9–10).

Giggling and Doting

At fourteen—just at the beginning of one of the great events in the Roman Church, the Vatican Council II—Gordon (and the changes in her body) changed her mind about being a nun: the outside world seemed much more interesting than sainthood. She quit putting thorns for penance and suffering in her shoes; she quit trying to stop shopkeepers from selling girlie magazines. Citing a Stevie Smith poem that questions an adolescent's giggling and doting and answers: "I'm fourteen . . . I giggle and dote in season," Gordon has commented on the healthiness of her being "properly irreligious" during puberty and her beginning to think of herself as a poet. Moreover, in the midst of "learning about great art," she was repelled by guitars and Peter, Paul, and Mary tune adaptations during Mass as well as the 1960s confusion in the Roman Church ("Getting Here," 51).

By a gradual series of events and decisions, Gordon opted for a life outside and unlike that of her mother's family. She had not forgotten those journeys into the city, and she insists that "I could never have become a writer without the idea of the city. For it gave such courage and it held such promise."[11] That became apparent just after she began high school at the Mary Louis Academy. One Saturday, as Gordon has described it, she and her two best friends made their first trip alone into Manhattan. Not knowing any non-Catholics and not meeting, as they had fantasized, an intellectual Jew who, like Seymour Glass in *Franny and Zooey,* could introduce them to all the right places and gestures of sophistication, they (rather frightened by this time) ended up at the Museum of Modern Art. Their fright ended in a room of Monet's water lilies. Gordon recalls, "And something lifted in the three of us; some dark shutter was pulled up; this was it . . . And we could do anything we wanted with our lives, anything that any of these people in the museums, on the streets, could do. We didn't have to grow up and live near our parents. We would remember Monet's water lilies, and do what we liked" ("Looking," 32).

The Barnard and Syracuse Years

A seventeen-year-old Gordon and those two best friends (to whom Gordon has subsequently dedicated works) entered Barnard College in the fall of 1967. Based on her brightness and economic needs, Gordon received a four-year regent's scholarship. Commenting on her willfulness at that time and her mother's supporting her decision to go to Barnard—despite others' objections that it wasn't a Catholic school— Gordon has surmised, "I think she felt a great mandate from my father to take my intellectual life seriously. She had great respect for intellectual life. . . . And also there was something in her that trusted my intellect" (Bennett interview, 14). Gordon also has laughed about her *Franny and*

Zooey obsession as having led her to Barnard; she thought she would meet the Glasses (who attended Columbia) there.

At Barnard and in Manhattan, Gordon found her milieu. Moreover, she found herself surrounded by professors who took her under wing. Three were special mentors to the young poet: Anne Prescott, Janice Farrar Thaddeus (now at Harvard), and Elizabeth Hardwick. The latter, with whom Gordon studied writing during her senior year, was the first person to insist that she was a fiction writer, not a poet—advice Gordon was reluctant to accept. While reading Virginia Woolf, however, a certain confirmation of Hardwick's judgment had begun to germinate; Gordon remembers, "I was a poet then, and prose seemed to me a rather baggy and encumbered thing, fine in its place, but its place was not the highest. I remember the phrase in *Mrs. Dalloway* that did it to me: 'trophies of nuts and roses.' There was a click like the snap of a broken bone; for something in me broke, broke apart. It was six years before I had the courage to try fiction." [12]

For the first two years—turbulent years in which Gordon also was involved in antiwar demonstrations and student protests at Columbia—she commuted from Valley Stream to Barnard; she admits now that even in the midst of seizing a building at Columbia, she would find herself worrying about catching the train home to Long Island (Robertson interview, C8). During her junior and senior years, she lived in Manhattan. When asked about her love life at the time, Gordon answered, "Well, I seem to marry WASPS, but before that I was almost exclusively in love with Jews. Catholics I've never been in love with" (Bennett interview, 13).

After graduating from Barnard in the spring of 1971, Gordon and a friend spent the summer in Europe. Years later, a short story and two essays would reflect Gordon's having been raped in Wales. That fall she enrolled in the writing program at Syracuse University, chosen because she wanted to study with W. D. Snodgrass and because they offered her a scholarship. She soon realized that Snodgrass was an unfortunate mentor-choice; some of the reasons appear in the opening of her essay "The Parable of the Cave; or, In Praise of Watercolors." Only much later has she recognized that "working-class panic" drove her to Syracuse and that she had lacked the kind of middle-class security that would have allowed her to step offtrack for a time to work in Europe.

Finding Syracuse to be a depressingly sexist enclave of male professors (only one emeritus woman professor was on the faculty then), Gordon and several other women in the program organized a writing group outside the regular workshop. In this group, Gordon (whose poems were becoming more and more narrative) was encouraged to attempt a short story. When Gordon protested, "I can't do that. Stories are too long; I lose control of the language," one of her friends in the group suggested, "Well, you're very good at taking exams, so pretend it's an exam. . . . We'll sit you in a classroom for two hours. You'll pretend you're taking an exam and at the end of two hours you'll give me a story" (Bennett interview, 6–7).

The result was Gordon's first work of fiction, a story based on a verbal exchange with James (Jim) Brain, a British-born anthropologist and professor with whom she had just become involved. Fiction notwithstanding, she completed her creative thesis, a collection of poetry, and received a master's degree in 1973, the same year in which her first publication, a poem, "To a Cow," appeared in *New American Poetry*. By then, she already had enrolled in the PhD program in English at Syracuse, where she soon began research for her dissertation on Virginia Woolf, more precisely, the split between Woolf's vision of and for women in fiction and nonfiction.

More Upstate and Manhattan Years

In 1974, Gordon married Jim Brain, then and now a State University of New York at New Paltz faculty member whose anthropological fieldwork centered on Tanzania. She joined him in Poughkeepsie, where she began teaching English at Dutchess Community College while continuing to work on her dissertation. In that same year and after twenty years of regarding herself as a poet, Gordon also began *Final Payments*. What she already had learned from Woolf was proving to be invaluable, particularly "the rhythms of those [Woolf's] incredible sentences—the repetitions, the caesuras, the potent colons, semicolons" ("Getting Here," 171). Other early models were the dense prose, extended sentences, and imagery of Elizabeth Bowen, and "the possibilities of a moral tone that was contemporary, ironic, and unsentimental" in the novels of Margaret Drabble (Gordon, "Hum," 28). Encouraged by the works of these three English women writers and other novelists encountered in her reading, Gordon began.

While sketching out *Final Payments* in 1974, she also wrote a short story, "Now I Am Married," which appeared the following summer in the *Virginia Quarterly Review*. This story, Gordon's first published piece of fiction, received a Balch Award in 1976, the same year in which another story appeared in *Redbook*. These initial successes coincided, however, with a period of personal trauma during which she and Jim Brain separated in 1977, and she moved to New Paltz. The separation was not only provoked by her having fallen in love with a faculty colleague of Brain's: Arthur Cash, an English professor and biographer of Laurence Sterne. Gordon had become increasingly unhappy in her marriage. What she had perceived as a remarkable fusion of intellectual and political interests and physicality had turned into a relationship she has described as "colonialism." As she admitted in 1995, her 1982 short story "Safe" reflected Brain in the narrator's account of her first husband who "thought of me as if I were colonial Africa: a vast, dark, natural resource, capable, possibly, of civilization. As it turns out, I did not want his civilization—a tendency colonialists have discovered to their sorrow" (Bennett interview, 18).

Ironically, Gordon's unhappiness led to an encounter that would change the course of her writing career. In 1976, while in London, where Brain was doing research and where she divided her days between mornings of writing and afternoons of Woolf research at the British Museum, she saw a BBC program featuring Margaret Drabble. On an impulse, Gordon wrote her, in care of the BBC, a note that described her lonely, unhappy days and her thinking of Drabble. The distinguished novelist— whom Gordon still considers "one of the best human beings that has ever lived"—responded with an invitation to dinner. Subsequently, Drabble introduced the twenty-six-year-old writer to her agent, Peter Matson, who became and continues to be Gordon's agent. Looking back at those encounters, Gordon continues to emphasize, "Talk about luck; that was luck" (Bennett interview, 23).

In the meantime, she was wrestling with *Final Payments:* it took three drafts with two separate endings (all read by Elizabeth Hardwick at Barnard College) to complete the novel that Matson sent first to Viking and then Knopf. Both publishing houses rejected it. At this point, Elizabeth Hardwick suggested that Gordon shift the narration from third to first person. That change completed, *Final Payments* was published by Random House in 1978. The critical and popular success of the novel led to a contract with Ballantine for a paperback edition that appeared later that year. By the end of 1979, some 1.25 million copies of the paperback edition alone had been sold.

These responses to the novel ended any efforts by Gordon to complete her doctoral dissertation on Woolf. Still, Gordon was completely shocked by her first novel's success. She remembers asking Anne

Freedgood, her editor at Random House, "Do you think there's a chance I'll get reviewed in the *New York Times?*" This, Gordon hoped, might help her get a teaching position at a regular college rather than at the community college where she had been teaching for four years (Bennett interview, 22). Reviews of *Final Payments* appeared in major newspapers, magazines, and journals throughout the country. Then the novel was named one of the outstanding books of 1978 by the *New York Times Book Review,* was nominated for the National Book Critics Circle Award, and received the 1979 Janet Heidinger Kafka Prize for best novel written by an American woman. Within two years it had been published in eight languages.

Gordon's enjoyment of the novel's success was preempted by her guilt and unhappiness surrounding the pending divorce from Brain. To her surprise (since hers was the first divorce in her mother's extended family), her mother did not question either the divorce or her relationship with Arthur Cash, whom her mother adored. In 1979, Gordon divorced Brain and married Cash. That year, she began a one-year appointment as a visiting professor at Amherst College and continued to work on her second novel, *The Company of Women,* the working title of which was *Fields of Force.* The publication in 1980 of *The Company of Women* (which earned Gordon a second Kafka Prize) coincided with the birth of Mary Gordon and Arthur Cash's first child, a daughter Anna Gordon Cash, a coincidence mentioned, along with Gordon's unmistakable joy, in several interviews at the time.

Gordon has suggested that the success of *Final Payments* was, in part, accidental: her timely, innovative focus on Catholics and Catholic women and the literary world's needing an occasional bright, new talent who, in 1978, happened to be her. However, she is quick to point out that "what I've done after that: that was no accident" (Bennett interview, 23). Certainly by 1984, with two published novels and a third nearing completion, with an O. Henry award for a story, "The Only Son of the Doctor," with almost four dozen published essays, stories, reviews, and introductions/prefaces, as well as numerous lectures, readings, radio and television appearances, and the first of several honorary doctorates, Gordon's career was in full stride.

By 1984, her and Arthur Cash's family also was complete. Gordon had lost a baby in 1982 during her fifth month of pregnancy. In the following year, however, their second child was born, a son David Dess Gordon Cash (Dess being Cash's mother's maiden name). Having never been around infant boys, Gordon greeted David's birth with initial trepidation and then profound joy, responses that eventually turned up in her essay "Raising Sons."

Gordon has summarized her New Paltz life: "Years passed, marriages, and babies: I found myself living in the country for many years. It was the right thing for a while, a quiet time, when my focus was turned inward, toward my children rather than the world."[13] What she does not include is obvious: a lot of writing. Certainly, the decade between 1984 and 1994 proved to be a highly productive and rewarding period in Gordon's career. Her third novel *Men and Angels* was published in 1985, the same year in which she received a Literary Lion of the New York Public Library Award. Two years later (and now with Viking Penguin), twenty of her short stories were published as the collection *Temporary Shelter*. Since 1985, she also had been working on her fourth novel *The Other Side,* which appeared in 1989. During 1988, she began teaching as an adjunct professor at Barnard College. Two years later, Gordon was appointed Millicent C. McIntosh Professor of Writing at Barnard. That same year she also was appointed Adjunct Professor in the writing division of Columbia University's graduate school. As she describes it, "A miracle happened! I was offered a job at my old college. I moved back to the city. I went home" ("Coming Home," 136). Gordon's 1991 collection *Good Boys and Dead Girls and Other Essays* was followed, two years later, by *The Rest of Life: Three Novellas.* During this same period, she received two more honorary doctorates, as well as a Lila Wallace-Reader's Digest Writers' Award, and a Guggenheim Fellowship. These latter awards allowed her to take a semester away from teaching, during which she completed research for *The Shadow Man.*

In 1995, while talking about these particular years of her career and her family, Gordon observed that the happiest and unhappiest events of her life usually coincide. She then elaborated: just before David's birth and while Gordon was approaching the final stages of her third novel *Men and Angels,* her mother, at Gordon's insistence, retired at the age of seventy-five, sold the family home on Long Island, and moved to a house in New Paltz two blocks from the Cashes'. What promised to be an ideal arrangement turned into disaster: her mother, who had worked in the same law firm for fifty-five years and lived in the same community all her life, grew angry and depressed—a depression that soon became severe. Five days after David's birth, she fell and was incapacitated. Taking care of her during the next seven years became increasingly difficult, and in 1990, when Gordon accepted the professorship at Barnard, she had to move her now senile and invalided mother to a nursing home in Manhattan (Bennett interview, 6–7). Once again, happiness and unhappiness coincided.

While many writers discuss and draw from their experiences, Gordon has done so to such a degree that her life and family have become an integral part of her public discourse as a writer. A conspicuous case in point is an essay Gordon completed in late 1994, an unflinchingly honest description of her mother's aging and senility and of her own complex grief and responsibilities. Accompanied by a full-page cover photograph of her mother and other full-page and smaller photographs, the essay appeared as a feature article in the *New York Times Magazine* in March of 1995. Gordon has explained, "One of the reasons I published it where I did (and in some ways I knew it was an exposing act to my mother and myself) was that I knew a lot of people were going through the same kinds of issues, and I thought it was important to speak truthfully about all the ambivalence—to me, the wild ambivalence—that one feels about this kind of degeneration" (Bennett interview, 34). This kind of private mandate typifies Gordon's public candor and her ability to shrug off responses to her work. But in the midst of both encouraging and hostile reactions to "My Mother Is Speaking From the Desert" in March of 1995, nothing could daunt Gordon's joy when, in that same month, her daughter Anna, a ninth-grader, was featured in a Wendy Wasserstein article in the *New Yorker*.

Life-in-Progress

Gordon's published observations about her husbands, children, father, mother, relatives, and friends reflect her attention to intimate relationships as well as a writer's astuteness about the dynamics within those relationships. Nevertheless, trying to balance her commitment to writing with an equally fierce commitment to her family, friends, and teaching remains a struggle. She talks ruefully about this struggle in terms of a daily splitting: a desire for a pure, uninterrupted life of the mind and spirit versus "a life of ordinary happiness," filled with her family and friends, daily exercise, local volunteer work at a senior center, and board of directors' meetings of such organizations as Catholics for Free Choice.

In the midst of all this, she has no doubts about her and her children's pleasure in living in Manhattan. Although the two households in Manhattan and New Paltz create weekend commuting, Gordon, a self-described "city person," is most content in their upper West Side apartment where she writes—always in longhand with a particular brand of felt-tipped pens and in bound notebooks from England.[14] From the apartment she can quickly reach her office and classes at Barnard, and she also can easily go to the Metropolitan Museum of Art, where, when she hits a writing snag, she goes to look at two particular paintings (Vuillard's *Interior with Woman Sewing* and Bellini's *Davis Madonna*) and to write.

Gordon is a piercingly intelligent, winsome, unpretentious, and witty person. At the same time she is profoundly serious. But, as she articulated in a lecture at the New York Public Library, events and influences during her childhood taught her that "life was serious," that she was "supposed to be a saint," that "everything mattered terribly and that you could never do enough." Then Gordon added, "But this is not such a bad thing for an artist. For the life of the working artist is a perpetual reminder that everything you do matters. Nothing is enough" ("Getting Here," 39, 40).

Perhaps the most striking example of this is her 1996 memoir-biography, *The Shadow Man,* in which Gordon as a daughter, a literary critic, scholar, and artist comes to terms with a man who was a writer, an anti-Semitic Jew and Catholic, and her adored father. Its conclusion, a series of journal entries written in 1995, documents her having her father disinterred (from his unmarked grave in the Gagliano family plot) and reburied in a recently purchased Gordon-Cash plot. This action and the entire project-in-writing about her father symbolize the courage of her public discourse, the ways in which Gordon lives and works, and the ways in which she attempts to connect "the differing passages of existence." After the wrenching task of *The Shadow Man,* she was relieved to return to fiction and her work on two novels (entitled *Her Muse* and *Pearl*) and on three more novellas. Thus the life of this working artist moves forward.

Chapter Two

Offices of the Dead and Living:
Final Payments

The year 1978 was, like every year, a complicated one. Its events included the Camp David Agreement, three Popes in quick succession, the murder of former Italian Premier Aldo Moro by the Red Brigades, the discovery of a hominid's 3.6 million-year-old footprints, the birth of the first "test tube baby," the Jim Jones-Peoples Temple cult's mass suicide in Guyana, the publications of John Irving's *The World According to Garp* and Herman Wouk's *War and Remembrance,* the Bee Gees' *Saturday Night Fever* release, and the New York Yankees' defeat of the Los Angeles Dodgers in the World Series.[1] In the midst of all this and with considerable literary fanfare, Mary Gordon's first novel, *Final Payments,* was published in March.[2]

From the first review onward, it was clear that *Final Payments* had surprised critics. As Nan Robertson underscored in the *New York Times,* "All of a sudden, this first novel called 'Final Payments' has surged up out of the 'me generation' of self-absorbed, navel-contemplating dropout American children, and has knocked the critics for a loop" (Robertson interview, C1). The plot itself was not the surprise. The story begins at the funeral of Joseph Moore, an archconservative Catholic intellectual whom his daughter Isabel has cared for during his last eleven, stroke-ridden years. Determined to "invent an existence" for herself, thirty-year-old Isabel leaves their parochial neighborhood and Queens to pursue her adulthood and a job in Ringkill, New York. After a confused affair with her best friend's husband, she falls in love with Hugh Slade, a veterinarian who is a fine person but who is also a married man. When publicly humiliated by Hugh's wife, Isabel recoils in guilt from her new life, breaking off contact with Hugh and her friends. She tries to emulate her earlier life with her father by taking care of the one person she has always despised, Margaret Casey, the former housekeeper for Isabel's father. After months of physical neglect and psychological numbness, Isabel gives Margaret her inheritance and reclaims her own life.

On its most basic level and like any number of novels, the plot moves through a closed—open—reclosed—reopened sequence that would not in itself attract critical interest. Critics were struck, instead, by Gordon's remarkable mastery of language and her unusual treatments of Catholicism and sacrifice. In hindsight, what remains equally remarkable about the novel's success is the provenance of Gordon's rapid maturation as a writer, which is documented in her earliest publications.

In 1973, a poem had appeared in *American Review;* that year (the same year in which Gordon began her switch to prose), five more poems were included in *New American Poetry.* In 1974, Gordon began work on *Final Payments;* a year later, her first fiction, a short story "Now I Am Married," appeared in the *Virginia Quarterly Review* and earned Gordon a Balch award. From 1976 until July of 1978, Gordon also published seven other stories in popular magazines, such as *Redbook, Mademoiselle, The Ladies Home Journal,* and *Ms.,* as well as in scholarly journals and magazines such as *Granta, Antaeus,* and *Atlantic.* These and other unpublished short stories and poems thus developed alongside *Final Payments,* which marked her major literary debut.

The popular success may have reflected, in part, what Gordon has described as "tasteless" television advertisements for the novel.[3] Undoubtedly, much more of the novel's popularity can be attributed to its critical success. Even before the book had been released, prepublication remarks by novelists Margaret Drabble and Mary McCarthy had set the stage for critical attention. The subsequent reviews were prominently placed and lengthy.

Maureen Howard's April 16 review [4] began on the first page of the *New York Times Book Review.* The novelist Wilfrid Sheed[5] wrote two full pages about the novel in the *New York Review of Books.* These reviews and many others were full of accolades. For example, in his April 4 *New York Times* review, John Leonard describes the novel as "a splendid balancing act of the intellect and the emotions on a high-tension wire" and the novelist as "a first-class writer [who] declares herself with knowing art."[6] Edmund White's review for the *Washington Post* suggests, "It is the most intelligent and convincing first novel I have read in years, one that combines the high moral seriousness of Doris Lessing and the stylistic elegance of Flannery O'Connor."[7] Frances Taliaferro's review in *Harper's* magazine begins: "*Final Payments* is Mary Gordon's first novel, and it is a beauty. It is the least pompous novel imaginable on the largest possible subject" and ends: "This versatile, original novel defies summary and stereotype. Read it."[8] Bruce Allen's review goes further to name Gordon as "one of the most gifted writers of her generation."[9] Within two years, John Auchard's encyclopedia entry about the novel and the critical flurry that surrounded its debut would begin by pointing out: "Mary Gordon appeared on the literary scene, not as a promising apprentice but as an accomplished and mature writer deserving of the extraordinary amount of critical attention her work received."[10]

By this time, the novel and the critical attention itself had spawned an inevitable wave of dissenting critical responses that, in the long run, added the kind of controversy that guarantees a writer's next work will be closely monitored. For instance, Paul Ableman wound up his negative review (in which he described the character Isabel Moore as a "Pharisaic monster") by confirming: "Readers will rightly suspect by now that I didn't much enjoy this book. It seemed to me to be theology posing as fiction, a hybrid form which compounds the tedium of the former with the imprecision of the latter to the advantage of neither." Then, after acknowledging Gordon's strengths as a writer, Ableman advised: "My own hope is that next time her voice will be less that of a casuist than of the novelist."[11] James M. Rawley and Robert F. Moss, in a joint three-novel review, had shared Ableman's criticism when they described *Final Payments* as a "sturdy hybrid: a relatively trashy plot, marked by contrivance and sensationalism, but handled with the tools of high art, specifically a technical sophistication and an allusive, savagely ironic tone."[12]

Even in the positive reviews, certain criticisms of Gordon's work had surfaced. Benjamin DeMott, after praising Gordon's handling of her character Isabel's Catholic milieu, complains, "Unfortunately, the plot of the book takes a series of excessively contrived turns. An ungainly but very likable first novel."[13] Similarly, in the course of his long review, David Lodge points out that *Final Payments,* "so firmly and freshly written at the outset, threatens to turn soft at the core, like a sleepy pear."[14] Both favorable and critical reviews praise Gordon's memorable vignettes of the elderly individuals Isabel visits in her new professional career; likewise, almost every critic mentions Gordon's strong male character, Joseph Moore, and her weak depictions of the novel's secondary male characters and of sexuality itself, a novelistic weakness that Gordon admitted from the start and which, as we will notice, she ameliorates somewhat in her third and fourth novels but conclusively in her novellas. Still, the split judgments continued. In 1981, for example, James Wolcott's review of Gordon's second novel *The Company of Women* begins: "I thought *Final Payments* was foolishly overpraised—Isabel's friends and lovers were lukewarm dumplings, and Gordon had no flair for writing about sex—but the first sixty pages or so had a weight and assurance rare in a first novel. When Gordon wrote about Isabel's love for her father, the prose was hushed, unforced; the sturdy sentences themselves seemed to shoulder grief."[15]

The range of criticism is offered as a sampling of the kinds of issues that critics have addressed in *Final Payments* and in Gordon's later works. The sampling also indicates a common denominator in responses to *Final Payments:* few critics or scholars failed to praise this first-time novelist's mastery of language. In addition to her exceptional language skills and her use of humor, critics invariably addressed her treatment of Catholicism and of sacrifice. All four of these components are explored in this chapter. To facilitate further studies of this and Gordon's subsequent novels, the chapter also examines various approaches to the complex, structural, and metaphoric systems that Gordon layers in *Final Payments.* As Gordon pointed out in 1979, in a burst of frustration at being asked repeatedly "What is your book about?": "any novel is at least as much about its language and its structure, as its plot and characters."[16]

Partially following Gordon's lead, the chapter now moves to a brief review of her language, its syntactical sophistication, and her use of humor as a ludic salvation. The second section examines Gordon's novelistic treatment of Catholicism and is followed by a study of the novel's structural and metaphoric systems. The chapter concludes with a lengthy exploration of Gordon's preoccupation with sacrifice. These four sections, in turn, serve as the initial platform for the chapters that follow.

Shortly after the publication of *Final Payments,* Diana Cooper-Clark asked Gordon about the function of a novel, to which she answered, "If it's accidentally instructive, that's all to the good. But its main function is to be beautiful, and in some sense, true in a very large way I can't even begin to explain. . . . I am very attracted to formal beauty. I like a well-made piece of work. I like balance, so that's very important to me. I'm by nature a Classicist. I am by nature anti-Romantic." Then in her answer to the interviewer's subsequent question about what Gordon liked best about her writing, she was much more specific: "sometimes I think I write really smashing sentences."[17]

The first three sentences that make up the opening paragraph of *Final Payments* give us clues about her syntactical sophistication: "My father's funeral was full of priests.[18] Our house had always been full of priests, talking to my father, asking his advice, spending the night or the week, leaving their black shaving kits on the top of the toilet tank, expecting

linen towels for their hands. A priest's care for his hands is his one allow-
able vanity" (3). The first deceptively quiet sentence, with its alliterative
f's, *l*'s, and *s*'s, suggests both her risk-taking, her ear, and the emotional
import of the novel's subsequent plot. The accreting precisions within
the second sentence's catalog of details and the wavelike repetitions of
short phrases begin a boiling motion below the surface, which then
explodes into the pithy wisdom of the third sentence. The next paragraph backs away into a quiet exposition of theological details. The third
paragraph is sharp, intense in its overt precision, a further shift which
suggests that a helpful way to understand Gordon's control of and sen-
sitivity to the pacing of her paragraphs is to study the first sixteen or so
of the novel. Such a study will lead invariably to more examples of
Gordon's penchant for aphorisms, which might be described as single-
sentence explosions or mini-epiphanies and which the critic John
Leonard has included in his discussion of Gordon's "electric prose" ("Kill-
Joy," 31).

Occasionally, such aphoristic explosions introduce a sequence. For
example, when Isabel Moore is having dinner for the first time in the
home of her new professional colleague, the patrician Lavinia Hartman
suggests that Isabel's years with her father "must have been damned
hard." Gordon delays Isabel's answer with a charged paragraph of interior monologue that begins with one of those "electric" sentences, soon
moves to an analogy, and then ends with the kind of thick word exploration we come to expect from Isabel: "Lavinia said 'damned' like a
Protestant, like an American. I felt put on the spot. . . . I would have to
win Lavinia to my life as you have to introduce someone to eating arti-
chokes, slowly, and with a combination of tact and salesmanship. I
would have to explain about my father to someone to whom the word
'orthodoxy,' for example, might be utterly foreign, for whom the concept
of authority was either public or menacing" (154).

Another of Gordon's syntactical skills appears in exchanges of logic
and debate that step briskly along and then break off suddenly, leaving
their subtle resonances for the reader to think about. One such sequence
occurs in a dialogue between Isabel Moore and her friend Eleanor Lavery
as they swim at a motel in Ringkill. The dialogue follows Isabel's confession of her lifelong hatred of Margaret Casey:

> "That's why I feel I ought to love her. It would be one of those pure acts."
> "Why do you want to *conquer* yourself? And why pure acts? Freud tells us
> there are no pure acts."

"And no jokes."

"What?"

"Freud says there are no jokes."

"And no accidents."

"God, what a life. Who wants all that control?"

"Yes, but we have to *pretend* there are jokes and accidents, or life is unbearable."

"And pure acts of love?"

"Yes," I said, diving under the water (116–17).

Gordon's sentence rhythms reflect her years of training as a poet. For example, in musings that describe her father, Isabel's sentences could easily be divided into poetic lines that rise and fall and push forward to the last word: "My father's life was as clear as that of a child who dies before the age of reason. They should have had for his funeral a Mass of the Angels, by which children are buried in the Church. His mind had the brutality of a child's or an angel's: the finger of the angel points in the direction of hell, sure of the justice of the destination of the souls he transports" (4).

This and several of the other cited passages also demonstrate her seemingly instinctive turning to metaphors and similes to augment her characters' thoughts, points, or characteristics. This metaphoric penchant provoked criticism from James Rawley and Robert Moss, who claim that "The similes range from fair to excellent, but there are far too many of them, almost all are obviously reached for. Consider the following: 'Eleanor and I wept until our faces felt fragile as balloons'" ("Pulp," 686). Conversely, other critics have cited Gordon's metaphors and similes with particular approval; John Leonard, for instance, singles out and announces the following passages as examples of "electric prose": "On beer: '. . . a perfect drink for John Ryan. Its gold was a male color; no woman's hair ever shone like that. And its structure was right for men, too: clouded on top, then clear to the bottom. For women, it would have to be the opposite arrangement.' On sexual technique: 'He handled my breast as if he were making a meatball'" ("Kill-Joy," 31). Gordon has talked about her novelistic uses of these literary devices in relationship to her early work in poetry: "Perhaps more than anything else, poetry has given me a sense of metaphor as being centrally important. Metaphor and simile do some of the work of explanation in a more efficient and profound way than other narrative techniques. I include them when something needs to be made more concrete, more physical" (Gorman interview, 225). Gordon's subsequent novels reflect a gradual reining-in of her metaphoric dependence, but its presence continues in multiple contexts.

A final consideration of Gordon's language in this novel must address her use of comedy. Occasionally, Gordon has made passing comments on (and wry demonstrations of) comic relief. In a 1987 article in *U. S. News & World Report,* for instance, she remarked, "Even though life is quite a sad business, you can have a good time in the middle of it. I like to laugh, and I think all the unsung, real literary geniuses of the world are people who write jokes. Both the Irish and the Jews are very fatalistic, but they laugh a lot. Only the Protestants think that every day in every way, life is getting better and better. What do they know?"[19] A year later, in a lecture at the New York Public Library, Gordon pointed out, "The comedy of Catholic life. It comes, of course, like all other comedy, from the gap between the ideal and the real" ("Getting Here," 38).

Gordon's published comments have not specifically addressed the venerable British tradition of comic fiction, in which comedy and religion are deliberately linked, but her inseparable linking of the two in *Final Payments* suggests the degree to which she has continued this tradition. As Robert M. Polhemus has pointed out in his study *Comic Faith: The Great Tradition from Austen to Joyce,* "novelists are trying, by means of wit, humor, and satire, to fulfill at one time or another all of these missions [which he had listed] of religious faith. For Meredith near the end of the nineteenth century and Joyce in the early twentieth century, belief in the power of comic insight and the inclusiveness of comic form becomes itself an explicit faith. The emergence of such comic faith deserves attention."[20]

Polhemus's comment and, in fact, his entire book are helpful when we consider the ways in which Gordon's characters, Isabel, Eleanor, and Liz, maintain the bonds of their lifelong friendships. They do so through a web of jokes, satire, and profanities drawn from their shared childhoods and introductions to religious faith and rituals and to parochial traditions. As adults they no longer practice their religion; nevertheless, their comedic treatment of faith acts as its resolute replacement, a surrogacy of faith that all three depend on, particularly at junctures of relational and psychological crises. In the case of a tension-filled scene in which Liz Ryan confronts the more vulnerable Eleanor, Isabel sees Eleanor's desperate glance at her as a petition: "I am drowning. Save me" (122). Isabel thinks, with increasing urgency, "I felt the full weight of my responsibility. I had brought these two together: something must be salvaged of the day. . . . The past, I thought. We all share a past. I must fish up something of the past, something brilliant, something glittering, or the day will be ruined." Then Isabel finds a humorous mediation: "Sister Adolphus is supposed to have a radio program on Sundays called 'Sister Says.' Can you believe it? That jerk. She has debates with rabbis about situational ethics." Isabel sees Liz beginning to relax, so she continues: "I saw her on TV. Can you imagine that idiot on TV and here I am moldering in obscurity. She was saying, 'I am a *nun*. My business is *love*.' And she was carrying this terrible pocketbook." One by one, Liz and Eleanor join in the repartee, and finally all three end up laughing. As Isabel observes, "None of it was that funny, but we laughed. . . . I breathed normally for the first time in twenty minutes. . . . It was possible to go on living" (122–23).

That the main characters use such exchanges as crisis mediations points both to Gordon's comedic timing and her penchant for witty salvations that move throughout the novel. This first becomes conspicuous in an early scene in the novel, in which Isabel, a few days after her father's funeral, begins to weep when she opens the refrigerator, only to face stench and liquefied broccoli. At this point, Liz telephones her and asks, "What's wrong, dear? Is it your father?" to which Isabel answers, "No, it's a broccoli, I said, and then I began to laugh. I could hear Liz laugh in relief on the other end" (41). The character Isabel acknowledges this as "a quirk of my own soul . . . I thought jokes were more important than medicine" (131–32). However, when she adds: "Or at least I preferred talking about them" (132), we see that Gordon is drawing attention to the pleasurable aspects (what, on page 78, the character Liz enjoys as a sophisticated game) of such exchanges, as well as the pleasurable, repressive habit of avoiding more serious verbal exchanges. Isabel gradually recognizes this habit as "some hollowness, some wrongness" (216). Nonetheless, this is one more aspect of humor's complex healing power and its ability to substitute for religious faith; the most singular example of this appears in the novel's final scene, in which Eleanor and Liz arrive before dawn to take Isabel away from Margaret's house and from Isabel's self-destructive reenactment of religious sacrifice. As Isabel walks dazedly from the house and toward the car, Liz, with her typically acerbic quick wit, delivers the ludic salvation, the comedic blessing: "Who did your hair? Annette Funicello?" (297).

Gordon's use of comedy is not limited to such mediations. It moves through the entire novel. As Wilfrid Sheed, for instance, has noticed, "The heroine's chaste bitchiness adds a little something to each miserable character until we have comedy: as Austen made comedy of the puddingy gentry of western England. And when the characters flag, Gordon takes over herself, like Austen, and *makes* them funny" ("Defector's," 14). Examples of this abound, but a typical sample is Isabel's private description of Margaret Casey, who served for eleven years as housekeeper for Isabel and her father: "I wondered how she managed to keep the house so tidy and yet look so inevitably germ-ridden herself. . . . Her feet were flat as a fish, except where the bunions developed like small crops of winter onions" (28).

But Wilfrid Sheed adds a crucial observation regarding Gordon's humor, which he begins by citing a number of passages, such as: "Father Mulcahy was clean as a piglet bathed in milk. His black hat was brushed as smooth as the skin of a fruit; his white hair, so thin that the hard, pink skull showed beneath it like a flagstone floor, looked as though the color had been taken out of it purposefully through a series of savage washings" (91). Then Sheed comments: "The cadences are graceful, unfacetious: a tragedy could be written in such prose. It is as if the jokes are being paid for even as they're being made. Even at her most carefree, when she has one of her old ladies cheerily piping, 'blow it out your ass,' Gordon's effect is reverberantly sad" ("Defector's," 15). Sheed, in other words, is confirming Gordon's premise that life is sad, but she deserves the last comedic advice regarding the sadness: "you can have a good time in the middle of it."

All this is to suggest something of the richness, the natural and learned gifts of Gordon's language, something of the bases for Bruce Allen's claim that her "spectacular verbal skill allows her heroine to express complex emotional and intellectual attitudes with great precision" (Allen, 616). And that skill also allows Gordon to create other characters and vignettes within the novel that, once discovered, remain distinctive and usually troubling. As John Leonard's review affirms, "With the exception of the veterinarian [Hugh], Mary Gordon's characters are so strong and rounded that one flinches in their presence; even the old people are allowed to be various. She is as good on the Catholic Church versus women as Marina Warner; as good on class and style and modern attitudinizing as Mary McCarthy; and as good on friendship as Jane Austen. That should be enough" ("Kill-Joy," 31). Gordon would never allow herself to bask in such certainty, and in *Final Payments,* she certainly does not allow any such comfort to Isabel, who recognizes, "What I had was either too much, things that would smother me, or nothing at all, nothing to break my fall. I wondered if it would be possible to walk through some moderate landscape, populated yet expansive, and blessedly to scale" (38). Her language and her inquiry lead directly to the immoderate Catholic landscape that shaped Isabel's life as well as her father's.

Catholicism as a "Framework of Language"

Gordon's literary preoccupations with her and her family's past reflect a universal proclivity noticed by her favorite poet, W. H. Auden: "Man is a history-making creature who can neither repeat his past nor leave it behind."[21]

Even the most cursory perusal of her novels, stories, essays, and the memoir-biography *The Shadow Man* will suggest something of how Gordon has utilized and transformed a past, as interesting as it is complex. Nowhere is that novelistic transformation of the past any more overt than in Gordon's setting up Catholicism as, in her words, a "metaphoric rubric" for her first two novels, *Final Payments* and *The Company of Women.* As she explained in a 1981 interview, "The metaphors of Catholicism, the Catholic way of looking at the world, these are in my bones. It is my framework of language."[22] When asked more recently about her use of the word *rubric,* Gordon explains it in terms of a template: "The structure was there, the form was there, the ritual was there, the shape was there. So it's both the shape and the terms" (Bennett interview, 24). Elsewhere, Gordon has observed that the daily Latin Masses she was carried to as a child were an ideal training ground for her future life as a novelist. Her father, we recall, had her memorize the Latin Mass at the age of five. Therefore, for the young Mary Gordon, the hour-long Mass—with its imagery and repetitions; its Old and New Testament narratives and poetry; its alternating literary types and patterns; "its mix of official and passionate language" and diverse worshipers; and its main event (the Eucharist) "way after the middle"—proved to be lessons in observation, rhetoric, poetry, style, and structure, as well as contemplation and faith ("Getting Here," 31–33). Her acute awareness of the literary advantages within those lessons has become a hallmark of her approach to writing and her insistence that a novel's language and structure are as important as its characters and plot.

Moreover, as Gordon has pointed out, "One of the greatest treasures a novelist can have is a secret world which he or she can open up to his or her reader. When I turned from poetry to fiction in my mid-twenties, I had a natural subject—the secrets of the Catholic world. And since the door had not been very widely opened before I got there, I was a natural" ("Getting Here," 34–35). Thus, at the start of her career, Gordon found in the preconciliar (pre-Vatican Council II) Catholicism and the parish life of her childhood an enclosed secret world that was "the perfect size and conformation" for her fictional and nonfictional literary explorations ("Getting Here," 33).

Part of the excitement generated by Gordon's first novel is due to her daring to take on an enclosed secret world, since, as Mikhail Bakhtin has pointed out, "A sealed-off interest group, caste or class, existing within an internally unitary and unchanging core of its own, cannot serve as socially productive soil for the development of the novel" unless that core is "shifted somehow from its state of internal balance and self-sufficiency."[23] In Bakhtin's qualification we see directly into what Gordon realized as a novelist's enormous advantage: the shifting of Catholicism's tectonic plates after Vatican Council II, with its significant changes in the liturgy and language of the Mass and the sacraments, its ecumenism, its emphases on laity participation and on socioeconomic and political problems. Both *Final Payments* and *The Company of Women* address the gap between preconciliar and postconciliar world views.[24]

Despite this and the other novelistic advantages, Gordon has paid a certain price for choosing Catholicism as subject and setting for her first two novels. Almost two decades after the publication of *Final Payments,* for instance, Gordon is still having to clarify her subject choice and her metaphoric use of Catholicism; this obviously would not be necessary if she had chosen a more generic context. In fact, beginning with her third novel, *Men and Angels,* Gordon has shifted away from a Catholic milieu. Yet in critics' still-persistent attempts to marginalize Gordon as a religious or Catholic novelist, we see a residual unease with novelistic treatments of Catholicism—an unease attributable, in part, to the subliterary and didactic nature of that genre's history—which I address at the end of Chapter Three.

Another factor may be critics' and readers' inability to differentiate between the religious dimensions of this novelistic subject and those of the novelist herself. Even as she acknowledges, for example, an essential tonal connection between her religious and literary lives, Gordon has no such problem. What's more, she resents what she describes as a voyeuristic tendency in critics and interviewers who probe into her highly private and complex religious life with a kind of indelicacy they would never employ if asking about her equally private sex life.[25]

Perhaps a more problematic and more central factor may be our culture's inability to distinguish between a work of art (reflecting a religious subject) and a religious experience itself. Gordon does not confuse the two, and she is quick to articulate those differences: "To my mind, an experience to be properly religious must include three things: an ethical component, the possibility of full participation by the entire human community, and acknowledgment of the existence of a life beyond the human. Art need do none of these things, although it may" ("Getting Here," 49). It is easy enough to apply her "although it may" to a Bernini altarpiece in Venice, Beethoven's *Missa Solemnis,* Rothko's large canvases in the Rothko Chapel in Houston, or even to Annie Dillard's *Pilgrim at Tinker Creek.* It is more difficult to judge how one applies these lines of demarcation to a novel. And that difficulty, along with cultural divisiveness about religion itself, remains problematic for many novelists— Salman Rushdie being an obvious case in point—who choose a religious subject or context. Such problems notwithstanding, the fictional transformations of Gordon's childhood religious milieu demonstrate the fecundity within Catholicism's rituals and its linguistic, aesthetic, structural, and parochial traditions. Those transformations (and Gordon's subsequently more oblique considerations of the spiritual dimensions of contemporary life) also serve as reminders that feigned surprise or knee-jerk marginalizations are inappropriate responses to novelists of the 1980s, 1990s, and twenty-first century, who claim the freedom not only to make spiritual inquiries but to break through, redefine, or manipulate traditional genre demarcations.

Given all these factors, however, it is important to keep in mind that the Church was by no means the only literary catalyst within Gordon's early work as a novelist. The Barnard College mentoring of Anne Prescott, Janice Farrar Thaddeus, and novelist Elizabeth Hardwick was crucial, as was Gordon's subsequent doctoral research on Virginia Woolf. Another factor was the encouragement Gordon received within a small graduate school group of women writers at Syracuse. Then, as her shift from poetry to prose became focused on her idea for a first novel, Woolf, Elizabeth Bowen, and Margaret Drabble's novels became models for Gordon. All these factors combined to give her a second formative stage of influences that coexists with the earlier liturgical and parochial stage.

To grasp the Church's formative role in Gordon's work, it is equally important to keep in mind that the Catholicism which serves as the metaphoric rubric of her first two novels is a pre-Vatican Council II world of language, formality, ritual, and parochial life that, by and large, had disappeared before she began writing *Final Payments.* As Father Mulcahy, one of Gordon's characters in that novel, laments, "Look at the

Church. I can't get used to it. . . . . They [older parishioners] feel like someone's broken into their home and stolen all the furniture. I feel that way myself" (101). Gordon herself, when discussing this phenomenon, cites Gertrude Stein's remark about Oakland ("There is no there there"). Gordon then adds, "So what do I do? I write my fictions. And my relation to the 'there' that is not there I make up each day, and it changes each day as I go along" ("Getting Here," 52–53). What has not changed—even after she shifted away from Catholic subject matter—is her intense interest in aesthetic standards and circumscribed social systems that she first experienced within the Catholicism of her childhood.

Structural and Metaphoric Systems in *Final Payments*

Final Payments shows how that material evolved into an intense exploration of what Gordon has described interchangeably as closed or enclosed social systems, particularly those within preconciliar American Catholicism, an exploration she continues in her second novel, *The Company of Women* (1980). After 1980, when Gordon shifted away from Catholic subject matter, her fascination with enclosed social or relational systems takes on various guises in her subsequent novels, novellas, and stories.

The central task of both *Final Payments* and Isabel, its main character, is an attempt to come to terms with systems that have governed her life: Isabel's intense relationship with her widowed father, an archconservative, Catholic theology professor whom she has nursed for eleven years until his death; Catholicism with its liturgical richness and order, its ambiguities toward the body, sexuality, and women, its focus on sacrifice; and, finally, a parochial circle of strong friendships and enmities.

Isabel's struggles within this fifteen-chapter novel form a quadripartite study of closed—open—reclosed—reopened systems that revolve around her earlier life with her father until his death, her search for a new life, a self-defeating retreat, and a resolution in which Isabel reclaims life. The experiential and psychological motions of these death—life—living death—life sequences bring to mind the word *office*, in the ecclesiastical sense of a ceremony, rite, or service intended for a special purpose, such as an ecclesiastical order's rite for the dead or a local congregation's devotional service. Thus, in addition to its obvious death-life imagery, my assigning the phrase *Offices of the Dead and Living* to this chapter is meant to draw attention to the novel's intimate, ceremonial, and incremental nature. Moreover, the phrase—with its suggestion of enclosure (in an intimate circle or group), closure (as in death or a process), and openness—serves as a framework for both the novel's core components and Gordon's metaphoric use of Catholicism.

Gordon sets into motion any number of venues in which these four structural stages can be explored. Of the sixteen that will be discussed, three have already been introduced:

Closed	Open	Reclosed	Reopened
Death	New life	Living death	Life
Death of Joseph Moore	Isabel's new life	Her retreat from life	Her reaffirmation of life

Other closely linked summaries of the novel's metaphoric structure might be expressed as:

Old existence	Inventing new existence	Retreat to old existence	Reclaiming new existence
Stasis, or stillness	Tentative motion	Stasis	Resolute motion

More conventional structural analyses could include those of:

Innocence	Initiation	False innocence	Complex maturity
Dependency	Fledgling independence	Dependency	Independence
Safety [and loss]	Danger [and loss]	False safety [and loss]	Partial safety that affirms danger and loss

The last seven of these approaches (variations, in effect, of the closed—open—reclosed—reopened framework) introduce the multiple layering Gordon sets into motion within each stage of *Final Payments*. Among the many other metaphoric and structural strata, several warrant some discussion. For example, at one of its most obvious levels, the novel combines a sociological and theological tracking of Isabel's life. Thus, her story moves from a self-contained Catholic parish to a secularized, mainly Protestant, outside world; back to an isolated, self-contained, but truncated Catholicism; and finally back out into the mainstream, with tentative, but important vestiges of a partially reclaimed Catholicism. If this paired tracking is expressed in developmental terms,[26] Isabel's unfolding story might appear as:

Unification of self with child and parent	Attempted unification of self with self and others	Negation of unification	Unification of self with self, others, and divine

Traditional theological terms to track Isabel's spiritual struggles might include:

Public affirmation of faith; secret negation of faith	Negation of faith	False reaffirmation of faith	Tentative reaffirmation of faith

   What is clear from the start of the novel is Isabel's commitment to her father and to the community's approval of his radical devoutness and her sacrificial, caretaker role. Equally clear is her no longer sharing his faith; each Sunday during his long illness, Isabel has deceived him into thinking she is attending Mass, when, in fact, she spends those fifty minutes walking. After her father's funeral, when faced with an overwhelming desire for "something I was sure of . . . something outside myself, and larger," she instinctively starts to pray but then recognizes, "having given up the rigors and duties of belief, I had no right to its comforts" (64). Moreover, to move out into the adult world requires Isabel's giving up the clarity and complex comfort of her role as martyr to the demanding, childlike absolutes and "impossible goodness" shared by Joseph Moore, her father, and Father Mulcahy (65–66) and mandated by the parish.
   In light of Gordon's conspicuous juxtapositions and sociological-theological pairings of the presence or absence of clarity alongside absolutes, perhaps a useful structural approach could first address Isabel's:

Old clarity	Search for	False old	Newfound
and absolutes	new clarity	clarity and	clarity about
via her father's	without	false use of	life and
clarity	absolutes	old absolutes	absolutes

Certainly, clarity is a standard by which Isabel judges herself. Her frequent use of the word and of "unsureness" confirms this preoccupation. Even at her father's funeral, for example, she chides herself for noticing details about the people around her: "I knew I was wrong to do it; I knew the clarity of my mind was unseemly. They lowered the body of my father. I would never see him again" (3). Later, as she starts on a weekend trip to Liz Ryan's home, Isabel is unnerved even by the purchase of a hostess gift: "I felt again that new unsureness, as if I were walking on ice of uncertain thickness, brown water and mud just below the surface, bubbling at the pressure of my step. I thought of my father and his sureness, his body in the bed at the center of the room, and I wanted to cry out, 'I am terribly alone,' in the midst of the summer travelers in Grand Central Station" (67). It is something she begins to hate in herself: "my own uncertainty, my lack of authority, my concern for what people thought and felt about me" (102).

Soon, however, one becomes aware that her need for clarity carries an attached subtext. Despite incremental steps away from her father's sureness, from her "new unsureness," and toward self-actualization and a new clarity, what Isabel cannot shake off is a lingering, stubborn belief in guilt and an inevitable retribution for "advantages" in intelligence, love, sexuality, and money, in pleasure and autonomy. Such advantages contradict her former, self-abnegating, absolute model of sacrifice, of "being a good person" and "not hurting people" (242).[27] Not surprisingly then, after Hugh's wife confronts her, Isabel shatters psychologically and decides to abandon her new life. As she tries to explain to Hugh: "You see, we've been given these gifts—looks, intelligence, charm—and what did we do with them? Used them to snare each other, not to make people happy, people who don't have as much as we do" (237); "I liked those things [sex, beautiful objects, their walks, etc.] disproportionately. I made mistakes. I made people unhappy. I made my father ill; I nearly ruined your marriage with my selfishness" (241). The only option Isabel can envision is to return to her "old, childhood certainty" (240), her former "goodness," which would require the ultimate sacrifice, in Isabel's mind: going to Margaret's home.

By the time one tracks these juxtapositions from the fierce absolutes of Joseph Moore who, as Liz remarks, "signified all over the place" (77), to the end of the novel where Isabel—walking back to Margaret's house on "clever legs" (293)—affirms a complex reintegration of death, life, faith, love, friendships, it becomes apparent that Gordon has created a correspondence between clarity and articulation:

Isabel's clarity and muteness: circumscribed by role with articulate father	Fledgling clarity and partial muteness: circumscribed by sexuality	False clarity and muteness: circumscribed by Margaret	Hard-won partial clarity: and openness to others' and own articulation

The numerous examples surrounding these stages (such as those found on pages 3, 163, 261, and in the novel's last sentence) reveal that Gordon's pairings of clarity and speech move far beyond Isabel to inform the actions and circumstances of other characters and relationships as well as episodic settings. Gordon's attention to light and darkness and to characters' minds, eyes, and bodies transforms these descriptive components; they actually provide much of the formal and emotional momentum in the story that unfolds between, on the first page, Isabel's knowing that "the clarity of my mind was unseemly" (3) and, on the last page, her leaving Margaret's home in the queer light of predawn, savoring, as a miracle, the three friends' laughter, the "cutting edge" of Liz's joke, and Isabel's knowing, "there was a great deal I wanted to say" (297).

There is, of course, a great deal more one can say about the structural and metaphoric ways in which Gordon energizes her first novel. One such exploration entails an anthropological reading of *Final Payments* as ritual and social drama. Such a reading is supported by Isabel's final sentence and by anthropologist Victor Turner's insisting, "it is not enough to possess a meaning of oneself; an experience is never truly completed until it is 'expressed,' that is, until it is communicated in terms intelligible to others, linguistic or otherwise. . . . made available to society and accessible to the sympathetic penetration of other 'minds.'"[28] Moreover, an anthropological analysis is suggested by Gordon's grounding in rituals and social dramas that, despite her culture's technological sophistication, are similar to those (equally rich and complex in terms of religion and art) observed, for example, by Victor and Edith Turner among the Ndembu of northwestern Zambia. In fact, as the next paragraph shows, *Final Payments* contains a double pattern of:

Conflict,	Slide into	Seclusion,	Redress,
breach	crisis	separation	reincorporation
		from community	into community

—the highly charged stages of the Ndembu social drama that, according to Turner, "besets us at all times, all places, and all levels of sociocultural organization" (*FRT,* 11). It is particularly interesting to test detailed components of the novel's structure against a typically elaborate Ndembu ritual for an infertile woman (and thus, for their society, an incomplete woman) who must again take on the role of a novice. Like her earlier experiences as a puberty novice, the woman must move apart from the community and relationships to a seclusion hut; this is the first step she must take to remedy the crisis, to be "regrown into a woman."[29] As the ritual tunnel through which she later will move is dug, medicines are gathered and prepared; symbolic animals and tokens are assembled; and a ringed, sacred space is created.

Almost voluntarily, the reader of *Final Payments* will recall Isabel's two life crises: her father's discovering her in bed with his student (and her father's subsequent stroke) and, some twelve years later, her public humiliation by her third lover's wife. After each breach-crisis, Isabel moves into seclusion: the first, in her father's home, where, in an unnatural, postpuberty-novice status, she remains for eleven years; the second, in Margaret's home, where she retreats in an attempt to redress what she perceives as sexual and relational failings. The differences in Isabel's two periods of seclusion also echo Ndembu rituals, in which, as Turner describes them, "what has been undone by the curse has to be done all over again, although not in precisely the same way, for life crises are irreversible. There is analogy but not replication" (*RP,* 21). Of course, in light of the encircling community, the ritual's sacred circle, and its healing usage of bones and derisive laughter, one also recounts circles of friendship, enmity, and community around Isabel as well as her move to a community named Ringkill, and on the novel's final page, the signal of Isabel's return to adulthood, to a more complete womanhood: the healing laughter that, in Isabel's mind, "stirred the air and hung above us like rings of bone that shivered in the cold, gradual morning" (297).[30]

An examination of other ritualized components reveals multiple resonances within *Final Payments*. For example, witch personae and ritualized uses of intense verbal abuse suggest Margaret and then Hugh's wife; magical, healing words and healers suggest Father Mulcahy, Eleanor, Liz, and Hugh; and, as mentioned before, the woman's required periods of inarticulateness, as well as liminal, transitional processes of isolation within the seclusion hut and the tunnel all suggest Isabel's months at Margaret's house and the eleven years in her father's home. Given Gordon's particular, twentieth-century background in parochial and religious traditions and structures, such echoes of more ancient ritual patterns should come as no surprise. As anthropologist Monica Wilson has pointed out in her field research on religion in Tanzania, "Rituals reveal values at their deepest level . . . men express in ritual what moves them most, and since the form of expression is conventionalized and obligatory, it is the values of the group that are revealed. I see in the study of rituals the key to an understanding of the essential constitution of human societies" (cited by Turner, *RP,* 6). It may, I suggest, also be a helpful key to the constitution of a novel such as *Final Payments* and something of its author's artistic, theological, and sociological preoccupations.

Gordon's handling of structure and sacrifice in this novel proves her mastery of transforming rituals and community and familial patterns, observed and memorized in childhood, into multivalent fictional structures. As Turner reminds us, "When we act in everyday life, . . . we act in frames we have wrested from the genres of cultural performance. . . . when we enter whatever theatre our lives allow us, we have already learned how strange and many-layered every life is, how extraordinary the ordinary." Citing W. H. Auden, Turner concludes, "We then no longer need in Auden's terms the 'endless safety' of ideologies but prize the 'needless risk' of acting and interacting" (*FRT,* 122), which is precisely what the character Isabel Moore comes to understand at the conclusion of *Final Payments.*

Final Oblations

Some fifty years ago, the literary theorists Max Horkheimer and Theodor Adorno argued that "the history of civilization is the history of the introversion of the sacrifice."[31] The validity of their argument can be documented in ongoing studies of such rituals as suicide, dieting, bulimia, anorexia, fitness obsessions, self-immolation, unprotected sexual intercourse, political and religious fasting, and, of course, terrorism. Thorough research might also suggest complex aspects of this phenomenon, on a broader spectrum, in our penchant for and frequent championing of unmediated, deadly confrontations among individuals, races, regions, and nations; and, on a more specific basis, in our current debates on abortion and in our highly selective eagerness to sacrifice money and food for starving masses (especially those outside our own nation's boundaries) and our unwillingness to intervene in mass genocides. Whatever examples one might choose, it is clear that an active factor in the success of Gordon's first novel is her having tapped into one of our society's best-hidden arenas of confusion: sacrifice.

Throughout *Final Payments,* as well as her second and third novels, *The Company of Women* and *Men and Angels,* Gordon addresses the intricate properties of and introverted dangers within sacrifice. All three novels are essential to an understanding of her persistent questions about and partial answers to the meaning and purpose of self-negating and -sacrificing acts. Gordon's attention to the relationships between her sacrificer and sacrificed characters not only links these novels; it also reveals how astutely she understands the dual nature of sacrifice. As Roberto Calasso has observed, "The basis of sacrifice lies in the fact that each one of us is two, not one. . . . The revelation of the sacrificial stratagem—that sacrificer and victim are two persons, not one—is the dazzling, ultimate revelation concerning our selves, concerning our double eye."[32] We see Gordon's novelistic awareness of this "double eye" most clearly in the character pairings and mirrorings of Isabel and Margaret (*Final Payments*) and Anne and Laura (*Men and Angels*). As I discuss in chapter four, Gordon further complicates her incremental approach to rituals and systems of sacrifice by testing them in a more thorough and severe way against *caritas,* the Latin word for an all-embracing, selfless love for others that is embodied in the New Testament usage of the Greek word *agape.* Still, Gordon's prioritizing of such questions and answers in *Final Payments* establishes a starting point from which her subsequent inquiries and resolutions evolve.

The novel begins and ends with overt gestures of sacrifice: Isabel's eleven-year care of her invalid father and her failed care of and subsequent gift of her entire inheritance to long-despised Margaret. That one could describe Gordon's approach to sacrifice as multivalent suggests something of her techniques and that adjective's chemical, combining, and displacing strengths. *Multivalent* is an even more useful modifier when the word *oblation* is substituted for the generic *sacrifice,* for an oblation indicates the sacramental offering of the bread and wine to God in the Eucharist as well as any act of offering something in a sacred service or to a church or parish. Moreover, the word *oblate* describes, in its respective roles as noun and adjective, a layperson who attaches him- or herself to a monastery or cloister and turns his/her possessions over to it, and a geometrical flattening at the poles of a sphere.

A typical example of Gordon's conflating all these definitions occurs early in *Final Payments,* when Isabel's lawyer, who calls her "a saint of God," suggests that his priest friends can find her a new career as a paid companion to invalids (45). Isabel, recognizing in horror the similarities between herself and Margaret, muses about "the interminable history of good daughters who cared for their parents" and the plight of those women who endured somehow when "the object of all that sacrifice was gone." She moves to the conclusion that "charity is tedious, and sacrifice is not, as Christ deceived us into thinking, anything so dramatic as a crucifixion. Most of the time it is profoundly boring" (46). Here, within less than two pages, Gordon simultaneously sets into motion the parish community's approval of Isabel's and other single women's oblations, Isabel's nausea regarding oblation itself, and her displacing Christ's sacrificial example with her own terms. To these, Gordon adds Isabel's rejecting an oblatory (a flattening) option for her new life and choosing instead to buy a copy of *Vogue* magazine that will help her move into the outside world and her adult physicality.

Isabel's decision alerts the reader to pay keen attention to Gordon's shifting body foci. The four major focus-shifts include:

Joseph Moore's body and Isabel's neglect of her body	Isabel's body rediscovered and reaffirmed	Margaret's body and Isabel's extreme neglect of her own body	Isabel's body reclaimed

Within and between these shifts and Gordon's fierce attention to bodies—fit, unfit, corpulent, wasted, strong, fragile, soft, hard, diseased, robust, elderly, young, immaculate, ill-kempt, loved, and unlovable—the reader can recognize that Gordon has moved beyond descriptive details and what one usually thinks of as body language. She has, in fact, opened up an inquiry in which the bodies of her characters become a privileged form of speech, and the complex speech of their bodies leads the reader directly to Gordon's minihistory (borrowing Horkheimer and Adorno's phrase again) "of the introversion of the sacrifice."

Of course, the context of Gordon's novel reflects a larger history of sacrifice, which is an intrinsic part of Judeo-Christian rituals, scriptures, and traditions. Old Testament examples that come to mind are Abraham's willingness to sacrifice Isaac, and, from Psalms 51: "The sacrifice acceptable to God is a broken spirit; a broken and contrite heart, O God, thou wilt not despise." Within the New Testament context, one thinks of Christ's crucifixion, and such verses as "Take, eat; this is my body" (Matthew 26:26); "Christ our Passover is sacrificed for us" (I Corinthians 5:7); "For God so loved the world that He gave his beloved son" (John 3:16); and "Greater love hath no man than this, that a man lay down his life for his friends" (John 15:13).

More specifically related to Gordon's Roman Catholic context of sacrifice are the celibacy vows of Catholic priests and nuns (and the physical, psychological, and social distancing these create); the Church's depriviledging of the Virgin Mary's sexuality, and thus, all women's sexuality; the Church's privileging any unborn infant's life over that of its mother; and the Church's limiting the leadership roles of women and designating women as supportive servants to male authority and the parish community. This is the circle articulated in multiple ways by the bodies of Father Mulcahy, Margaret Casey, John Delaney, Joseph and Isabel Moore and their neighbors, and Isabel's friends, Liz O'Brien Ryan and Eleanor Lavery. And this is the circle in which Isabel first learns to love and sacrifice her own sexuality, to loathe Margaret's body and to block her out of any possible relationship with Isabel's father, to care for her father's aging and increasingly inarticulate body, and to understand what the poet W. H. Auden, in another context, has admitted: "The image of myself which I try to create in my own mind in order that I may love myself is very different from the image which I try to create in the minds of others in order that they may love me."[33]

The tension between Auden's two images is a helpful way to approach additional agenda within *Final Payments.* For Gordon is concerned not only with the ways in which characters' bodies articulate their efforts and conflicting pressures; she is also interested in optional models of articulation. This becomes especially clear when the character Isabel moves out of the parish body into the equally articulate, outside world's body, where her own body attempts an articulate mediation between those two contexts.

In the outside world, she meets some of "the other's" forms of physical and verbal languages—Quaker, Protestant, Jewish, young, elderly, professional, governmental, lesbian, and heterosexual. Gordon's depictions of the latter's physical language and intercourse itself have been criticized in this and her second novel; there are cogent grounds for the criticism. Nevertheless, few can fault the way in which Gordon sets up Isabel's body as a means of verbalizing some of the profound social, theological, and ethical confusions that drive our culture's private and public, self-sacrificial and -destructive embodiments. The novel's most dramatic example of such confusions is Isabel's decision to retreat from verbal and sexual articulations (thus embodying vows of silence and celibacy) to take care of Margaret, the only person she has always loathed physically, intellectually, and emotionally. This guilt-driven retreat from Hugh and her friends (prompted by Hugh's wife's attack on her and thus on *her* sexuality rather than Hugh's) and her eating binge at Margaret's home demonstrate what Maud Ellmann has pointed out: "the social stigma against women's sexuality has now transferred itself to women's fat with unabated persecutory intensity" (*Hunger Artists,* 7). Isabel's self-persecutory transfer is a complicated one: in what Ellmann describes as an infantile, cannibalistic regression state (49–50), Isabel is devouring her newfound selfhood and sexuality at the same time her body is articulating its introversion of "the word became flesh" and the Eucharist's transubstantiation. Her fat is the primary text of her oblation, one that ritualizes an obeisance to her father's world and faith; in effect, her fat keeps him alive and thus blocks her acceptance of his death. Moreover, her expanding body, shorn hair, and silence internalize Margaret. Isabel *becomes* Margaret, the very transformation she has always feared (*Final Payments,* 58), and in doing so she devours Margaret: she takes on Margaret's selfhood and body.

As if to prepare the reader for the severity of Isabel's transfer, Gordon has included a horrific prefigurement in Isabel's approach to Margaret's house. At the Ramona bus station, we recall, Isabel sees a rather crazed elderly woman who, she notes, is reading *Pride and Prejudice.* Isabel's descriptions of the woman's hair and eyes, which "focused on nothing," anticipate the later, self-destructive transformations of Isabel's hair and eyes. When Isabel admits to herself, "I thought how easy it would be to kill a woman like that. . . . To watch her die would be perfectly enjoyable" (252), we see directly into the internalized rage and what Maud Ellmann has described as Isabel's "gynophagous relationship with Margaret" (*Hunger Artists,* 52). Everything about this prefigurement and its gradual actualization is disturbing; as John Auchard has pointed out, "Since Arthur Dimmesdale laid the lash to his body in *The Scarlet Letter,* few books have presented a more complete lust for self-punishment than *Final Payments*" (*American Novelists,* 110).

Gordon does not leave Isabel in such a state. However, alongside Isabel's decisions to leave Margaret and to give this unloved and unlovable person her entire inheritance, we see that Isabel must now sacrifice fat itself. The impetus for this final oblation comes through the words of Father Mulcahy and Hugh, male representatives (one should note carefully) of her two worlds. Her devoted friend and surrogate parent, Father Mulcahy, points out that her bodily neglect is a slow death that violates the fifth commandment: "Thou shalt not kill" (287). Then Hugh's short letter articulates his physical desire for her body, words she perceives in ritualized terms: "But I had heard Hugh's voice now. That was a curse . . . Now the mark of him was on me. He had written to me" (277). In other words, Hugh's words had written *on* her body, and to rejoin him will require that she first get rid of the fat, the embodiment of the kind of neglect Hugh will not tolerate; Isabel admits, "For I knew, and in knowing this, I hated him for a moment, that without my beauty he would not love me" (291). Rejoining Hugh also will require Isabel's losing the fat that embodies her truncated grief for her father and her misguided attempt to embody his world; in other words, she must give up finally both his body and Margaret's.

With such admissions, Gordon demonstrates again her feminist attention to the intricate ways in which women's sexuality, desirability, and roles are conflated with male authority. Intimately linked to that, as Maud Ellman has pointed out, is the fact that, "Having initially relinquished words for food, she [Isabel] turns full circle in the end and resolves to diet in order to replace her fat with speech. . . . What the novel shows is that language is a sacrificial order, exacting every pound of flesh, and that it is woman who is doomed to make this 'final payment'" (*Hunger Artists,* 53).

Gordon adds more components to such conflations when Isabel juxtaposes aesthetic standards and wonder. Isabel, in an epiphanic moment, begins to think of the human body in terms of great art: the art of the body is its constant articulation of and possibilities for metamorphosis. What's more, in thinking of Hugh's aesthetic standards for bodies, she knows, "Without that judgment he could not be the man I loved; he would be nothing like my father. And I needed a man whom I could love for his rigor, for the challenge, and the sense of having been carefully chosen after a consideration that was not hasty" (291). Thus, at the end of the novel, Isabel chooses another male authority system. She expresses no interest in autonomy; she wants to move physically and mentally back into community, into relationships, into the pleasures, risks, and (she now accepts) inevitable losses. A number of critics have faulted this resolution, as well as the last third of the novel, as being imperfect, excessive, even melodramatic. Still, the strength of the protagonist's final decisions (and thus the novelist's) lies in Isabel's hard-won ability to redefine those systems and standards that will govern her life. Isabel, for the first time, has begun at least to differentiate her own values system.

This final stage reminds the reader that the novel's first three body foci reflect severely myopic, all-or-nothing models of sacrifice or pleasure that are finally redefined, reintegrated, and thus sacrificed. However severe each shift may be, its dramatic role is never simple. These shifts, for example, are an intrinsic part of Gordon's inquiry into value. This is expressed in a struggle not just within Isabel's understanding of the value of oblation-sacrifice itself but also between oblation versus pleasure as value. The four distinct phases of that struggle are obvious:

Sacrifice as value	Pleasure as value	Sacrifice without value	Complex values that combine sacrifice and pleasure

What's more, Gordon creates multiple episodes in which sacred, sexual, and ludic aspects of Isabel's struggle are juxtaposed. For instance, at the end of her first day at work in Ringkill, while trying to mingle at a party for college students who have volunteered for her program, Isabel catches herself looking for a sad face among all the healthy, happy students. She realizes, "I was angry at myself for making the equation, my father's equation, the Church's equation, between suffering and value. I would have some more beer; I would enjoy myself" (134). That enjoyment includes her sleeping with John Ryan, her best friend's husband, a man she can't stand, and discovering a complex, new equation of pleasure and value that includes possibilities of sacrificing moral surety as well as a lifelong friendship.

At the point of Gordon's introducing these possibilities, one is reminded again of how often she inserts humor in the juncture between pleasure and pain. However, a significant contradiction to these tripartite intersections emerges as the novel proceeds. Isabel's love relationship and pleasure with another married man, Hugh, lead to her being tested by the pragmatic effects of her "pleasure equals value" equation: pleasure also can entail hurting others and being hurt, loss, risks, and humiliation. Guilt-stricken and unable to cope with these ramifications, Isabel reverts to a severely truncated version of her earliest oblation: she sacrifices relationships and herself to being Margaret's companion.

In this phase of Isabel's struggle, all humorous mediations disappear. Nevertheless, by the evening of Good Friday, she has decided on two radical countermeasures: she will give her inheritance to Margaret and leave her home. For Isabel, these decisions represent a fledgling integration of values—one that affirms inevitable hurts, risks, sacrifices, and deaths alongside life-enhancing pleasures, work, and the "luxury of our extravagant affections" (289). These are demonstrated in Isabel's new understanding of pivotal New Testament episodes and her own relationships and physicality. And the novel closes with ringing laughter and a sacrifice of sacrificial absolutes.

Chapter Three

"radical closeness":
The Company of Women

In a 1988 interview, Gordon mentioned that "Somebody wanted to buy *The Company of Women* for a movie, but she [the interested party] said, 'Felicitas has to leave. She has to go back to New York at the end of the movie with her daughter.' And I said that she missed the whole point of the book in a very radical way. It's not *An Unmarried Woman*. It's not somebody who goes through a rough patch and pulls herself up by her bootstraps and goes and works for *Ms.* And most people do have severely limited lives. I mean, life does not always get out of the way so that we express ourselves to the fullest."[1]

The tone and points of this spirited barrage, and the movie option itself, are apt introductions to Gordon's second novel, which was published in 1980, two years after her first novel's commercial and critical success and which *The Company of Women* gave every sign of matching commercially: within months of its publication, it appeared in a condensed version in *Redbook,* it was a Literary Guild dual main selection, it had garnered a lucrative paperback contract with Ballantine, and within a few more months, it had received the Kafka Prize.

Not unexpectedly, comparisons of the two works filled the reviews, most of which were accompanied by new photographs of Gordon and, in the case of James Wolcott's review in *Esquire,* by a caricature of Gordon as the Pope at a typewriter. Clearly, the second-time novelist was being treated as a "writer to watch," and she was being measured against the quality of her first novel. Francine Du Plessix Gray, for example, begins a long review of *The Company of Women* with the comment that "If there was any doubt that Mary Gordon was her generation's preeminent novelist of Roman Catholic mores and manners when she published her remarkable first novel, 'Final Payments,' it is dispelled by her new book."[2] The editor of the *Washington Post Book World,* Brigitte Weeks, starts off with: "A first novel may show 'promise' but the second novel must sustain that promise and build on it. . . . So here we are, watching, in fact reading *The Company of Women* to see where her [Gordon's] talents will take us. Happily, her new novel is both a variation on the themes of *Final Payments* and a clear step forward, deepening and expanding our view of her astonishingly detailed, purposely circumscribed landscape."[3] Similarly, Barbara Grizzuti Harrison's review admits she approached *The Company of Women* fearing "the slackening of powers one so often sees in second novels," but this is not, she claims, the case.[4]

However, to read straight through some two dozen major reviews of the novel is to discover serious questions about the novel, such as Du Plessix Gray's: "Is Miss Gordon's craft as a novelist keeping up with the grand and virginal boldness of her vision?" ("Religious Romance," 1). William O' Rourke's scathing (and, ultimately, condescending) review insists, "*The Company of Women* is not an advance—as I hoped it would be—over *Final Payments:* it stands alongside it. And though I am all for (relatively) young writers being encouraged, in this case, bad notices will not affect the novel's fate since it is already a success. . . . Nonetheless, *The Company of Women* is a disappointing piece of work that inexperienced readers may enjoy (not knowing the same ground has been covered so much better so many times before)."[5] Christopher Lehmann-Haupt's review and questioning are more cogent: "why, if the two novels resemble each other so strongly, is 'The Company of Women' such a falling off from the high level of 'Final Payments'?" He immediately posits two possibilities: "The answer could well be that in trying to probe deeper into the psychological situation that underlies both novels, Miss Gordon has bumped into something she can't yet resolve. But I'd prefer to believe that the problem is simply that the new novel is technically more ambitious than the earlier one."[6] The latter suggestion seems especially appropriate; in fact, many other critics' discussions end up reflecting more on the ambitious scope and complexity of Gordon's second novel than they do on the novel's strengths and weaknesses or the critics' acumen and biases, as interesting and helpful as these are. What's more, to review the reviews is to reconfirm the initial impression *The Company of Women* leaves: Gordon made no attempt whatsoever to play it safe with her second novel. Her innovations and the places in which those innovations occasionally seem to outreach themselves must be addressed, but first, certain continuities between the two novels need to be reviewed.

Even though it is sadder than its predecessor, *The Company of Women* matches the intensity of Gordon's first novel. With the exception of a curious enervation in the middle section, that intensity moves through the novel's three parts, organized around the years 1963, 1969–70, and 1977, fourteen years in the lives of the characters: Felicitas Maria Taylor (from age 14 to 28); an ultratraditionalist priest, Father Cyprian Leonard; and a group of five working women, including Felicitas's mother, Charlotte (a character based on Gordon's mother, to whom this novel is dedicated), Elizabeth McCullough, Clare Leary, Mary Rose [née Costello], and Muriel Fisher.

The Company of Women also continues thematic preoccupations begun in *Final Payments:* a widowed parent; a daughter's search for her own life; sacrificial, female devotion to a male champion of conservative Catholicism; and a circle of female friendships and enmities. These are the basic continuities, but there are a number of more specific thematic resonances. Christopher Lehmann-Haupt, for instance, has cataloged: "Felicitas and the heroine of the first novel, Isabel Moore, are spiritual prodigies of sorts, who are protected from 'real life' by their relationships with older men. Both older men, Father Cyprian and Isabel Moore's father, are fiercely conservative Roman Catholics who expect their girls to follow in their spiritual paths. Both suffer breakdowns of their health . . . which are apparent consequences of rebellious acts by Felicitas and Isabel, for which the girls blame themselves unconsciously. Both Felicitas and Isabel get into sexual messes as a result of breaking free from their 'fathers.' Both end up seeking refuge with 'mothers'" ("Company," C28). A more sardonic take on the novels' similarities emerges in William O' Rourke's review, which suggests that "both [novels] employ the Rip Van Winkle, Time Machine, Wild Child of Borneo principle: a character emerges from a grossly sheltered existence into a 'new' world, appearing to be a primitive faced with outlandish customs, similar to the Japanese soldier found in the jungle decades after World War II who is then whisked off to modern Tokyo" ("Father Father," 245).

"Wild Child" or no, the thematic similarities form the first level of resonances between the two novels. The second level is their plot structures, both of which evolve within a closed—opened—reclosed—reopened pattern: Part I (1963) of *The Company of Women* introduces the closed company of women and Father Cyprian, the history of their individual and collected lives, and the childhood and youth of the only child in their circle, the novel's protagonist, Felicitas Taylor. In Part II (1969–70), the enclosure is forced open by Felicitas who, at Columbia University and its Manhattan environs, tries to build a life for herself outside the group. Her attempts end up in double enclosures: moving into the apartment-commune of her first lover, Robert Cavendish, and her eventual pregnancy by either Robert or their neighbor Richard, after which she returns to her mother's home, which is the resounding confirmation of reclosure. Part III (1977) reflects an unexpected type of reopening, which is revealed in seven first-person monologues, the first of which is by Felicitas, who begins with one of the most remarkable openers Gordon has ever written: "It was because of the bats that I decided to marry" (239). Except for Clare Leary, who will join them when she retires, and Mary Rose, who has finally married Joe Siegel, the entire group is now living in Orano, New York: Felicitas, her young daughter Linda, her mother Charlotte, Elizabeth, Father Cyprian, and Muriel. Felicitas, trying to build a different sort of life for herself and her daughter, has decided to marry a quiet, steady, local man, Leo Byrne. If Felicitas's adult life is nothing like what she and the rest of the little group expected for her, she nevertheless demonstrates a hard-won clarity and control with which she is shaping her and her daughter's lives, as well as those of the now elderly group. Still, she reminds us of Gordon's comments about the novel: "most people do have severely limited lives. I mean, life does not always get out of the way so that we express ourselves to the fullest." With this brief review of the two novels' similarities in place, the ambitious innovations in Gordon's second novel can be examined.

As Robert Towers has pointed out, "Though it is to some degree a reworking of the themes of the earlier novel, *The Company of Women* is, in its structure and scope, a very different sort of book."[7] The most obvious structural innovations occur in the third part of the novel, where, as mentioned earlier, Gordon shifts to a series of seven first-person monologues. (Only Mary Rose, who has recently married and begun a new life with Joe Siegel, does not speak. Instead, Linda, Felicitas's young daughter, is the seventh and final speaker.) Gordon's third and fourth novels demonstrate more sustained versions of this multivoiced, structural experiment, and there is a much earlier precedent of Gordon's using this technique in her first published short story, "Now I Am Married." Still, in *The Company of Women,* the individual monologues of each person within the main circle of friends achieve important results; even William O' Rourke concedes that "the last section is the novel's strongest" ("Father Father," 246). The characters' first-person immediacy surprises, then augments, what the reader knows about the group as a whole, and finally makes the reader privy to much more of each character's interior life. In essence, on page 239 Gordon is removing a kind of remaining scrim that separates the reader and the closed company with its Catholic milieu. The resultant "close encounters" with the characters are so private that the reader may forget to differentiate between him- or herself and the "other world." This possibility, in itself, seems well worth the risks Gordon takes in making the abrupt voice shift.

Another structural innovation is Gordon's attempt to develop a second enclosed circle that, with its polemics and circle of sexual and political devotion, will act as a radical, secular mirror image of Father Cyprian and the five women. Felicitas is, of course, the common denominator between the two as she visits her professor and first lover, Robert Cavendish, in his sleazy Amsterdam Avenue commune-apartment, and eventually moves in with the rest of the apartment's denizens, one of whom has a child. On the most fundamental structural level, Gordon succeeds: Felicitas flees her formative circle only to find herself ensconced in another. And Madonna Kolbenschlag has suggested that "Robert is in many ways . . . a shadow-self of Cyprian. Both men collect women, but they attract them for different reasons; they control and use them in different ways. . . . They require women as totems of their own inner life. They require a chorus of women to reinforce their own dramatic conceptions of themselves. Above all, they require women as an audience for their monologues."[8] Nevertheless, the dialogue, details, character developments (particularly Robert's), and sexuality in the middle section's counterculture cannot hold their own against the expertise and informed energy with which Gordon developed the Cyprian circle in the novel's Parts I and III. And critics were quick to point out various details of the weaker development that even the most positive of reviewers, such as Barbara Grizzuti Harrison, recognize as the novel's "grave structural defect—the middle sags alarmingly" ("Eccentrics," 62).

The strong criticism directed at this section may reflect the high expectations regarding Gordon's skill. And Gordon may have had her reasons for writing it as she did: first of all, perhaps much of the radical 1960s polemics *was* characterized by such linguistic paucity (a possibility that creates more than a little discomfort for this reader), and second, perhaps the superficial commune clichés are meant to demonstrate, by contrast, the profound richness of a rhetorical tradition and system of faith that is being, if not destroyed, then popularized during this same decade. But these are reaches; critical judgments of many of the dialogues, the sexual episodes, and the character Robert Cavendish, in particular, will probably stand. In Gordon's own account, the latter elicited a certain disbelief from Elizabeth Hardwick, one of Gordon's Barnard College mentors and her main reader for *Final Payments:* "He's [Cavendish] just too awful. *No one* would sleep with him the way you've written about him" (Bannon interview, 274). A year before *The Company*

of Women was published, when questioned about her responses to critics'
attacks on her younger male characters in *Final Payments,* Gordon laughingly had admitted, "I'm not very good at young men, men who have a
sexual identity. And I wish I were better. . . . I can't write sympatheti-
cally about a normally sexed man" (Cooper-Clark interview, 272). As any
reader of her three novellas knows, Gordon subsequently has mastered
the problem. Still, the 1960s drugs-sex scenario in *The Company of
Women,* as well as the dialogues and character developments within that
scenario, seem (in comparison to Gordon's otherwise apparent finesse)
strangely superficial, even awkward.

Nevertheless, Gordon's including the commune circle points to
another of Gordon's ambitions for the novel: its broad sociological scope
that unfolds incrementally. The novel is set in the 1960s and 1970s,
when institutions, traditional authorities, and social and sexual mores
were under attack. Initially removed from such inquiry, the plot moves
across paradigm shifts in the American Catholic parochial world, discussed at length in the last section of this chapter. In Part II of the novel,
the plot includes broader paradigmatic shifts in North America regarding women's rights, illegal abortions (in a pre-pill, pre-*Roe* vs. *Wade* context), sexual revolution, and a new generation's virulent, highly politicized protests against traditional authorities.

In hindsight, additional resonances between the first two novels
seem apparent. Like the enclosed circle of devotion with which Gordon
begins *Final Payments,* the even fiercer devotion of this novel's small
"company of women" had already become a theological as well as a
sociological anomaly, for the most part, by the early 1960s. But in the
second novel, Gordon goes much further in her explorations: she sets
up such anomalies within the small group as a metaphor for all that
will be ruptured and questioned during the 1960s and 1970s. Her
attempt to track these ruptures across the novel's evolving plot and
characters reflects one of the most distinctive challenges Gordon sets
up for herself. Examples of these are varied, but although most of the
political context is removed from Part III, the final section of the novel
contains the novel's most poignant examination of the paradigmatic
shifts in American Catholicism. This appears in Father Cyprian's private monologue, in which he traces his career and what he perceives as
the rupture of his profession's piety, self-discipline, reverence for
authority, as well as the new tackiness that surrounds the Church. At
the same time he confesses his arrogance, his refusals to change, his
professional failures, and his understanding the Incarnation, only now

in these failed circumstances, only through the company of his long-
time women friends.

In other examples throughout the novel, however, Gordon highlights
societal and theological shifts by placing them in juxtaposition. Such
examples range from Cyprian and Felicitas's fights about politics; to Mary
Rose and Joe Siegel's visiting Felicitas in the Amsterdam Avenue apartment; to the group's strained Christmas gathering in Orano, New York,
and Muriel's silent criticism of Felicitas's sitting "in that most unladylike
way . . . saying, 'These people should be shot'" as she reads the *U. S. News
& World Report* (164); to Robert's suggesting that Felicitas write for the
radical newspaper *Sub Rosa:* "'She writes a clearer prose than any student
I've had in this place in ten years. . . . As a matter of fact, I think the
three women in this room could be at the vanguard of the new movement. Felicitas the head, Sally the hands and Iris the heart.' The mystical
body of Christ, Felicitas thought, but said nothing" (144).

In the latter example, Gordon is demonstrating what, by this point in
her career, had already become a noticeable stylistic device in her writing: a simultaneous treatment of opposites. As the next chapter will
explore, Gordon's third novel, *Men and Angels,* transforms this penchant
into a full-blown, thematic and compositional counterpoint. Still, in *The
Company of Women,* Gordon is testing the limits of such juxtapositions,
and when she does so, she frequently uses surprising pairings. For
instance, "When he [Robert] touched her arm to open the heavy door
for her, she was afraid and hopeful that his fingers had left a mark on her
clothing, like the shroud of Turin or Veronica's veil. She felt the burning
of her flesh beneath his fingers, which had rested there for no more than
an instant. And when, after a second, he took his hand away, she felt the
strongest deprivation of her life" (108–9).

Fields of Force

A year and a half before the publication of *The Company of Women,* Mary
Gordon, in a *New York Times Book Review* summary of her work in
progress, gave its working title as *Fields of Force* ("Work in Progress," 14).
Gordon's choice of this particular scientific phenomenon as a working
title can inform one's reading of the novel, for a *field of force* is "a region
of space throughout which the force produced by a single agent, such as
an electric current, is operative" (*American Heritage Dictionary,* 501).

Applying this definition as a broad approach to *The Company of Women,*
we see that Gordon places in unsettling proximity multiple force fields

whose agencies—religious faith and rituals, a Catholic priest, female friendships, a Columbia University professor, and sexuality—drive the plot, structure, imagery, and thematic considerations of the novel. Gordon's use of these "fields" allows the reader to view a range of radical strengths and weaknesses within closed and enclosed circles. Moreover, within each of these fields or systems, Gordon sets up a prescribed set of standards to which one instinctively reacts; these reactions, in turn, gradually lead both her characters and the reader into examinations of authority, faith, sex, family, friendships, and language in terms of love and truth.

Gordon signals her systems (fields) and standards approach in the novel's epigraph, twenty-one lines from the poem "The Common Life" by W. H. Auden.[9] The lines begin: "What draws/ singular lives together in the first place,/ loneliness, lust, ambition,/ or mere convenience, is obvious." Likewise, *The Company of Women* opens with explanations of why the women and Father Cyprian have been drawn together. Beginning with the early 1930s, Father Cyprian has given the five adult women assistance and comfort when each was attempting to cope with traumas such as the death of a husband, father, or child; brutal or abandoned marriages; sole care of aging parents; and various other difficulties and disappointments. During the subsequent decades, the friends share unwavering parochial trust in Cyprian's advice. For his part, as Father Cyprian's ultratraditionalist rigidities cause him to be more and more marginalized in the rapidly changing, post-Vatican II Catholic world, his parish eventually contains only this tiny band. Thus, the "why" of their coming together is clear.

However, it is in Gordon's explication of the "how" and "what" the group builds together that we see reflected the more crucial second point of W. H. Auden's poem, the point of miracle and mystery: "how they create, though, a common world/between them, like Bombelli's/ impossible yet useful numbers, no one/has yet explained. . . ." Sometimes, the characters come close to articulating the mystery of their little group's significance. Charlotte Taylor, Felicitas's mother, is one of these spokespersons. For example, she knows that she will never forgive Father Cyprian's saying to her, when his best friend, Frank (Charlotte's young husband and Felicitas's father), had died: "'Do not speak to me of your sorrow. Your sorrow is nothing to mine.'" "Still," Charlotte reminds herself, "there was nobody like Cyp, which was why she came up here [to Orano] every year. There was something between them, between all of them. They were connected to something, they stood for something. They were not only themselves, secretaries and schoolteachers, people who took care of their mothers, ushers in movie theaters, the lame ducks no man wanted. When all of them came together, they were something" (18).

The more urbane Clare Leary, on the other hand, recognizes that all the rest of the group, except herself, center their professional and private lives so completely on the Church that they "lived in a virginity far more radical than their intact physical states" (24). Theirs, in other words, is a virginity of standards within an enclosed system of faith and devotion that isolates them, as a sort of remnant, from the questions, events, and changes of the 1960s and 1970s. Young Felicitas has absorbed the group's radical devotion and high standards with a single-minded relish that isolates her, in turn, from potential friends her own age and, until she leaves the group, from her own generation. Her mother recalls that "Even as a child, Felicitas, frightened by other children, wept and begged to be let in the house. When Charlotte ordered her to stay outdoors, she would see Felicitas, huddled, miserable" (149).

Gordon reveals only gradually the damage this radical devotion is doing to the only child in the circle. Felicitas's superb mind and spirit are bound up in the group's expectations; the women and Cyprian, in fact, place all their hopes for the future on her. Father Cyprian, whose orthodoxy has reduced his career to this group, takes comfort only in Felicitas, his surrogate daughter; she, in turn, adores him and feels closest to the center of God when she is worshiping with Cyprian at Mass or riding in his pickup truck. Despite her mother's and the others' occasional private worries, Cyprian is grooming Felicitas in Latin, logic, and theology for a future without a man, marriage, and motherhood. He wants no "womanish" life for her. As the scholar Anita Gandolfo has pointed out, such training reflects "pre–Vatican II dualism. It is an education in the exclusive virtue of reason" (*Testing the Faith,* 173). Just as in Isabel's training by her father in *Final Payments* (who wants her to be "a Theresa of Ávila, not a Thérèse of Lisieux" (28), or to use New Testament nomenclature, Mary instead of a Martha), *The Company of Women* makes clear that such patently rational equipment and the cloistered intensity in which the young girl learns it create rigid parameters against which her fledgling autonomy will eventually shatter. By the time such shatterings begin, the reader has long since recognized that Felicitas, without adequate emotional and integrative equipment, is severely crippled. Even her mother Charlotte has recognized that Felicitas does not know how "to bend in the wind" (197). Therefore, crises are inevitable, and the damage these inflict on Felicitas will be directly proportional to the unmitigated rationality and ill-equipped emotionality with which she approaches them.

Before moving to the next section, it is important to keep in mind that these contexts serve Gordon's major focus (which she assumes the reader shares): a profound interest in the inner life of a character. As she explains it, "every novelist has to believe that character is more important than outside events, or he or she would not be a novelist—unless you were someone like Gorky. Even with Defoe, or Fielding, or Tolstoy, or Thackeray, who include a lot of the outside world in their books, the reason we read the novel is to find out about the inner workings. As the outside world impinges, it impinges on that particular individual, whom we know in a very inner way" (Bolotin interview, 232). Gordon makes particularly clear both her novelistic "inner" priority and this impinging "outside" relationship in the character Felicitas.

Radical Love, Radical Damage

At Felicitas's baptism in May of 1949, one of her three godmothers had joked that the virgin martyr's name given the infant suggested "some hope for ordinary human happiness" (3). There was, as mentioned earlier, nothing ordinary in Felicitas's subsequent childhood and youth. Gordon herself has often chosen the word "radical" to summarize the love, expectations, and damage that surround Felicitas. The same adjective is appropriate for this novel and Gordon's next, *Men and Angels.* Her interest in extreme systems and sacrificial gestures was apparent in her first novel, in which the character Isabel finally opts (after a miserable attempt at depersonalized charity) for a much more tempered life of "ordinary human happiness." In her second and third novels, however, Gordon intensifies her questions about the nature of *caritas* (the highest form of self-sacrificing love and charity, in the sense of love as represented by the Greek word *agape* in the New Testament). Gordon also intensifies her questioning of the extreme dangers inherent in one's giving, receiving, or demanding radical love. As the adult Felicitas recalls the unusual circle of love that surrounded her childhood, she remembers, "Adoration is addictive. It is also corrupting; there is no way out of it except a radical life" (257).

If Part I of *The Company of Women* tracks the development of radical love, Part II tracks the results of such love. For example, by 1969, Felicitas's relationship with Father Cyprian has ruptured. She has become as rigid and verbally tenacious as her mentor. As Cyprian notices (not recognizing himself in his protegé), "But what had she become? Full of anger, full of argument, as convinced in her opinions as any of the smart alecks he had had to talk to in the parishes" (162). When the twenty year old, about to transfer to Columbia University, briefly joins the group's annual retreat in Orano, New York, her opposition to the Vietnam War provokes another fierce argument with Cyprian, an argument that, in turn, triggers his heart attack. Despite his serious illness, Felicitas leaves Orano immediately. She is exhausted by his rages, by the group's pressures on her, and by the women's constantly propping up Cyprian's ego. She vows to change her life but is not equipped to deal with her own emotions, sexuality, contemporaries, and life outside the little group. At Columbia, Felicitas promptly falls in love with her political science professor, Robert Cavendish, who pursues, deflowers, and adds her to his apartment-commune of sexual and radical political groupies.

As discussed earlier, many critics have attacked the Columbia University scenario as being the least convincing sequence in Gordon's novel. Bill Greenwell, one of this number, suggests: "rot sets when we're skipped to 1969–70 . . . Marcuse. Bad Karma. Dynamite chicks. . . . 'The root problem is monogamy. I think you should be fucking other people.' A promising novel collapses."[10] Nevertheless, the sequence succeeds in what seems to be its primary structural goal, for Felicitas, in effect, recreates a secular version of the only model she knows: she is back inside a circle of women (one with a young child named Mao), devoted to a man who sets their lives' patterns. Attempting to revive Robert's waning interest, she (at his suggestion) sleeps with their downstairs neighbor Richard, an unattractive, awkward character who remains memorable only because of his dogs' names: Ho, Che, and Jesus (names changed to Jo, Jay, and Peaches after Felicitas leaves Manhattan with them in tow). Made pregnant by either Robert or Richard, during this pre-pill and pre–legal abortion era, Felicitas goes to an illegal abortion clinic. Horrified by the setting and the ordeal she and the other women in the waiting room are facing, she flees the clinic (and an abortion), Robert's circle, and her studies. Her and the Cyprian group's extraordinary expectations disintegrated, a shattered Felicitas returns to her mother's home, knowing that she has been unable to sustain autonomy, academic achievement, friendships, and sexual relationships. In a discussion of Father Cyprian and Felicitas, Gordon has confirmed: "an extreme life doesn't breed happiness" (Keyishian interview, 73). Nor can

Felicitas find an adult life as a woman who, in Gordon's words, will not "suddenly buckle to the authority of a male mentor, whether it's a priest or professor or a lover."[11]

If Columbia University becomes a symbol of Felicitas's failed autonomy and adulthood, it (along with the women around Cyprian) also symbolizes a crucial aspect of a failed, or, at the very least, flawed womanhood. One of Gordon's central feminist preoccupations in this novel is women's unquestioning abdication of responsibility to male authority: father figures, priests, lovers, professors, and the male-dominated institutions each represents. Obviously, Gordon affirms the comfort and assistance Father Cyprian has given to his five women devotees, and she has elsewhere emphasized, "The positive side of people like Cyprian is that they stand for a kind of absolute standard and passion and uncompromisingness and some notion of the ideal. Without which I think life is very impoverished" (Schreiber interview, 26). However, Gordon shows that it is through her adult women characters' *unquestioning* surrender of their and young Felicitas's spiritual, intellectual, emotional, and social lives to Cyprian that very real damage occurs. While each of the five women confesses, sometimes to herself, sometimes to Cyprian, a candid rebellion against his pronouncements, none acts against his advice. An example is Mary Rose, once a nightclub dancer, and, at the opening of the story in 1963, an usher at a Broadway movie theater run by her Jewish friend Joe Siegel. But, accepting Cyprian's advice, she does not marry Joe for fifteen years, that is, until after the death of her deranged husband, Burt, who has been institutionalized for decades. Likewise, Charlotte, who grew up in a large, lively family, knows that she is not providing a normal childhood for Felicitas; however, she entrusts her daughter's development to Cyprian's charge—a trust that no one really questions, certainly not Charlotte. As she watches Cyprian and Felicitas drive away in his old pickup truck, "she thought quite simply, knowing she did not exaggerate, 'For those two I would die'" (19). Not surprisingly, when Felicitas later attempts to establish a life for herself, the damage created by the group's unchecked adoration and trust is obvious.

Felicitas's eventual re-creation of a healthier life for herself and her child demonstrates the difficulty of such a task for any contemporary woman. Of course, we also recognize that Felicitas's pregnancy in the midst of the 1960s sexual revolution addresses the specific, pragmatic dilemmas that women faced in a pre-pill and pre–legal abortion context. Gordon's attention to such dilemmas, moreover, is heightened by Felicitas's (and Gordon's) interesting decision to keep the identity of the father of her child unknown. On the one hand, it suggests Felicitas's unconscious replication of her own childhood's model: an adored child of an absent father, surrounded by an unusual circle of expectations. But, despite her efforts to give Linda's childhood all the normality she herself never experienced and despite the six-year-old's secret worry about being the daughter of "one of two men," Felicitas's decision is perhaps the only healthy way that she can negate their permanent, accidental presence in her life. Still, her decision seems to augment rather than displace: the unknown, the unnamed retains a strange potency.

Nonetheless, it is certain that Gordon's second novel, completed at the beginning of the 1980s, is intended as a reminder that women's rights regarding their own bodies and well-being remain vulnerable to decisions imposed by men and by male-dominated institutions, both legislative and ecclesial. At the same time, however, Gordon extends her commentary on authority by showing (through Cyprian, in particular, and Robert, to a lesser degree) that men's unquestioning presumptions of authority and/or adherences to authoritative structures invariably restrict their own lives. Of course, Cavendish is such a cad that most readers would say he deserves any available restrictions, but Cyprian is another case altogether. His obdurate refusals to change precipitate ever-tightening circles of reductiveness in his priesthood. By 1969, his parish has shrunk to his faithful, tiny company of women who, during their visits to Orano, observe mass (in Latin, of course, for which he had to obtain special dispensation) with him in the room next to his kitchen, which has been designated as the chapel and filled with the traditional cast-off furniture of parish churches that have modernized their accoutrements. Even near the end of his life and surrounded by and relishing the daily love of the small group, he continues to struggle, still longing for the detached surety of the austere priesthood to which he had committed his life, still wanting the life of the ideal abstraction.

Gordon's exploration of the ways in which absolute authority damages males' lives has been overlooked by critics, especially the male cadre, and perhaps with good reason: as Peter Prescott has warned, in the midst of praising Gordon's strong female characters in *The Company of Women,* "It's been clear for at least a decade now that men who read novels by women had better get used to hunkering down in a defensive posture. The relief column isn't in sight and probably hasn't been formed. For the foreseeable future we can't expect much good news about ourselves. . . . And yet . . . may we not hope that this generation of feminist fiction may soon evolve into another in which women are allowed to mature in a world where men are themselves seen as independent, complex creatures?"[12] By the time Gordon completed her novellas in 1993, Prescott's hoped-for evolution had taken place. Nevertheless, from the early years of her career, many potential male readers have presumed that Gordon's novels are "for women only," a presumption that continues to gall the novelist. In a conversation about this problem, Gordon recalled going up to speak to a man at a reception after one of her readings. He gave a quick disclaimer about making any response to her work by saying, "I'm here with my wife; she reads all your novels." To this, Gordon wanted to reply (but did not), "Just read them, damn it. Read them."[13]

The fact remains that *The Company of Women* and Gordon's other novels, so far, do focus primarily on the difficulties and limitations women often face in and impose upon their decisions about sexuality, marriage, motherhood, careers, and, most important, personhood. To varying degrees in all four of her novels, Gordon also introduces such questions in tandem with equally important questions about the moral and spiritual dimensions of contemporary women's lives. Her linked inquiry tests imposed and self-inflicted boundaries at the same time it explores collisions of transcendent visions of life, such as those of feminism and Catholicism. And in her fourth novel, Gordon adds immigration and workers' rights to that inquiry. While such inquiries remain, for the most part, focused on women, Gordon's questions clearly are intended for men as well. No male character in her novels demonstrates this more thoroughly than Gordon's remarkable character Father Cyprian, whose life continues to be as complex a yearning for and struggle with boundaries as that of Felicitas's.

Nevertheless, we pay most attention to the boundaries that impact Felicitas, and Gordon makes sure that we track those from the young protagonist's childhood to the end of the book. We recall, for instance, that as a child, Felicitas admits to herself that she does not mean the prayer "Domine, non sum dignus" [Lord, I am not worthy]; she sees herself worthy enough, her soul important enough, to "take God in" (6). She also is capable of ridiculing Cyprian's disapproval of, for example, Jane Austen's novels, which Elizabeth McCullough and Felicitas adore; she whispers to Elizabeth, "He doesn't know everything. He's not God" (76). Still, Felicitas and Elizabeth, wary of displeasing Cyprian, whisper, and Felicitas's sense of self-worth (which equals Cyprian's) will prove to be as dysfunctional as her mentor's. Seeking independence, Felicitas, as we have discovered, subordinates herself to another man, who, with his selfishness, arch-liberalism, and female coterie, is a secular mirror image of Cyprian's stance (the kind of mirroring technique that Gordon explores much more fully in *Men and Angels*). Nonetheless, Felicitas's traumas result as much from the older adults' unquestioning, radical nurture of her sense of specialness as they do from her and the older women's unquestioning capitulations to male authority. These unquestioning and radical components remain the novel's most singular warnings. The challenge, as the adult Felicitas finally recognizes, is in finding healthy ways to put all of life together, to discover and encourage a robust, well-integrated sense of self that can declare "Sum dignus" (I am worthy) in the midst of life.

By the conclusion of the novel, we know that her daughter Linda is well on her way to such a declaration, and we see that Felicitas is trying to ensure that her child will not suffer from the kind of radical love that had surrounded her own childhood. Thus, even though the novel begins and ends with a young girl surrounded by love, as the wonderfully chosen Mary Cassatt painting on the book jacket emphasizes, it will be different for this child. For not only is young Linda well-rounded, keenly intelligent, and sociable; she is moving out into a world beyond the rigidities that formed her mother's world. And Linda, for example, who has decided that she wants to be a priest, has convinced even Father Cyprian to pray that her vocational choice will be possible. As the elderly Cyprian admits to himself, "I thought of all the foolish, mediocre men who were permitted ordination because of the accident of their sex. And I thought of this child, obviously superior to all others of her age in beauty, grace, and wisdom" (288). Still, if the reader has followed Linda's mother into the core of her own struggle, a further subtextual warning remains clear: as Gordon expressed it in 1985, "The history of women is the history of a great deal of thwarting. It's very wicked" (Bolotin interview, 232). As the following section explores, another, even more stubborn, subtext of the novel counterbalances that warning: as Felicitas's mother has explained: "When all of them came together, they were something" (18), and that "something" is not only their shared religious faith, but, as the next section explores, the novel's best-kept secret.

"the subaltern should be truth": the Countersystem

Both *Final Payments* and *The Company of Women* explore beauties and dangers within systems and standards of Catholicism and the pre–Vatican II parochial world. In *The Company of Women*, however, Gordon goes much further in exploring the precarious balance of truth (systems and standards) and love, terms suggested in the powerful conclusion of her novel's epigraph by W. H. Auden:

> and always, though truth and love
> can never really differ, when they seem to,
> the subaltern should be truth.

In light of the final line, it is helpful to reread a review by Barbara Grizzuti Harrison. Trying to get at the essence of *The Company of Women,* she points out that the novel is "so richly layered and textured that it is nearly impossible to say what it is about: It is 'about' human love; it is 'about' divine love; it is 'about' the redemptive power of suffering, about illusions, resilience, and delusion." She tries a second listing in her conclusion: "it is about instinct and reason, submission and authority, the holiness of the flesh, and the awesome power of love to diminish, enrich, and immortalize." Earlier in the review, however, after listing several optional interpretations of the novel, she turns away to a more succinct summary: "Little Matter. *The Company of Women* tells a story; it tells truths" ("Eccentrics," 62–63).

Harrison's generalized use of the word *truths* and her lists are a fortuitous segue to a countersystem that becomes clear in Part III of the novel and that also undermines my two previous sections, putting them into their proper, secondary roles. Nevertheless, Harrison's "truths" need to be examined in the context of her catalogs of what the novel is about, since, in the novel's epigraph by Auden and in Gordon's conclusion for the novel, there is a clear differentiation between the Letter of the Law and the Spirit of the Law—in other words, between truth and love. And the latter is privileged, just as it is in Harrison's circuitous approach. Still, it is impossible to ignore the fact that the novel privileges three "truths": an absolute, idealized system of thought, faith, fellowship, and life, as well as divine and human love. But in its final judgment, the novel affirms human love over all the rest, an affirmation that is revealed most specifically by the elderly Father Cyprian: "It is only now that I am close to death that I acknowledge the great kindness of my faithful friends. For years, I thought of them as second best. They could not speak to me of the spirit of God; they could not counsel me in my growing bitterness. I could not share with them the great transcendent beauty of a life of consecrated men. . . . I saw them as simple and myself as complex" (282). "I have had to learn the discipline of prosperous love,

I have had to be struck down by age and sickness to feel the great richness of the ardent, the extraordinary love I live among. I have had to
learn ordinary happiness, and from ordinary happiness, the first real
peace of my life, my life which I had wanted full of splendor" (284). As
Gordon mentioned in the broader context of a CBC interview, "there
was a subtext there, a subversive subtext—though they didn't realize
it—of women who did not play the game according to the rules that
men set down for the female body. I think there is a way in which
Catholic women do have models that are helpful, in a strange way, in
counteracting the enormous repression of a church run by celibate
males."[14] Further along in the interview, after describing herself as being
"pathologically obedient" as a child, she points out the gifts of having
"two funny parents," despite their stark differences. Then she adds, "But
my mother also had a real interest in the dailiness of life that my father
didn't have. I think that, too, was a gift to me as a writer" (Wachtel
interview, 270–71).

In the dramatic intensity of *The Company of Women,* it is easy to overlook the evidence that the women around Cyprian, excepting Muriel,
have always been capable of working out this balance, one that opts for
daily, ordinary, rather than radical, human happiness. In other words, the
cloistered circle has always masked its own contradiction, a subversive
countersystem that has developed within the system represented by
Cyprian and their submissive roles as women-in-retreat. This contrapuntal distinctiveness is its *inclusive* impulse that counteracts the more obvious exclusiveness of "radical virginities" and rigidities of minds, spirits,
and lives that fill the novel. It is precisely this inclusiveness that Cyprian
does not recognize or appreciate until the end of his life and that the
adult Felicitas finally begins to explore as she restructures a life for herself, her daughter, and the now-aging group. But the less-apparent
counterpoint has been in operation from the start of the novel; it is not a
sudden reversal or mellowing at the end. To follow it from start to finish,
we have only to begin to trace several of the women's strong capabilities
for friendship, problem-solving, business transactions, humaneness,
humor, cultural passions, and daily celebrations of life and love. Perhaps
one of the most singular examples of this occurs quietly in the painful
scene of Felicitas's telling her mother that she is pregnant. Suddenly, the
angry mother says, "We'll have to go away someplace and have it." As
Felicitas recalls, "This was the beginning of her entirely appropriate use
of the first person plural in relation to my pregnancy. Over time, she
took on all but the responsibilities it was physically impossible for me to

relinquish" (246). Elizabeth and Charlotte both retire from their jobs, and their friend Clare Leary's pragmatic wisdom, love, and financial success make it all possible: for many years, she had secretly supported Cyprian and then given him the money for his retirement home. She also had paid for Felicitas's college fees. Now, she arranges for a first-class doctor for Felicitas, she pays for a house that Cyprian will help to build for Charlotte, Elizabeth, and Felicitas in Orano, and she pays the hospital costs for Linda's birth. Remembering Clare's and the others' reactions to her pregnancy, Felicitas realizes, "They could, in the course of helping me, have insulted me, condemned me, made my misery deeper than it was. But they didn't. They stood by me and defended me. I no longer believe in looking too closely into people's motives. Kindness is a rare thing, and having been saved by it, I no longer choose to mar its luster by too close examination" (249–50).

To trace these seemingly competitive impulses of religious devotion and human love throughout *The Company of Women* is to recognize the subtle as well as overt energies represented by Gordon's working title for the novel: *Fields of Force*. Still, Gordon's final title for the novel suggests that the women's countersystem—particularly that being fashioned by Felicitas at the end of the novel and already reflected in young Linda—points to the novel's search for wholeness, what novelist and critic Margaret Drabble describes as Gordon's "reaching for . . . a way of connecting the different passages of existence" ("Limits," 31).

Certainly the novel's denouement—the 1977 monologues—explicates the ways in which Gordon's characters subordinate their individual perceptions of universal truths to the particularities of their ordinary life and love. If, as critic Susan Bolotin has suggested, Gordon's first two novels are "full of absolute judgments about what makes a life well-lived" (Bolotin interview, 232), these seven monologues anticipate the less-absolute judgments Gordon offers in her third novel *Men and Angels.* Moreover, in the concluding less-absolute context of *The Company of Women*, all the characters are, as Sally Fitzgerald notes, "except hopeless Muriel, happier than they have ever been in their lives."[15] Fitzgerald then supports her point with a quote from Charlotte's monologue: "There they are, five old women waiting for an old man to die, living in the country with a young woman and a kid. When you put it that way, it sounds pretty goddam flat. But you can always make your life sound wrong if you try to describe it in a hundred words or less" (266). The same is true, of course, of such daily human fellowship and love as Gordon and Auden ultimately privilege.

The conclusion of *The Company of Women,* delivered by Linda, epito-
mizes both that privileging and the shift toward permeability that
increasingly characterizes Gordon's voice in her later novels and novellas.
After carefully differentiating between each member of the group's varying capacities for love, and after worrying about her friends knowing her
"father was one of two people" and about her fear of the aging group's
deaths, young Linda suddenly moves toward both the ambiguity and the
women's countersystem of love: "I am running toward them. They are
standing under the apple tree. My mother picks me up and holds me in
her arms. My grandmother is laughing. My mother lifts me up into the
leaves. We are not dying" (291).

Through Linda's final words, Gordon shows us how it's done, what a
novel's conclusion can do: the character's radiant embrace of love and
ambiguity plus the reader's recognition equals a lowercased incarnation,
that "scandal of the particular," brought to life. This is the novel's high
achievement.

Final Payments and *The Company of Women*
Within the Tradition of Religious Fiction

In a 1980 interview, Gordon was asked to define the religious novel.
Before she could answer, the interviewer went on to describe the theolo-
gian Paul Tillich's defining *religious* in terms of honesty and concern and
his suggesting a Cezanne Postimpressionist painting of a rock was more
religious than a German painter's sentimental depiction of Christ on the
cross. Mary Gordon's forthright response struck directly at the core of
much contemporary confusion: "I think it's nonsense because it devalues
both the religious experience and the experience of Cezanne. All beauty
is not religious in its nature, and all aesthetic or heartfelt responses are
not religious, and I don't like that kind of sloppiness." With those critical demarcations in place, Gordon moved to a definition: "For me the
religious novel would be something which had a relationship to God at
the center of it. No, I don't think swimming in the ocean is as religious
an act as contemplative prayer, which is not to say that one is more valuable than the other. If you call everything religious, then nothing is religious" (Cooper-Clark interview, 270).

Gordon's answer gives us a freeze-framed glimpse of her logic and her
ability to articulate the differences between a religious experience and a
work of art that reflects, in varying degrees, a religious subject,
metaphor, or iconography. Both characteristics are a part of what has

made her novels and essays so intriguing to American and European readers and critics. Both characteristics are also decisive components in the ways in which her first two novels (as well as several early essays) helped to generate new dialogues about spirituality and metaphoric and sociological components of that spirituality within the North American literary mainstream, in general, and the novel genre, in particular.

Such clarity, however, has never precluded Gordon's nuanced attention to the ways in which differentiations between art and religious experiences might, at times, overlap. In 1985, for example, Gordon pointed out three essential conditions for a "properly religious" experience and then set them alongside art: "an ethical component, the possibility of full participation by the entire community, and acknowledgment of the existence of a life beyond the human. Art need do none of these things, although it may" ("Getting Here," 49). By and large, however, contemporary cultures, with their religious divisivenesses and confusions and their novelistic expectations, are not equipped to follow these kinds of nuances to their logical conclusions. As a result, novelists such as Salman Rushdie and Gordon, in vastly different arenas, have found themselves and their creativity caught in the throes of our "sloppinesses," our metaphysical, intellectual, and aesthetic confusions. Having to clarify these was never a role Gordon envisioned as she wrote her first novel. But even before *The Company of Women* was published and took its place alongside *Final Payments,* Gordon found herself being singled out and simultaneously marginalized as the hot, new "Catholic novelist" and spokesperson for what can only be described as the subliterary, parochial, "religious novel" tradition in North America. In order to understand the critical and cultural contexts that surrounded her first two novels, perhaps it would be helpful to review briefly the evolution of American Catholicism and the "religious novel" tradition it spawned here.

Catholicism in North America began as an immigrant church that offered to waves of immigrants and their progeny a shared language and ritual of worship and thus, some semblance of continuity, order, and "place" within a familiar hierarchy. Moreover, the parish, in its role as a neighborhood's religious and social focus, fostered a strong sense of identity and belonging. Such advantages also fostered insularity. As Mary Gordon has mentioned often, until she enrolled at Barnard College, she knew only a few non-Catholics, who were merchants or professionals in her community. Such parochial insularity was never one-sided. Established populations (including well-established minority, immigrant groups) habitually, perhaps chronically, have resented and feared mass immigrations. Moreover, non-Catholics often viewed with particular suspicion and prejudice Catholics' large families, their Latin Mass, their personal and ecclesial European connections, their Church's hierarchy and its priests and nuns. These suspicions were intensified by the Catholic Church's rigid policies regarding its members marrying non-Catholics, divorce, and birth control. Such suspicions and resentments (on both sides) spawned certain invisible ceilings for Catholics, despite the North American Catholic Church's strong endorsement of education and prosperity for its followers. Few of those first- and second-generation Catholic immigrants with initiative, expertise, and/or education achieved financial and professional parity with their successful, non-Catholic counterparts. For example, the historian Thomas J. Archdeacon has pointed out that before World War II, "if you [a Catholic] were a doctor, you were not associated with the most prestigious hospitals. If you were a lawyer, you were not with the most prestigious law firms."[16] Of course, if you were a politician, you could be a party boss, but you could not— until John F. Kennedy's election in 1960—be the President of the United States. As Gordon in *Final Payments* has Isabel notice, while passing through a Catholic neighborhood enroute to Margaret's drab home, "The houses of servants. Frightened of grandeur, frightened of the banker around the corner. And they were right to be frightened; they were right to build their small, unimportant houses, risking very little in design" (253).

Much of this, including Catholic insularity, was transformed by World War II and, especially, by the G. I. Bill. David C. Leege, director of Notre Dame's massive study of American parish life, suggests that "The G. I. Bill may have had more of an impact on the Catholic Church than the Second Vatican Council" in the early 1960s ("Being Catholic," 64). Two generations of American men who had served and then studied together—and their wives, many of whom had worked or also served together during the war—moved out on more equal terms and mutual trust into the American mainstream; many of them also moved from their old neighborhoods, parishes, towns, and identities to live as neighbors in the new suburban communities that were springing up across the nation. Of course, problems of class and advantages did not disappear. As Gordon has pointed out, "Working-class parents bring up children to think the world is a dangerous place and 'they'll get you.' . . . The middle and upper classes assume that the world is theirs and they should go out and take it. . . .Who are working-class kids going to talk to? Are they going to ask their mother who works in K mart how to write a jazzy application that will get them into Amherst?" ("Growing up Catholic," 74).

Despite such continuing disparities, the post–World War II educational and suburban integrations of Catholics and non-Catholics mark an important sociological stage in the breakdown of Catholic insularity and non-Catholics' prejudice. Within a decade, the decisions implemented after the Second Vatican Council also would set into motion the final shattering of such insularity as well as the universal Latin Mass and many of the mysteries, traditions, and musical treasures surrounding that ancient ritual. In 1987, Joseph Berger was puzzled by Mary Gordon's still thinking about "the loss of fictive material that may result from the homogenization of Catholics." He goes on to quote Gordon as saying, "Nobody wants to write about yuppies. It's much more interesting to write about a closed, slightly secret, marginal group" ("Being Catholic," 65)—comments that come as no surprise to the readers of her first two novels, which address radical love, devotion, and sacrifices within surviving anomalies of this parochial insularity during the 1960s and 1970s.

Her working across these paradigmatic shifts in Catholicism was, in fact, one of the things that made Gordon's first two novels so timely. Moreover, as novelist and critic Wilfrid Sheed pointed out about her first novel, "Mary Gordon's *Final Payments* is much more than the latest thing in Catholic novels . . . it does show brilliantly the effects of the new dispensation on American Catholic fiction. It gives a picture of certain Catholic lives . . . more ambiguous than anything either a loyalist or a heretic would have had mind to produce a few years ago. In the European manner, the Church is seen not as a good place or a bad place, with batteries of the best lawyers to prove both at once, but as a multilayered poem or vision which dominates your life equally whether you believe it or not: which doesn't even seem to need your belief once it has made its point" ("Defector's," 14). Thus, before a secret world within that "multilayered poem or vision" had disappeared completely, Gordon opened up and explicated (for Catholics and non-Catholics alike) both the struggle within the new integration into the American mainstream and the pain inherent in relinquishing an unusual, radical innocence that insular world had nurtured and the outside word had demanded. In other words, these major shifts in American Catholicism also had masked the beginning of the breakdown of the American Catholic culture's role as last defender of the stubborn American myth of its nation's and citizens' innocence.

"American innocence" (frequently and nostalgically linked to such cultural rituals as baseball, parades, high school bands, and children's birthday parties) is a label intellectuals have assigned to this idealization phenomenon. And any reader who has seen such 1940s and 1950s films as *The Bells of St. Mary's, Joan of Arc, Going My Way,* and more recently, *Sister Act* (with Whoopi Goldberg), knows how this cultural expectation works. Anita Gandolfo, in her fine study on the new Catholic fiction in America, addresses Catholicism in her definition of "American innocence" as "a structure of values in the American culture that corresponded closely with the dominant Roman Catholic *weltanschauung* [world view]: belief in a rational cosmos and an objective moral order in nature, confidence in progress, and a preference for didacticism in art forms, especially in literature" (*Testing the Faith,* 2).

For the purposes of differentiating Gordon's work from the "religious novel" tradition in America, Gandolfo is particularly helpful in establishing the links between American innocence fantasies, the American (immigrant) Catholic Church's "strong devotional life that represented an entire religious heritage" (7), and the didactic requirements of the subliterary "religious novel." That Gordon, from childhood, seems to have been aware of and interested in such linkings is apparent. She has spoken often about the religious tracts (including one on the Trinity and another entitled "What Is Prayer?") she wrote as a young girl as well as about reading stories about the lives of women saints, and of her pious acts of trying to wear thorns in her shoes and reprimanding neighborhood merchants who sold girlie magazines. Nevertheless, her first two novels make clear her antipathy to the didactic, sentimental, tacky, and anti-intellectual aspects within Catholic devotional literature and accoutrements. In *Final Payments,* for instance, the thirteen-year-old Isabel's hatred of Margaret is symbolized by the housekeeper's little prayer books: "Perpetual Novenas, Devotions to St. Anthony, St. Jude, The Little Flower" (31). At the same time, Margaret's subliterary devotional tastes support Isabel's feelings of superiority, since Isabel, like her father, uses only the Latin missal for her own devotional life. Much later in the novel, Isabel's antipathy to all their former housekeeper represents is embodied in Margaret's Lourdes 1968-calendar dish towel, pious plaque, elaborate evening recitations of the rosary, and in her love of simplistic romances and dislike of *Jane Eyre.*

Gordon continues this kind of literary and iconic differentiation in *The Company of Women.* When young Felicitas is hospitalized, for example, Father Cyprian and the circle of women all bring her things to read. The bitter-spirited Muriel Fisher, typically choosing the wrong thing for Felicitas, gives her three pamphlets: "So You Think It's All Right to Go Steady," "TV for Teens," and "St. Peggy of the Tennis Court." After plowing through the latter, Felicitas "knows one thing, that Peggy was the kind of girl who made her puke. She would rather be herself than Peggy. Even if it meant she couldn't be a saint" (62). Cyprian's gift, a book about women saints entitled *Quartet in Heaven,* also leaves her cold: "she thought she would go mad if she read one more word about picking up straight pins in silence for the love of God. And she had promised herself that she would not read any more about Latin Americans who had visions" (63). Only Elizabeth's gift pleases Felicitas; *Pride and Prejudice,* she discovers, is "the book she wanted most to live in" (65). Elizabeth Bennet is the person she wants to emulate.

In such novelistic steps, Gordon makes clear her attitude toward the anti-intellectualism that has been a traditional component in American Catholic literature, a stance stringently underscored in Irish Catholicism in America by what Gordon views as central aspects of the Irish character: sexual puritanism, fear of exposure, and self-protection through concealment and silence—characteristics Gordon learned about firsthand. For example, within her familial circle, she has had to face disapproval, precisely because of her mainstream literary achievements. As Gordon has described it, at a beloved uncle's funeral in the late 1980s, another uncle told her, "I just want to tell you I can't stand your books. None of us can. I tried the first one, I couldn't get past the first chapter. The second one I couldn't even get into; I didn't even want to open it up. I didn't even buy it; I wouldn't waste my money." The most honored person in the family, a cousin who is a nun, said, "Mary, I just think your books are dreadful. . . . They're just too worldly for me" and later told one of Gordon's aunts, "She didn't really want to put all that sex in those books. The publishers made her."[17] Elsewhere, Gordon has pointed out that the Irish-Catholic world of her childhood and youth discouraged questioning and independent thought: It "might get you out of the neighborhood and you might never come back again" ("Being Catholic," 64). One result of such attitudes, as Gordon has recognized and discussed at length, is a conspicuously small contribution to American literature. She suggests, "It would make good sense to teach a course in the American Jewish Literary Experience, or in American Black Literature. But a course in American Irish Literature would take up barely half a semester." Outlining a tentative course syllabus for the latter, she starts a little list, full of qualifications, and finally comes to William Alfred, Elizabeth Cullinana, Maureen Howard, and William Kennedy; then she admits, "After that, there would be nowhere to go" ("Can't Stand," 203).

Such comments and her first two novels have helped expose this Irish immigrant literary phenomenon, as well as the gap between an artist's free inquiry and the paucity of traditional, North American "religious novels" and devotional subliteratures. Nonetheless, the fact that Catholics and non-Catholics alike continue to marginalize Gordon as a "Catholic novelist" suggests that her audiences retain a residual critical murkiness about her novelistic treatments of Catholicism and her place within the tradition of the novel genre. Some critics have no such problem; for example, while citing the ways in which Gordon has given "everyday shape" to eschatological concerns, Frances Taliaferro recognizes that "*Final Payments* is a Catholic novel in the same way that *A Portrait of the Artist* is a Catholic novel, which is to say both completely and not at all" ("Final," 84). And other critics demonstrate an easy familiarity with the generations of twentieth-century novelists who have wrenched the "Catholic novel" away from its subliterary forebears; the opening of Doris Grumbach's review, "Two Catholic Firsts," is a case in point: "Books in the tradition of what we sometimes call 'the Catholic novel' are relatively few. The designation refers to fiction that either is written by authors who happen to be born Roman Catholic but whose scope is outside the tradition (Flannery O'Connor, Mary McCarthy) or is Catholic in subject matter (works by such authors as J. F. Powers and Edwin O'Connor)."[18]

Still, for the general readership and critics alike, any attempt to place Gordon in either category is also something of a murky operation, a small percentage of which may have been created by Gordon's own comments. One such example might be Gordon's explaining that *Final Payments* is not "a religious novel in the way that one of Mauriac's would be, or one of Bernanos's, but I think that Isabel is searching, trying to come to terms with her religious life. I would not say that her path of self-identification is a religious path, but in that she is so formed by religion and really sees everything in metaphors of Catholicism so much, I think it is" (Cooper-Clark interview, 270–71). And certainly, some confusions have been augmented by her religion-related essays, reviews, and forthright newspaper comments (all of which are discussed in chapter seven). For example, during a North American visit by Pope John Paul II, for instance, Gordon declared in the *New York Times,* "I think a

Pope could make a difference in the moral life of America, but not this Pope. . . . I think he thinks we Americans are all Protestants in disguise, all fat cats and self-indulgent children, and that it is his job to play the father. . . . Like Ronald Reagan, he could have had a career as a B actor. . . . It seems to me we have the same papacy as we have a presidency. It's all for the media."[19] Precisely because of her candor and because Gordon gives herself the freedom to address whatever subject interests her deeply, it remains helpful to keep reminding ourselves that she does not think of herself as a "Catholic novelist." In a wry comment during a 1993 interview, Gordon suggested, "When they start calling John Updike a 'white, male Protestant writer,' they can call me a 'Catholic writer.' The norm is still male and Protestant; anything else is considered remarkable" ("Gordon Wants," E10). The analogy is convincing; perhaps it is time for a moratorium on scholarly and critical uses of the term "Catholic novelist." At the very least, well-informed qualifications and contexts should surround its use.

More recently, when asked about this labeling problem and how she would describe herself, Gordon has pointed out, "I think it's kind of like what Sartre says about being a Jew: that you're a Jew if somebody calls you one. And so a lot of the time you have a label if people give it to you often enough. But what kind of label would be internally created by myself? (long pause) I think gender is important to me. . . . I think . . . because I'm still read in a gendered way that, in all honesty, I have to call myself a 'woman writer.' I won't call myself 'a Catholic writer.' That's too limiting. I just won't do it because it makes me sound like this Graham Greene, Evelyn Waugh, Flannery O'Connor . . . I feel no affinity. I don't feel that was how I was formed. But I do think I was formed as a writer by my femaleness" (Bennett interview, 33). This self-assessment clearly informs her third novel, *Men and Angels*.

Chapter Four

the art of dangerous limits:
Men and Angels

Men and Angels,[1] published in 1985, reflects a kind of seismic shift in Mary Gordon's techniques and purposes. One of these changes is established in Laura Post's chilling opening monologue in the novel: Gordon has shifted away from a Catholic context. Discussing Laura's twisted fundamentalism, Gordon has explained: "I was interested in the perversion of the religious impulse, because I had used the religious impulse differently in other books" (Keyishian interview, 71). Then when we begin to read the words of Anne Foster in the novel's second chapter, we discover in Selby, a New England college town, a completely nonreligious, second female protagonist, an art historian, who will lead the novel's explication of "the failure of love" which, Gordon has pointed out, "is certainly a religious theme" (Bolotin interview, 232).

The novel opens with a pending entrance: Laura Post's transatlantic flight from England to the United States and her vague expectations of finding a new job as an *au pair* in her home country. The next chapter explains an exit: Anne Foster's husband Michael has left Selby to begin a sabbatical year in Europe. During this year Anne has opted to remain at home with their two young children in order to complete an important exhibition monograph on Caroline Watson, a deceased, *fin de siècle,* American-born woman painter. Thus the novel focuses on Anne, her obsessive devotion to their children, her research (and Caroline Watson), and Laura Post, an unattractive, young religious fanatic who (despite Anne's instinctive reservations but because of her inherent charity) becomes the children's *au pair.* From the start, Anne feels that Laura's presence is somehow a threat to her and her children's happiness; in light of Laura's secret mission to persuade them of the meaninglessness of human love, Anne's nebulous fears are well grounded. Still, because she recognizes Laura's neediness, Anne's growing resentment makes her question her own goodness. Laura, on the other hand, is blind to Anne's struggles and sees in her a surrogate, loving mother. When Laura's negligence almost kills the two children, Anne fires her; Laura responds by committing suicide in the Fosters' home to show Anne how much she loves her. Their colliding obsessions thus end not just in "the failure of love" but also in death and the permanent alteration of Anne's, Michael's, and their children's "safe" lives. Gordon then adds a somber epilogue that documents Anne's hard-earned wisdom about the whole of life.

As in her first two novels, Gordon moves the story from an enclosed world to an opened world, then to two irrevocable closures that necessitate a risk-filled reopening. Likewise, the novel is filled with radical love and rejection. However, *Men and Angels* reflects Gordon's most powerful study of *caritas* (self-sacrificing love, or charity), which is the novel's overriding obsession.

Evolving Innovations

Despite Gordon's seemingly abrupt departure from a Catholic focus in her third novel, her readers have been prepared for this and other innovations in "Part Three: 1977" of *The Company of Women*. First of all, that section endorses a definition of love in terms of everyday exchanges that counter those more exclusive, abstracted theological standards that presumably have governed the group's history. The same movement from exclusiveness to inclusiveness is reflected in *Final Payments*. Gordon's third novel, however, intensifies this movement by alternating inclusive and exclusive patterns and interpretations of love.

Second, the third-person narration of *The Company of Women* is replaced in that novel's final section by a sequence of seven characters' first-person monologues. Thus, it is less surprising when Gordon decides to alternate third-person voices—those of Anne Foster and Laura Post (and by her journals and letters, Caroline Watson)—throughout the twelve chapters of *Men and Angels*. The alternations control the pace of the novel, while Gordon's fastidious crafting of each chapter's opening and closing paragraphs emphasizes the unique nature of each protagonist's character and language.

A number of scholars and critics have pointed out that the voices mirror each other in important ways.[2] Interestingly enough, Gordon's treatments of the Laura-Anne voices resemble the Baroque contrapuntal devices of Johann Sebastian Bach's so-called mirror fugues. For instance, the thematic melody and note intervals of the first fugue are duplicated in the second fugue. However, everything in the second is inverted; every note and interval moves in exactly the opposite, or contrary, direction. In other words, the second mirrors the first. This sounds like a complicated analogy for Gordon's techniques until one notices, for example, that in the first two chapters of *Men and Angels,* Laura's intense rejection of familial love and her expectations of charity (chapter one) are mirrored in Anne's intense endorsements of familial love and her worries about charity and goodness (chapter two). Another mirroring in those same two chapters is seen, respectively, in Laura's obsessive devotion to the Spirit and Anne's obsessive devotion to her children. With these "contrary" obsessions, both somewhat self-deluding, Gordon puts into conflicting motion the novel's prototypical voices of "angels" (spiritual preoccupations) and "men" (human preoccupations).

A related mirroring device that musicians call "contrary motion" is suggested when Gordon, in the subsequent chapters, has two voices (such as Anne's and Laura's or Anne's and Caroline's) *simultaneously* addressing the same problem or subject. The voices, just as the two hands of a pianist, begin to play the same theme, but they move in opposite, or "contrary," directions. However one explains them, the mirroring motions of these voices are conspicuous, especially in the case of Anne and Laura, whose "mutual struggle," as John Costello describes it, "allows each one to assume simultaneously the guise of 'monster of persecution' and 'angel of self-sacrifice.'"[3] And with the addition of Caroline's tertiary voice (which, like that of Laura, moves across the novel intrinsically connected to that of Anne), Gordon has the means in hand by which the novel's structure, plot, and themes are driven.

A fourth innovation in *Men and Angels* is hinted at in Part III of Gordon's second novel. There, Felicitas's preoccupations with her young daughter Linda and the now-aging group around them prepare us somewhat for the maternal preoccupations in the third novel. By this point in Gordon's career, her readers and critics had come to expect her intense explications of small enclosed groups, particularly those within Catholicism. Nevertheless, perhaps because of the dominant father figures in her prior novels, Gordon's decision to expand maternal preoccupations into obsessions in this novel came as something of a surprise. To a number of critics, this was not a welcome surprise; as one woman writer suggested with particular viciousness, "Women will never be free until Mary Gordon's picture appears on a milk carton."[4] Others continue to disagree. For example, Judie Newman, in an important essay on Mary Gordon and Alison Lurie, insists: "Because women are not mirrored in culture in ways that provide us with adequate self-definition, the creation of full-blooded, substantial identities and strong female representations remains an important project for the woman writer."[5]

One of the most interesting aspects of the novel's focus on motherhood is Gordon's continued circumvention of the subject conventions observed by most contemporary novelists of her rank. First, it was Catholicism, now, motherhood. Furthermore, her development of these choices remains detached from postmodernism, which, according to Judie Newman, "has tended to offer only games for the boys" ("Telling," 172). That both were carefully scouted-out choices is documented in interviews and essays. Concerning *Men and Angels,* for example, Gordon explained soon after the novel's 1985 publication, "I looked around in literature to try to find models for that kind of [maternal] passion—not intellectual, not moral, but just these bodies [children's]. . . . We love the way they look, the way they feel, the way they smell. The feeling is certainly as genuine as sexual passion and it can be obsessive and it can be misused."[6] That same year, feminist scholar Susan Rubin Suleiman, as she describes it, "went to hear Mary Gordon talk about the book and read excerpts from it at the Boston Public Library. 'Who has written seriously about the inner world of mothers?' she asked, uncannily echoing a question by Julie Kristeva that I had used as an epigraph for 'Writing and Motherhood': 'Que savons-nous du discours que (se) fait une mere?' (What do we know about the [inner] discourse of a mother?)."[7]

Four years later, Gordon admitted, "To write about women and children is to be immediately ghettoized, unless you're talking about women, children, and sex, and the way that children interfere with sex for women. . . . if you really are talking about women and children and you take a man out of the central focus, you're really ghettoized. They think you're writing for *Ladies Home Journal*" (Keyishian interview, 71). Gordon goes on to suggest such reactions are basically due to people's fears about the potency and demands of motherhood. This suggestion, in turn, confirms my premise that Gordon is attracted to subjects, such as religion and motherhood, that not only threaten us with their demands and power, but that also challenge the subjects of traditional and experimental novels alike. Whether or not such a premise is valid, it is apparent that nothing, not even possibilities of being marginalized as a writer, gets in the way of Gordon's pursuit of subjects that fascinate her. It is also clear that *Men and Angels* brings together motherhood and religion in unsettling ways that demonstrate Gordon's art of dangerous limits.

The testing of those limits is most conspicuous in the lives of
Gordon's main female protagonists, Anne Foster and Laura Post. That
there will be a collision of obsessions is evident from the start. In the
opening pages of the novel, Laura Post's silent prophecies follow the pattern of Gordon's carefully crafted introductions. The opening of *Men and
Angels,* however, has more dramatic weight than its more thematic predecessors. The reader senses immediate danger in Laura's bizarre interpretations of Biblical injunctions and divine love. How she begins to act
out these misunderstandings within the Fosters' home sets into motion
the dramatic crisis of the novel, one that Laura attempts to resolve with
a razor blade. Her suicide, in turn, actualizes the novel's fundamental
premise: human love (especially maternal love) means everything, rather
than nothing (as Laura had prophesied). Those who deny this—even
because of other, worthwhile priorities, even because "the Other" is
inherently unlovable, repulsive, or an intrusion—do so at their own and
others' grave peril. The *Doppelgänger* of this premise is seen in the perilous exclusivity by which other characters offer or seek maternal love.

In this inquiry, Gordon goes beyond the "sounding brass or a tinkling
cymbal" warning in the novel's New Testament epigraph, taken from
Paul's first letter to the Corinthians. She does expose shallow failures
within the words and gestures of her characters—these "men [and
women] and angels," whose pairing one might interpret as secular and
sacred or all too human and spiritual. But such failures, Gordon's novel
points out, can lead to death. She does not let us skirt this: unlike the
deaths that characteristically occur offstage in Gordon's novels, Laura's
suicide at the end of the novel is graphically center stage. To guarantee
that we do not try to rationalize this away, Laura's death has already
been prefigured by what Anne's research has revealed: the self-destructive death of another rejected child, Stephen, son of Caroline Watson and
husband of Jane, who drinks himself to death at the age of 28.

In hindsight, we recognize another of the novel's innovations: such
tragedies seem to be prefigured in the Vuillard painting (*Woman in a
Striped Dress*) featured on the novel's book jacket.[8] In the painting's fore-
ground, a pretty, young, well-dressed, red-headed woman stares down at
a vase of flowers; directly to her left, an auburn-haired, larger, far less
handsome, and plainly dressed woman (unacknowledged in the painting's title) stares down more vacantly and with less certainty into separate preoccupations. Just how astutely the Vuillard painting was chosen
is apparent when we reread sentences that first describe Anne's worried
awareness that people thought she was good because of "her white skin

and blue eyes . . . her light, straight reddish hair," and small-bosomed figure (10) and then describe Laura's "light blue watery eyes," thick glasses that cloud her eyes, her Ingres-like opulent skin, "too heavy, too carefully darned sweater," missionary-type sandals, and puritanically clipped, thick red hair (13, 15).

As one reads further, we recognize that Gordon has given *Woman in a Striped Dress,* by her favorite artist, a more specific role within the novel. When Anne Foster meets the deceased Caroline Watson's beloved daughter-in-law Jane, she learns that Jane was the chestnut-haired model of Watson's painting entitled *The Striped Dress.* Anne then realizes that the second chestnut-haired figure in the background is Watson herself. In other words, Gordon uses art with great subtlety to underscore the novel's pairings of love and rejection that lead to deaths.

To the advantage of her readers, Gordon has accounted for the germination of the novel in several interviews. Soon after the novel was published, Gordon had to address questions about her shift away from Catholic contexts. She insisted, "It isn't that I thought, 'Enough of that Catholic stuff.' The idea for this novel came to me."[9] Ten years later, Gordon has talked more expansively than in previous accounts about the accidental ways things came together in her imagination for this novel: her love of looking at paintings, her fantasy about what would happen if one of her former woman students at Amherst—an unlovable, poor, and psychologically needy person—collided with another much more fortunate woman she had known at Amherst. Gordon's imagination went on, she recalls, to associate this fortunate woman with the face of another woman who happened to be an art historian. In her typically forthright style, Gordon has insisted, "So it wasn't any extremely well-thought-out theory. But I thought it would be fun because I love paintings. I have less artistic talent than anyone who ever lived. And I thought, 'Well, these will be my paintings.' And I also love learning things, so it was fun to learn more about art history" (Bennett interview, 26).

The result of Gordon's research and the advice of Linda Nochlin and Alexander Martin[10] is the character Caroline Watson, a fictional, *fin de siècle* woman painter, a composite Gordon created from the lives, careers, letters, and journals of painters Cecilia Beaux, Mary Cassatt, Suzanne Valadon, and Paula Modersohn-Becker. The deceased Caroline Watson, in turn, becomes the focus of the protagonist Anne Foster's research. And Caroline's conflicted career and motherhood parallel the novel's examination of contemporary women's similar dilemmas. But as has been suggested earlier, Gordon's novelistic strategies further complicate this examination by linking it to more fundamental moral inquiries.

By the end of chapter two, we already recognize one of these questions: can and must one love the unlikable, the unlovable? As Gordon has pointed out in describing the factors that led to her characters Laura (the unfortunate young woman) and Anne (the fortunate, beloved woman), "the first thing that got me was (in a way it was still a religious thing) if you followed what Christ said to do literally, it would be completely unlivable" (Bennett interview, 26). Gordon's novelistic preoccupation with this problem is not a new one. In the climax of *Final Payments,* for instance, Isabel unsuccessfully tries to resolve just this when she moves into the home of Margaret, whom she despises. The new spin Gordon adds to her third novel is in having her female characters address this dilemma either with no theological orientation whatsoever or with a twisted, antilife mutation of Christianity. On the one hand, Anne Foster demonstrates a completely secular struggle with charity, or love, which presumably Gordon is considering in the New Testament sense of *agape.* For example, in the midst of resentfully making a birthday cake for Laura, who has lied to the children about her birthday, Anne Foster admits to herself, "she didn't like Laura. Liking—you couldn't will it: it wasn't a quality like courage or fair-mindedness that you could work for. And things could only get worse" (111). For Laura Post, on the other hand, charitable love is a means to an end, the means by which she can gain access to children and adults; it is also her "wise as serpents and innocent as doves" strategy by which she tries to cultivate people's love and then lead them to distrust human love and to trust only "the word of the Lord," "the Word of Love" (9).

"such a strange thing, motherhood"

Gordon pushes the dilemma of selfless love still further when she links it to motherhood. The questions boil up in the novel's text: what about those mothers (such as Caroline Watson, and Laura's and Anne's mothers) who do not, seemingly cannot, like their own child? Conversely, what about those adults (such as Caroline Watson, Jane, Laura, and Anne) who do not and cannot like their own mothers? The questions continue to emerge. For instance, Gordon's depictions of the artist Caroline Watson (who gave birth at the age of thirty-six to an illegitimate son, Stephen) and Mrs. Post (who was seventeen when her daughter Laura was born) ask what quality of maternal love can be expected from a woman who gives birth to an unwanted child whose presence she continues to resent profoundly? As the crude Mrs. Post expressed it, "She [Laura] never meant anything to me, not from the minute I saw her. She was always ugly. She was never happy. She tried to make me miserable" (227). The deathbed journal entry of the eminently more sophisticated Caroline Watson admitted, "I left my son to wither. I knew what he needed: warmth and care, and moist rich soil. And I left him in a stony place, a leafless place. He died still a boy" (199). Both mothers' children, we notice, self-destruct in their twenties.

Like Mrs. Post's, Caroline Watson's rejection of her unwanted child is severe and unrelenting. Such intentional maternal cruelty is unfathomable to Anne. As she works on the monograph for a retrospective exhibit of Watson's paintings, Anne wonders if Caroline's mistreatment of Stephen reflected "some deficiency of spirit, some inexcusable coldness at the center" (100). Novelist Margaret Drabble has convincingly pointed out that the contrasts between these two mothers create, in effect, a Bad Mother (Caroline) and Good Mother (Anne) scenario ("Limits," 1). Certainly in stark contrast to Caroline Watson's reactions, Anne views a mother's love as something instinctive, natural: "How primitive it was, this love of children: flesh and flesh, bone, blood connection" (100).

In studying Caroline's life, however, Anne Foster keeps running into a closely related knot of questions about a woman's privileging a career over parenthood as well as society's privileging a woman's maternal responsibilities over her professional work or capabilities—what feminist scholar Susan Rubin Suleiman has discussed in terms of the "maternal splitting" that Gordon explores within *Men and Angels.*[11] An unusual conjunction of the split is articulated by Anne's jealous sister, Beth, during a gathering at their parents' home. Mocking Anne's attempt to bridge this splitting, Beth says privately to Laura Post, "I suppose my sister's quite the taskmaster with her Mrs. Dalloway fantasy that you have to bring to life. Only, now she thinks she's Mrs. Dalloway and Virginia Woolf rolled into one. Very handy, with you to pick up the pieces" (151).

Anne, for her part, is trying to comes to terms with this dilemma for women artists, scholars, and professionals of any ilk; only now has she had the courage to pursue her own scholarly work instead of, for instance, accompanying Michael during his sabbatical year in France. She recognizes that motherhood (especially outside marriage) was even more problematic in Caroline Watson's hard-won life and career during the Parisian *fin de siècle,* a period in which no one thought of condemning a male painter's neglect of his children. Even more subtle but undeniable was Caroline's own awareness that in choosing to paint women and children—a choice Gordon modeled on Mary Cassatt and other women artists of the period—her work was not getting either the attention or respect that her male artists-contemporaries' more prosaic or revolutionary subjects were being awarded.

Michiko Kakutani, in the midst of praising *Men and Angels* as "a novel that marks a new turn in Miss Gordon's brilliant career," mentions a "minor quibble," the overt agenda in Gordon's amplification of such problems; Kakutani suggests that "Gordon's insistence on giving a feminist reading to everything from sex appeal to artistic achievement (Nobody cares, complains one character, 'if Monet was a bad father') becomes tiresome at times."[12] Kakutani's point may be valid. Still, we recognize in our own *fin de siècle* that the problems Gordon raises remain: a professional woman who maintains a demanding career may have difficulty in getting custody of her children in a divorce; a professional woman who wants and has children may be more frequently passed over for the highest administrative positions; and any woman writer, artist, scholar, schoolteacher, professor, or the like, whose work focuses on children or motherhood or women will not garner the same level of immediate respect that one automatically gives to other preoccupations. The catalog is a long one.

All this notwithstanding, Gordon's character Anne Foster cannot come to terms with Caroline's neglect of young Stephen, whom she left at her parents' home. Caroline's journal entries show that she resented her annual summer visits to the United States, presumably for Stephen's sake, as much as she resented her child. On this, Caroline was brutally honest: "I cannot love. I cannot paint. . . . I too despise my son for his slowness, his misery. My son. I know where he is. He sits outside my door, waiting for me to finish. I can hear his breath through walls a foot thick. His breath steals mine and blinds me. . . . Sitting out there, covered over with unhappiness, waiting only for the word, the touch I cannot give him . . . " (122). For both Caroline and Stephen then, there was no bridge between their respective needs; as Anne expresses the dilemma within this mother's professional drives and her child's personal yearnings, "There was no connection between art and life" (123).

That Gordon, herself an intensely doting young mother with a daughter, lost a second child while writing this novel about women's careers and maternal obsessions and neglect adds poignancy to the

novel's preoccupations (Bennett interview, 25). Yet she had begun the
novel in 1980 before her daughter was born, and completed it just
before her son was born in 1983.[13] Such personal details aside, Gordon
admitted in 1985 that this novel was more difficult to write than her
first two because "the metaphors, the private language, weren't at hand.
There'd been an advantage in writing about a closed society: you could
simply lay out information that was interesting to outsiders and absorb-
ing to those who belonged to it. . . . I didn't have the luxury of a small
world" ("Ah," 75).

One might argue that in *Men and Angels* Gordon continues the
process in the closed-world constructs fashioned, for varying purposes,
by Anne, Laura, and Caroline Watson. In lieu of a singular, enclosed
Catholic venue, Gordon opens up at least five enclosures: motherhood,
family units, careers, an artist's life, and Christian fundamentalism. And
regardless of whether readers consider themselves outsiders or insiders to
any or all of these, Gordon's enclosed treatments create dramatic pressure on readers to rethink each. Her choices of these particular intimate
enclosures reflect, on a more general level, one of Gordon's novelistic
goals. As she has explained, "The tendency of the novel is to get more
abstract and removed and cold, and we [contemporary women novelists]
are fighting that, on the whole" (Bolotin interview, 234). Thus her handling in *Men and Angels* of a number of private systems reflects both this
fight as well as her maturation during the seven years since her first
novel. The same dual reflections are seen in her intertwining multiple
enclosed worlds through an explication of motherhood and mother love,
which become metaphors for Gordon's overarching explication of the
power and powerlessness of love.

Compensatory Constructs

Gordon uses failed motherhoods and flawed parenting in *Men and Angels*
to establish links between Anne and other characters: her scholar husband Michael; their children's *au pair* Laura; the late artist Caroline
Watson; Caroline's son Stephen and daughter-in-law Jane; and the elec-
trician Ed Corcoran.

In the absence of adequate role models, these characters attempt, like
Isabel in *Final Payments* and Felicitas in *The Company of Women,* to "invent
an existence" for themselves within real or surrogate familial constructs.
In *Men and Angels,* Gordon occasionally allows the inadequate nurturers
themselves to voice an awareness of the ways the phenomenon works;

Anne Foster's mother is one such commentator when she admits to
Laura Post her lack of talent for and her boredom with motherhood.
Commenting on how much more domestic and maternal both her
daughters are, she then adds, "I guess every generation of daughters has
to reinvent family life" (150).

Usually, however, the "inventive" characters are the main spokespersons. Anne, for example, thinks about how dysfunctional her mother
and her husband Michael's mother were. Anne is aware of the role those
failed parentings play in her and Michael's marriage. She muses about
the secret bond between herself and Michael: "they had both been, as
children, mothers, both involved in the conspiracy at the center of their
lives as children of deficient parents, the conspiracy to keep from the
world this shame, this failure. . . . They had married early because they
wanted to reinvent domestic life. It was a romance dear to both of them"
(21). Later, when thinking about how wonderful Michael is as a father,
Anne wonders if Michael's never having known his father (who deserted
his wife and infant son) was actually an advantage; in other words, without an injurious father model, Michael could compensate for the
unknown with his own invention and demonstration of an idealized role
(44). Anne herself, reveling in their two children, thinks that motherhood "wasn't a skill: there was no past practice to be consulted and perfected. . . . there was no wisdom you turn to; every history was inadequate, for each new case was fresh—each new case was a person born,
she was sure of it, with a nature more fixed than modern thought led
people to believe" (17). She consequently treasures her children's individuality, bodies, voices, minds, and personalities. But masked within
Anne's mother-love and disclaimer of any need for a nurturing maternal
role model is an intense compensatory reaction to her mother's unsupportive precedent: Anne is obsessed with her children's safety. "The
whole shape of her life," she reminds herself, "must be constructed to
make her children safe" (132). Thus, when their *au pair* absentmindedly
jeopardizes young Peter and Sarah's lives, Anne's obsession implodes
around Laura's neglect.

Conversely, the compensatory romance the mentally disturbed Laura
Post embraces, in reaction to her parents' particularly cruel rejections, is
an aberrant Christianity. Hers is an ominous romance that masks a
bizarre quest for a surrogate mother. Just the reverse, however, is suggested by the novel's opening. Flying from Europe toward the United
States (and the Foster family), Laura reminds herself that "she no longer
said, 'If only they had loved me.' . . . Now she knew a parent's love was

nothing. She was the favorite, the chosen. . . . The way of the Lord was beauty, was the Spirit in the Garden. It was also fire. And it also was the sword" (5). Confident that the Spirit would lead her to children she could take care of and influence, Laura silently declares that "She knew what they needed for their lives: The knowledge of the Spirit, the knowledge that human love meant nothing" (5). Laura's self-professed negation of human love anticipates the ironic tragedy within the novel: the failure of her abstruse search for a mother and Anne Foster's corresponding failure (during the months when Laura works as a live-in, surrogate mother for Anne's children) to recognize Laura's quest and mental illness.

What results is a horrific version of the cross-purposed gift-giving depicted, for instance, in O. Henry's short story "The Gift of the Magi." In Gordon's version, however, the ill-fated gift givers, Anne and Laura, do not share a common agenda of love. What they do share, as the strangely astute Laura notices, is that "their families were just the same, their parents didn't love them" (146). Yet each woman is projecting her compensating love toward a different construct. Thus, when Laura's negligence almost kills Anne's children, the crossed purposes erupt into crisis. With a silent, raging desire to kill Laura and for the sake of young Peter and Sarah, Anne summarily fires Laura—an uncharacteristically decisive action that Anne views, with some satisfaction, as a sign of her own maturation. Faced with sudden, furious proof of Anne's love priorities, Laura is equally decisive: "She would cut her hands just at the wrists. The cut would be in the name of Anne. . . . She would shed every drop of blood she had for Anne, so Anne would see how much she loved her" (209).

Laura's suicide note to Anne explains: "I will show you his face [the Lord's] in my hands," to which Laura adds a passage from the Old Testament book of Isaiah. The final two verses of the passage promise that "Even these [mothers] may forget, yet I will not forget you. Behold I have graven you on the palms of my hands" (209). This passage, we suddenly recognize, is the one Laura reads to herself in the opening paragraph of the novel. And we also recall that in the novel's second paragraph (as Laura muses on the failure of family love and her own mother), Laura remembers: "Once she had tried it herself, tried to make herself carve her mother's name on the palms of her hands. She couldn't do it. . . . She did not have the courage for her mother's name" (3). Laura does, however, summon the courage for Anne's sake: "She could do it now. The final thing, the violent thing" (209). And as she does so, she describes her suicide plan and herself in light-filled terms: "snow-white garments," "the radiance of her face. Shining before the mountains of the Lord" (209). Conversely, the Fosters' individual and familial lives are darkened, marked by her act that is a kind of permanent stigmata, one that will guarantee, as Laura's suicide note declared, "I will never leave you" (209).

Gordon's gradual reversal of light and dark images suggests something of an artist's technique of defining and contouring an image by means of *chiaroscuro*. We recall, for instance, that our first introduction to Anne Foster is a light- and love-filled sketch of a young, attractive, doting wife and mother who, instinctively charitable, takes Laura into her home, despite an immediate recoiling when she meets the young *au pair*. In Laura Post's quirkily perceptive mind, Anne's spiritual failure occurs "because she looked out at the white sun in the clouds. The white sun in the clouds was not her safety. Or the strength of her husband's arms. Or the sweetness of her children's bodies. That was the error that Anne lived by . . . " (152). It is Laura Post's presence that increasingly shadows and, to use Anne's word, "poisons" Anne's life, home, and self-image. Thus, what begins as kindness (in Anne's hiring the disquieting Laura) darkens to equity, then decency, and finally hatred. On the other hand, the dark-spirited, heavily drawn self-perception we first see in Laura's introductory chapter lightens in direct proportion to the tension that drives Anne's increasingly difficult gestures of kindness toward Laura. Moreover, as Laura cleans every corner, drawer, and closet of the Fosters' home (leaving it in its most shining state ever), Anne feels Laura's cleaning as an invasive poisoning of their home. But for Laura, a birthday cake and lunch, boots, a dress, and a scarf are proof enough: Anne loves her. Laura, however, despite hers being the name of Petrarch's beloved, is not loved; Anne cannot bring herself even to like her.

Therefore, what each worries most about at the start of the novel— being perceived as good (Anne) and not allowing human love and joys to interfere with the Spirit (Laura)—is painfully, terribly justified by the novel's end. Anne silently admits to herself the truths she will never tell the investigating police: "She had closed her heart to Laura. She had driven her to death" (216)—a secret admission that Laura, just before her suicide, had recognized in her surrogate mother figure: "Anne's heart had hardened against her as her mother's heart had hardened against her" (208). But she, as one of the Lord's chosen, would enter "her head high in the light of God's own countenance" (209). And the Foster home that she had cleaned with water would now be cleansed by her blood.

But as Jane Watson points out to Anne after the suicide, Laura "missed the whole point of the Gospels": "That [as a child of God] she was greatly beloved" (231), a point that the nonreligious Anne also cannot grasp.

In the evolution of this light and shadow show, Gordon's control is so remarkable that her readers are pushed through their own reversal process. Walter Clemons has summarized precisely this achievement : "Most of the way through *Men and Angels* we're so partial to Anne that we want Laura exposed and punished. At the end we have to revise judgment. We're made to ache for Laura. This change in feeling is the work of a humane, masterly novelist."[14] Alida Becker's review makes a similar judgment: "It is a superbly crafted story, with characters whose strengths and weaknesses mirror each other in ways that prevent pat judgments about either."[15]

Such an achievement has its own provenance. Gordon, we recall, has explored this kind of reversal before, but in more contained and less tragic circumstances. In *Final Payments,* for instance, the unhappy Isabel Moore attempts an extreme gesture of charity by living with the despicable Margaret, who has always represented everything Isabel does not want to be. After months of physical neglect and secret food binges, however, Isabel looks at her bloated, unhealthy image in the mirror and recognizes that she has become Margaret, one of Gordon's female characters whom several scholars have characterized as a "wicked witch" persona, a dreaded Other and *Doppelgänger*. Likewise, in *The Company of Women,* Felicitas wants more than anything else to escape the dominance of Father Cyprian, his group of women devotees, and her life as the beloved child of the group. She tries to establish a new life, a new personhood, in Manhattan, but she ends up in a secular model of everything she wanted to avoid: a circle of women (one with a young child), devoted to a man, Robert Cavendish, who dominates their lives. It is fascinating to follow the maturation of Gordon's reversal techniques, especially when we note that neither of the earlier mirrorings changes our minds: we're *for* Isabel and Felicitas, and we're *against* everything Margaret and Robert represent. The duality holds. Not so in *Men and Angels.*

What Gordon's two earlier female protagonists do share with Anne, Laura, and others in *Men and Angels* is the lack of a viable, maternal role model. Both Anne and Laura make that clear in the first two chapters of the novel. Other characters gradually reflect the same. Jane Watson, for one, admits to Anne that Caroline Watson, Jane's mother-in-law, "was a perfectly murderous mother to Stephen, but to me she was a mother made in heaven. Whereas I felt no more for my own mother than I felt

for a rather distant cousin." Jane is frank in saying that she had married
Stephen "because I wanted Caroline in my life. I wanted a formal tie
with her, since I couldn't have a blood one" (167). Caroline, for her part,
also had rejected her mother; as her last journal entry confesses, "I have
been a bad daughter. Indifferent to my mother, I did not mourn her
death" (199). And in Jane, but not in her own son, Caroline discovered
her adored child. The child substitution is obvious to Anne as she compares Caroline's letters to Stephen and to his wife Jane. Letters to her son
are "perfunctory and short"; they reflect "none of the pride, the private
jokes, the motherly concern she showered on Jane" (68). Caroline, in
Anne's silent judgment, "had come close to both" Jane and Stephen,
"warming one of them, leaving the other ashes" (69). When one compares Anne's summary judgment of Caroline with her own contrasting
responses to Jane and Laura, a resonant parallel emerges: Jane's friendship becomes a warm center in Anne's life, but Laura's ashes are scattered by Anne. Equally ironic is the fact that both Caroline and Anne are
survivors who, wittingly or not, sacrifice young, intrusive presences in
their lives: Stephen and Laura, respectively.

Jane, in talking to Anne about her close relationship with Caroline,
confides that she had a breakdown after her mother-in-law's death. It
was not just a matter of grief. She had come to the realization that her
and Caroline's surrogate mother-daughter construct "crushed that poor
boy [Stephen] into the ground. We killed him as surely as if we'd poisoned him" (167). Anne had already pored over Caroline's responsibility
in Stephen's early death "at twenty-eight, miserable, a failure." Yet Anne
realizes he did not fail to leave something behind: "He'd left his wife and
mother to themselves" (69). That Laura's death will leave Anne and her
preferred children and friends to themselves is, of course, another of the
palpable ironies that evolve later in the novel.

It is interesting to watch Gordon's subtle development of a mother-
daughter surrogacy between seventy-eight-year-old Jane, a fourteenth-
century medievalist, and Anne, art historian—two scholars linked initially by the late Caroline Watson. One such example of this emerges
when Anne and her children visit Jane's apartment in Manhattan. When
Anne belatedly learns that Jane has arranged for Betty, an abusive
mother, to take care of young Peter and Sarah, Jane answers Anne's
shocked protest by observing, "Well, my dear, I knew you'd feel just as I
do. We're terribly alike; we could be mother and daughter" (129). In an
obvious parallel Gordon sets up to Anne's attempted rescue of the
unhappy Laura, Jane has taken in and is attempting to rehabilitate the

much abused and once abusive Betty. Other examples of the delicate surrogacy between Anne and Jane occur at Jane's country home. There, as Jane cooks for, serves, advises, and tucks her into bed, Anne observes that "no one could have been less like" her own mother (101). And later, after Laura's suicide, Jane steps in immediately to help Anne and her children in multiple ways, while Anne's own mother whines her way out of driving down to be with them. After the telephone conversation with her mother, the thirty-eight-year-old Anne weeps, realizing with a sudden finality, "that was what made the difference between adults and children. Adults knew they were alone; their solitude was final, and there was no rescue" (230).

Yet Anne's scholarship is in itself a kind of rescue. Gordon, in fact, develops one of the novel's most important surrogate mother-daughter pairings in Anne and the late Caroline Watson. It is a surrogacy that develops on multiple levels. First, Anne's research on Watson's paintings, journals, and acquaintances initiates her deepening, self-reflexive reexaminations of women's careers, parenting, and marriage; the Bad Mother, in other words, introduces the Good Mother to a broadening inquiry. The emerging research on Watson also establishes Anne's scholarly career and expertise; Caroline's lifework gives birth to Anne's. Most interestingly, however, the research itself brings the forgotten Caroline Watson back to life as painter and person—a "rebirthing" of sorts that Anne thinks of in maternal terms: "I know her almost as I know my own children" (45) and "now we are connected. In the bone. This woman, whom I know and do not know at all, is part of my life like my own children" (45). Anne comes to feel that "To do justice to the dead required an intimacy in which justice had no part. . . . you needed to embrace them with the unquestioning love with which you embraced an infant. You needed to be always on their side" (69).

In her essay on Gordon and Alison Lurie, Judie Newman offers a convincing biographical-fictional approach to these novelists and their characters who try to retrieve the life and work of a professional artist. Newman goes on to suggest that "in rescuing a forgotten or misunderstood woman, the author may be seeking, indirectly, to rescue herself." The process is, therefore, what Newman describes as "a double-mothering; both 'mothers' nurture not an infant but a woman, and for both nurturing is a sanctioning of their autonomy" ("Telling," 177). The epilogue to *Men and Angels* suggests a complex example of the process. Anne, holding her young son and thinking about all that has happened to their lives, knows that she can go back, at long last, to "the work of a

woman forty-five years dead" (239); Caroline Watson will reemerge from
Anne's new sense of autonomy in "hard words, formed words, white
stones that she could hold and separate" (239). Anne, in other words,
has come to exemplify those biographers who, according to Newman,
"recreate 'mothers' with whom they can integrate—and separate—more
effectively than from their biological mothers" ("Telling," 178). Gordon
goes one step further in suggesting that the act of "recreating" a surrogate mother also frees Anne who, "then, refreshed," can "dive back
down to the dense underworld, to her children" with a new understanding of life's awfulness and beauty (239). Gordon's choice of the word
underworld in connection to her children implies a mythic twist, one in
which the children's world seems to be one of death, while Caroline's is
the world of life. More likely, however, it is intended to suggest Anne's
finally working out a sort of maternal mediation between the worlds of
"men and angels" (i.e., between her children's and her down-to-earth
lives downstairs and the deceased Caroline's posthumous elevation
within "the house that she [Anne] would build" (49) for her in the
upstairs study).

These mother-daughter surrogacies extend the novel's complex study
of compensatory, familial constructs. That these constructs often move in
contrary motion has been captured in Alida Becker's cataloging expertise:
"Laura longs to live alone with Anne in a house by a lake, just as Anne
longs, through writing about Caroline, to 'build a house for a woman she
loved.' One impulse results in death, the other in new life for the work of
a forgotten artist. Anne hungers for friendship with Jane Watson, and her
wish is granted, while Laura, whose desires are just as fervent, remains an
intruder. Anne, a mother who would die for her children, fails to keep
them from danger, but Caroline, who neglected her own flesh and blood,
turns out to be 'a mother made in heaven' for Jane" ("Arts," 6).

The goal of each of these and other highly selective constructs is to
find and show love that, in some way, will provide both sanctuary and
compensation for one's life. But each of these familial compensations
contains serious flaws, serious limitations. One notices that Gordon, in
considering such limitations, has substituted familial constructs for those
of the parish, that "fiercely limited terrain," as she has phrased it.
Certainly Gordon, in tracking these self-limited, familial constructs of
love to their inevitable collisions, forces the reader to consider unsettling
propositions about closed and enclosed family systems, about family life
itself. Those propositions are well-delineated in a review of *Men and
Angels,* in which Margaret Drabble admits that the novel "disturbs,

rather than reassures, for it demonstrates that family life itself, that safest, most traditional, most approved of female choices, is not a sanctuary: it is, perpetually, a dangerous place" ("Limits," 31). Alida Becker has echoed this warning in her discussion of the novel's main female protagonists: "It's a stormy emotional sea that Anne and Laura have been launched upon, one that might be tamed by saints but is unmanageable for all too fallible mortals. And so their voyage together will end in tragedy, yielding a dearly bought and not very consoling wisdom" ("Arts," 6). As quoted earlier, Gordon had recognized, even as she began to formulate the story's plot, that Anne and Laura's coming together would require a New Testament-inspired *caritas* that was, in fact, "unlivable." In the course of the novel, the pressure this fact creates in the reader is suggested in critics who pragmatically note, for example, that Anne, in her rage at Laura's lackadaisically letting the children play on a thinly iced pond, did not consider psychiatric help for the *au pair,* or that Laura may have been beyond help even before she joined the Foster household. Such comments confirm how deeply Gordon's readers, even her critics, are drawn into Gordon's plot of strategic reversals and contradictions. Nevertheless, only Gordon's further exploration of the creative ambiguities within limitations mitigates the unanswerable questions about moral responsibilities and failures that she places at the center of the novel's focus.

"This is life. What shall we make of it?"

When interviewed about *Men and Angels* shortly after its publication, Gordon said, "I wanted to show the limits of love and the failure of love, particularly for a good person. Also, I'm very interested in the limits and realities of maternal love" (Mitgang interview, 30). Throughout the novel, Gordon underscores her premise that humans are not whole, love and life are often unfair and terrible. She does not stop at these limitations. In the denouement of the novel, Gordon puts forward a contextual redefinition of *caritas* that is far more ambiguous and porous than those with which her previous novels ended. It is also created within far more unsettling circumstances: the permanent transformation of Anne and Michael's "safe" family and their children's innocence by Laura's suicide and by Anne's and her young son's discovery of Laura's body in their water- and blood-soaked home. There seems to be nothing untouched by her death. Even Anne's books have been soaked; they too will serve, in Anne's mind, as *memento mori.*

If we assume that Anne and Laura are a complex mirrored pairing, then Gordon's development of Anne's response to Laura's suicide is a critical juncture in the novel, a denouement for which an astute observation by W. H. Auden may be germane: "Every man [and woman] carries with him through life a mirror, as unique and impossible to get rid of as his shadow. . . . Some [mirrors] magnify, some diminish, others return lugubrious, comic, derisive, or terrifying images. . . . We shall be judged, not by the kind of mirror found on us, but by the use we have made of it, by our *riposte* to our reflection" ("Hic et Ille," 93–94). Something of this nature seems to drive the novel's conclusion. There Gordon sets up a charged frame of judgment around how Anne handles Laura's death, her *Doppelgänger*'s death. Thus, Gordon has the reader follow Anne in her visits to Laura's parents (who want nothing to do with her body or funeral) and in her arrangements for Laura's funeral, at which her children hear their first religious words and whose Old Testament questions elicit Anne's first spiritual query. The twelfth chapter of the novel concludes with her scattering Laura's ashes and her silent promise to Laura: "I did not love you. But I mourn you. I will always mourn you. I can give you that" (235).

In Anne's brushing of a few last bone splinters into the creek before she rejoins her waiting husband and children and their transformed lives, we recognize that Gordon has created a resonance with the conclusion of *Final Payments* in which the three friends' solid laughter hangs above them "like rings of bone" (297), a symbol that healing and maturation have begun.[16] Furthermore, that resonance includes a healing conjunction of bone imagery and the protagonist's hard-won ability to reenter a world of words. Gordon actually creates double conjunctures of a symbol and articulation at the close of *Men and Angels:* the first as Anne scatters Laura's ashes and bone splinters and addresses her (235); the second, on the final page, when Anne realizes she is ready to reapproach her research: "She would write, 'It should be noted,' and 'The style demands.' Hard words, formed words, white stones that she could hold and separate" (239). Although a predawn sky surrounds both novels' endings, that in *Men and Angels* is darker than the first novel's, an appropriate match for the far more serious challenge Anne's healing process will entail.

Gordon's decision to attach an epilogue to the novel has been questioned by a few critics, such as Rosellen Brown, who, while praising the novel as "a beautifully written, passionate inquiry into many kinds of vulnerability and power, and an acknowledgment of the pain of trying to balance instinctual love with a more encompassing compassion," suggests that "the epilogue iterates too explicitly what we have seen, casting a skein of sentimentality over the rest that it doesn't deserve."[17] Brown's comments lead me back to reconsider the epilogue's role.

In the broadest sense, the epilogue brings forward Gordon's privileging of language and of communication. These hallmarks of the texts of all of her novels inform the conclusions of her first three novels in remarkable ways. The conclusion of *Final Payments*—"There was a great deal I wanted to say"—is joined by that of *The Company of Women,* in which young Linda, inside the house, sees and hears her mother and grandmother outside: "'Come out,' they say, 'Come out and talk to us. We're lonely for you. Tell us something.'" These motions outward toward communication and relationship are doubly augmented in the conclusion of *Men and Angels* as Anne looks out the window. She is ready to move back into two worlds of words and relationships: the "hard words, formed words, white stones" that will bring Caroline Watson and her own scholarship back to life; and the words she can bring to her children: "'This is life. What shall we make of it?'" Such a recurrent emphasis seems to suggest that even if the answers, for example, to Anne's rhetorical questions turn out to be percussive—"sounding brass, or a tinkling cymbal"—"the tongues of men and angels" are the only instruments in the orchestra.

On a technical level, the epilogue provides a time lapse so that the reader can judge, as W. H. Auden's lines suggested, Anne's *riposte,* her use of the dark-mirrored reflection of herself in Laura. By the end of the epilogue in *Men and Angels,* Gordon has stripped Anne both of her naïveté and of the hubris by which she attempted to construct a protected life for herself, her husband, and especially for their children. Their closed circle has been opened up to encompass the dead Laura. It also encompasses new freedoms within Anne's career and her recognition that mother love is a different experience for every mother and child and "was not all of life." Anne also sees now that a child's response to damage and parental limitations was not something that could be determined: "children throve or starved, and no one knew why, or what killed or saved" (238). Gordon further emphasizes that the family's encounter with violence and grief has led Anne to recognize that the highest impulses of human love, limitations and all, are those that one lives out in the midst of, not safely apart from, the "terrible," "beautiful" world in which "anything might lie and then uncoil and strike, in silence, in the darkness" (239). Thus, Margaret Drabble's judgment of *Men and Angels* is keen when she points out that in this novel's contrasts of "mutually exclusive ways of being and seeing," Gordon is "reaching for a sense of wholeness, for the possibility of inclusion rather than exclusion, for a way of connecting the different passages of existence" ("Limits," 31). Still, Gordon leaves much unresolved in her examination of love and its "real life" physical and spiritual limits, of the standards by which actual and invented family units are to be judged and valued. This lack of resolution reflects a powerful decision.

Chapter Five

a serious person's stories:
Temporary Shelter and Others

Some months after the 1987 publication of *Temporary Shelter*,[1] an interviewer suggested that Gordon didn't write many short stories, to which she replied, "I actually write quite a few. Not all of them do I consider publishable. So I have many of them in folders." Mentioning that *Temporary Shelter* has "twenty, written over the course of a lifetime, over twelve years," she then commented on the selection process for the collection, "I've only recently gone back over things I'd written ten, twelve years ago, reworked some, and thought, maybe—that's okay. Some were actually published, and I had to make decisions that I didn't want to include them in the collection" (Keyishian interview, 70). The effect of those decisions had already become apparent. In a 1987 review of *Temporary Shelter*, Paul Gray admitted that "Gordon's formidable reputation has not been won through short stories." But then he added a crucial revision, "At least until now."[2] Within a year of its publication, the collection appeared in Dutch and Japanese translations; in 1990, Gallimard released its French translation.

The stories vary in length and narrative voice. The shortest, "The Imagination of Disaster," is four pages; the longest, the five-part "Now I Am Married," is nineteen pages. Seven of the stories have first-person narrators, while the others (with the exception of the omniscient advice-giver in "A Writing Lesson") have third-person voices. Of the twenty stories, fourteen had been published earlier in a wide range of magazines and journals, such as *Ms., Mademoiselle, Redbook, Woman's Day, Atlantic, Antaeus, Granta,* and the *Virginia Quarterly Review.* But six of the collection—"Temporary Shelter," "Delia," "Watching the Tango," "Agnes," "Eileen," and "Billy"—appear for the first time. The stories in *Temporary Shelter* do not follow, as some readers mistakenly have assumed, any sort of chronological order. For example, in a 1988 interview, M. Deiter Keyishian wondered if the five-voiced story "Now I Am Married" "was an earlier version of *The Company of Women* or something you did after," to which Gordon had to explain that the story was "very, very early. . . . I think I wrote that in 1974" (Keyishian interview, 75). Likewise, in a review of *Temporary Shelter,* Rachel Billington, assuming a chronological sequence, erroneously second-guessed several of Gordon's technical and stylistic intentions.[3] For these and other reasons, it is unfortunate that either Anne Freedgood, Gordon's editor at Random House, or Gordon herself decided not to clarify the publication or completion date of each story. Those dates (which, if available, will be indicated in this chapter) reveal an important chronology of Gordon's themes, techniques, and career. For instance, "Now I Am Married," which was published in 1975 by the *Virginia Quarterly Review,* was Gordon's first fiction publication and her first prizewinner: it received the Balch Award in 1976.

An Overview

The year 1975 marks a starting place from which one can track Gordon's career in prose. For her, the ensuing decade was productive, rewarding, and complex. By the end of 1987 she had published some eight poems, nineteen short stories, twenty-seven articles, twenty-four reviews, and three novels, the first of which had been nominated for the National Book Critics Circle Award and had been named as one of the outstanding books of 1978 by the *New York Times Book Review.* Both *Final Payments* and Gordon's second novel, *The Company of Women,* had been given a Janet Heidinger Kafka Prize for best novel written by an American woman. And all three novels were critical and popular successes. Another of her short stories, "The Only Son of the Doctor" (1982), won an O. Henry Award in 1983. A year later, Gordon had received her first honorary doctorate, and in 1985, she was given a Literary Lion of the New York Public Library Award. By 1987, five of her stories and essays were in anthologies. During the same twelve-year period, as Gordon has described it, "Years passed, marriages, and babies; I found myself living in the country for many years" ("Coming Home," 136). What Gordon's summary does not include, of course, is the word "writing"—and a lot of it.

Because this chapter also will discuss her more recent stories, perhaps a brief review of the subsequent years in her career will provide a helpful context for those discussions. Since the publication of *Temporary Shelter,* Gordon's work has earned her a Guggenheim Fellowship, a Lila Wallace–Reader's Digest Writers' Award, three more honorary doctorates, a Barnard Woman of Achievement Award, and appointments as Millicent C. McIntosh Professor of Writing at Barnard College as well as

Adjunct Writing Professor at Columbia University. In the meantime, Gordon's intense work pace has continued. She has published a fourth novel, *The Other Side;* a collection of essays, *Good Boys and Dead Girls and Other Essays;* a book of three novellas, *The Rest of Life;* a memoir-biography, *The Shadow Man;* as well as some three dozen articles, essays, and book introductions; one poem; nine reviews; and five short stories: "Vision" (1989), "At the Kirks'" (1990), "Separation" (1990), "Walt" (1994), and "City Life" (1996). "Separation" was included in *Best Short Stories of 1991,* and, despite her protests (which I discuss later), "The Important Houses" (1992) was one of twenty works selected from U. S. and Canadian magazine publications and included in *Best American Short Stories 1993.*[4] This cursory list of her work during the first two decades of her career would be incomplete without some mention of Gordon's numerous guest appearances on television and radio shows as well as a number of important lectures and some eighty readings throughout the United States.

The list continues to expand rapidly. Some things, however, have not changed. And Gordon's selections for *Temporary Shelter* are important clues to the constancies that mark her earlier and more recent work, constancies that seem to mandate a triadic approach to the stories in the collection as well as several more recent stories. First of all, these stories provide an evolutionary mosaic of the distinctive thematic preoccupations that characterize all four of her novels as well as her more recent memoir, *The Shadow Man.* And even though Gordon did not include her early short story, "A Serious Person" (1977), in this collection, the author's thematic interests remain, as this chapter's title suggests, those of a serious person. Second, the stories serve as apertures into Gordon's technical experiments and maturation as well as her implicit, immovable trust in the art of literature itself; as Christopher Lehmann-Haupt has described them, "the shelter of artistic form" is "in Ms. Gordon's able hands . . . not in the least temporary."[5] Third, the stories open up a kind of forum on the nature of fiction itself, and more specifically, on how Gordon blurs the boundaries between fiction and nonfiction. Gordon herself vigorously resists this sort of inquiry. Despite her resistance, it is a question that her readers need to address if we are to understand the ways in which this writer, in the guise of very traditional approaches, has made some of her most important, radically innovative contributions to contemporary fiction. But we first need to ground that inquiry in a broader study of Gordon's thematic and technical preoccupations in *Temporary Shelter.*

Theme and Variations

A natural segue to the overarching thematic focus of the stories is Gordon's tributes to two women whose friendship and advice continue to give her personal and professional "temporary shelter." First, the collection is dedicated to Jan Zlotnick Schmidt, an important reader of Gordon's chapters and drafts from her fourth novel to the present. Schmidt, a professor at the State University of New York in New Paltz, has been a friend of Gordon's since graduate school (Bennett interview, 22). Second, "The Headache," the painting featured on the collection's book jacket, is by Gordon's close friend and confidante, the artist Helen Miranda Wilson,[6] daughter of Edmund Wilson. Like the literary genre to which it has been attached, the 1978 painting is both small (11" by 11") and intense. Moreover, the painting, with its austere, painstakingly selected details and palette, not only narrates a story of a woman with a headache, but its subjective treatment parallels the same kind of pressured concentration that one expects in any masterful short story. What makes the painting most appropriate for Gordon's collection of stories is, of course, that the woman's pain is being temporarily ameliorated by a man's massaging her head. Thus, Helen Wilson's painting serves as a well-chosen visual metaphor for *Temporary Shelter* on many levels, not the least of which is that the stories in the collection create and reflect a certain constant pressure on the brain or, to borrow a phrase Gordon once coined for another context, "the hum inside the skull." Gordon's ability to sustain that pressure within each of the diverse stories is, as Christopher Lehmann-Haupt recognizes, "a matter of art, for Ms. Gordon always strives for a point of view that simultaneously envisions the peace and catastrophe implicit in her material" ("Temporary," 25).

Gordon's balancing act of "peace and catastrophe" is reflected in the tension between the words *shelter* and *temporary*. What unites the stories thematically is human loneliness and an awareness that nothing or no one can assuage this condition permanently. The characters who come to understand this include children, adult sons and daughters, wives, young mothers, émigrés, widows, divorcées, and elderly persons. For example, in the story "Watching the Tango," a woman and her married lover rendezvous at a tango performance. Their adulterous secrecy, the woman realizes, leaves them oddly isolated, like "orphans" (and, one notes, like the tango dancers themselves). Emboldened by the sad, violent, middle-aged passion and grace of the dancers, they leave the theater holding

hands and kissing publicly, for the first time. Then, the lovers witness
a bitter argument between two of the dancers leaving the theater, and
she insists, "'Let's go now.' . . . She doesn't want to have to worry" (64)
or to face their realities and her own. Conversely, in the story "The Other
Woman" (1976), after a husband has poured out the story of the woman
(not his first wife) who had been the great love of his life, the man's
second wife soothes him knowing—and facing: "he would never know
what she was feeling, and knowing this, she had never loved him so
little" (156).

Gordon's more complicated story, "Out of the Fray," reverses this
process. It begins as Ruth, a science writer and divorced mother of two
children, flies to London with her fiancé Phil, a thrice-divorced man who
works for a human rights organization. Despite Phil's excitement about
their impending marriage, Ruth is privately much more detached and
bothered; she feels that they will be "standing before a judge, their fingers crossed behind their backs saying, 'I promise I will never leave you.'
When what they meant was, 'I will try'" (89). Her detachment begins to
shift during the course of their stay in London and their visits there with
the Belgian-born Sylvie MacGregor, Phil's close friend, whose life he had
saved years before when she tried to commit suicide after her husband
Jack, Phil's friend, left her for another woman. The life the now almost
fifty-year-old Sylvie has constructed for herself in London is just that: a
modest, frozen, smooth construct of piano lessons, theater performances,
prematurely assumed elderly clothing and habits, and her work at the
institute for the blind. Hoping that Sylvie will give her the kind of guarantees ("You'll be happy now . . . I promise") she needs for her second
marriage, Ruth realizes that Sylvie, in "the thin present in which she felt
herself required now to live" (93) cannot; her life, in a sense, had ended
long ago. By the time their last visit with Sylvie ends, Ruth's own ability
to stay detached has also ended. In the dark of their hotel room as she
watches Phil sleep, "she understood that if he left her it would be like
death and wondered when it happened how she would go on" (100).
The *if* and *when* are a devastating finale. In the equally sophisticated
ambience of the story "The Dancing Party" (1986), only one of the two
older women has learned to bridge the abysses within relationships and
lives; the rest remain caught in them. Gordon, at two points in the story,
sets up unusual cataloging sequences of the women characters' various
dilemmas, which include "The scientist thinks: I will live forever with a
man who hates to dance"; "The daughter of the hostess thinks: I love my
mother, but I will not live like her"; "The angry wife wishes she were not

angry"; and "Her friend thinks: If this man dies I will be once more alone" (183).

Gordon's 1994, twenty-page story "Walt,"[7] which opens and closes in the female narrator's famous food store, moves back for most of the story to the narrator's youth and struggle to get out of her working-class world and family and to her odd, unhealthy relationship with another N.Y.U. student, Walt, obsessed with Marxism but more intensely obsessed with the narrator. In the story's opening, Walt has suddenly shown up at her store; by the time the story ends, the reader knows enough about their long-ago relationship and about Walt to understand the narrator's fright: her fears are altogether different from the ones that conclude the previous paragraph. Hers are based on the ominous possibility that Walt (unseen for all these years) will never leave her life: "He might have pretended to have gone. But he was there, even if I couldn't see him at that moment. He was there; he was waiting for me. He always would be" ("Walt," 77).

Such impasses and juxtapositions reflect, as I suggested before, a serious premise, one that gains seriousness in Gordon's self-declared purpose for her short stories and novels: "What I want to accomplish is to tell stories about real people, to tell the truth about human beings in human situations, the way in which people live their lives" (Bannon interview, 275). Not surprisingly, Gordon's perspective on humanity has drawn critical fire. In her review of *Temporary Shelter,* Rachel Billington complains that "the keening of a frightened and suffering woman is never far from the surface of Mary Gordon's writing." Billington then goes on to describe the stories as carrying "the same atmosphere of fatalistic depression, of lives lived with at best lack of hope and at worst something dangerously threatening" ("At Bay," 8). Other reviewers, while acknowledging the profound loneliness within the stories, have recognized the other half of Gordon's human equation, the other factor that unites the collection: what Carolyn See describes as "the absolutely extraordinary heroic attempts that human beings make to alleviate that condition. . . . It's just that pain, that loneliness, that makes the decision to love so amazing."[8]

A Coterie of Dualities

Critics and scholars have not yet discussed the dualities within which Gordon's characters reveal their deprivations and brave, sometimes fool-hardy, always poignant decisions. This sort of dualistic approach is certainly nothing new. Ancient oral and written epics, psalms, parables, proverbs, tragedies, and comedies, as well as more recent novels, poems, plays, films, and short stories alike reveal storytellers' and writers' adroit manipulations of the tensions and narrative economies inherent within oppositions. However, with the exceptions of the stories of Turgenev, Hawthorne, Poe, and O'Connor, I can think of few short story collections (especially those selected by their authors) that utilize and sustain dualities any more consistently than Gordon does in *Temporary Shelter.* And she does so, as Paul Gray has noted, by returning "habitually, hypnotically, to a small number of predicaments" (Gray, 74). A list of her predicament pairings in these stories includes various and often layered combinations of the following dichotomies: female-male; child/children-adults; child-parent(s); elderly-young; Jew-Catholic; Protestant-Catholic; immigrant-established; crippled-noncrippled; unmarried/divorced/ widowed-married; underpriviliged-privileged; and unsophisti-cated-sophisticated.

What transforms this listing exercise is the possibility that it catalogs not only the thematic dualities within the collection but also the majority of the fictional and nonfictional preoccupations that Gordon has explored so far in essays, interviews, novels, stories, novellas, and the memoir-biography. For instance, because of Gordon's preoccupations in all four of her novels, we recognize (almost as old friends) Gordon's interest in Bad Mother/Parent types in the stories "Billy," "Temporary Shelter," "Mrs. Cassidy's Last Year" (1983), "The Magician's Wife" (1978), and "The Only Son of the Doctor" (1982). In the first of these, Billy's mother, Veronica McGovern, whom the female narrator loved, nevertheless "had ruined her son's life as certainly as if she'd starved him in infancy; he would probably have been much better off if she'd abandoned him at birth" (158). It was a case of Veronica's cloistering her son, telling him "the truth . . . too early, and too much," warning him that the world was hurtful, all of which he believed because "She was telling the truth; she was his mother" (168). But the narrator, whom Billy had always furtively and hopelessly loved, knows that she cannot be so truthful with her own sons. Like the young mother in "The Imagination of Disaster," who knows she "cannot pervert her [daughter's] life so that she will be ready for the disaster" (26), this mother explains Billy's death and life's cruelty to her frightened sons in a manner "that will let them live their lives" (168).

In the title story, "Temporary Shelter"[9] (1987), Gordon creates an intriguingly contradictory duality between a Bad Mother (who tells too much, too early) and a Good Father (who tells too little, too late). The contrast is between young Joseph Kaszperkowski's tough, foul-mouthed, Polish immigrant mother, Helen, and the widowed, erudite, wealthy, gentle, Jewish convert to Catholicism, Dr. Meyers (perhaps a fantasy version of Gordon's own father), who hired Helen as his and his infant daughter's live-in housekeeper when Joseph was two. Dr. Meyers showers on his daughter Maria and Helen's son Joseph equal love, education, and attention. He teaches Joseph about Cimabue and Simone Martini, table manners, poetry, history, and taste in clothing; he provides for both children those essential accoutrements of sophistication: piano, French, and tennis lessons; he takes them to movies and teaches them the art of eating cream puffs: "You must eat many cream puffs before you can truly say you know how to eat them *comme il faut*" (9). Helen, on the other hand, calls young Maria "a pig, a slut, a hussy, a disgrace" for being so sloppy and then, when Joseph takes Maria's side, tells him too much (like Gordon's character Veronica McGovern): "They're all alike. Fine ladies, with someone like me to clean up their shit. . . . They'll leave you in the end, don't you forget it. In the end I'll be the only thing you have" (7), a threat that leaves Joseph permanently wracked with terror and guilt. As the two young people enter puberty (at which point Joseph is going to be sent away to school and Maria wants desperately to become a nun), both adults—in their wildly disparate styles—acknowledge to Joseph not only the potential sexual problems but that Maria will never be allowed to be a nun because she is, in the Church's eyes, still a Jew. The latter is a truth that young Joseph knows he must protect Maria from; taking on a parental role himself, he silently vows to "make her want to marry him . . . before she could find out that because of her blood they would keep back from her heart's desire" (24). Gordon makes the reader fear that such sheltering intentions will prove to be tenuous, at best.

In the stories "The Magician's Wife" (1978) and "Mrs. Cassidy's Last Year" (1983), Gordon depicts parents whose love for each other excludes their child. As the first two sentences of "The Magician's Wife" set forth, Mrs. Hastings "did not think of herself first as the mother of her children. She was proudest of being Mr. Hastings' wife" (77). Despite her son Frederick's success as an architect and his kindness to his now elderly parents, she is upset that Mr. Hastings (who, after all, had once performed his magic for the Roosevelt family) is now known only as the son's father. For the narrator-wife, Mr. Hastings' magic tricks represent the specialness of her husband and of their life together, a metaphor that took shape on the fourth day of their honeymoon when he bought the materials for his first magic trick. But when his grandchildren and son Frederick insist that the now increasingly blind and feeble Mr. Hastings perform his magic show for the town's Fourth of July Town Fair, Mrs. Hastings becomes terrified that he will be humiliated. When, as she feared, the performance is full of failed tricks, she turns on her son in rage, despite and because of the sympathetic audience's standing ovation for Mr. Hastings. It is at this final point of the story that we suddenly become aware of the finesse with which Gordon has moved the story's tensions and details along; that recognition comes when Mrs. Hastings' son, for the first time, confronts her. Reacting to her fury, he remarks, "You know, Mother, Father is twice the person you are . . . Three times"; only then, with her son's compliance in her all-exclusive love, can Mrs. Hastings take his arm and look "at her son with something like love" (86).

The 1983 story, "Mrs. Cassidy's Last Year," contains a complicated nucleus of parental neglect and damage around which Gordon eventually developed her fourth novel, *The Other Side* (1989). By the time the novel was published, the elderly parents' names had changed, and their surly son Tom (who had always known that he had not been the best-loved, "most prized" son) had disappeared, only to be replaced by unloved and damaged daughters. Yet the elderly Mr. Cassidy's promise to his wife is unchanged, as is the death of their adored firstborn son, John, and the foulmouthed ragings of the now senile Mrs. Cassidy who, as in the novel, pushes her husband down and breaks his leg. In the short story, Mr. Cassidy understands his son Tom: a "self-made man, . . . Good time Charlie. Every joke a punchline like a whip" (198); he understands Tom's wounds, "Tom for whom there had been no time" (199). Even now, however, Mr. Cassidy will not allow Tom to intrude into his immovable commitment to his wife or to interfere with his promise made years before: that he will guarantee that she can die at home and not be taken "away" (198). As unattractive as Tom and his wife's personalities are, it is difficult to ignore the pain of this son who brings dinner each night to his parents and who, finally, is the agent for bringing his wandering mother back to her home and to his father, her now injured, but invincibly loyal husband.

Like these two stories, "The Only Son of the Doctor" (1982), which was reissued in *Fiction Magazine* in 1985 and in *Cosmopolitan* (London) in 1987, makes a circuitous approach to neglect. The story only gradually reveals that Henry Cosgrove's obsessive, philanthropic advocacies for the elderly and other causes have driven away his wife and shut out his son,

Eliot. The story, narrated by Louisa Altiere, Henry's lover, begins like a love story in its first celebratory stages. The idyll is interrupted by a visit from Eliot, Henry's rebellious, drifter son, whom Louisa resents. That resentment begins to erode when she realizes, "What would a child have thought, seeing that back turned to him, listening to the typewriter? For Henry needed no one when he was at his desk, writing his letters for the most just, the most worthy, of causes" (49). Eliot's understanding that "nobody's good enough" for his father leads to Louisa's recognition that "such a moderate man" as Henry "had to inspire radical acts" and a life posture like Eliot's (49). The story ends with her own little cosmetic rebellion against the tyranny of Henry's myopic, exclusive goodness. These rebellions are quieter but as inevitable as those of Isabel and Felicitas who, in *Final Payments* and *The Company of Women,* respectively, must react in radical ways to impossible, unlivable, radically exclusive love and standards.

The Good Mothers who narrate the stories "The Imagination of Disaster" (1985) and "Safe" (1982) remind us of Anne Foster in *Men and Angels,* as well as several of Gordon's essays (such as "On Mothership and Authorhood," "Explaining Evil," and "Raising Sons") and interviews. In the first of these stories, the young mother is obsessed with a sense of impending political catastrophe from which she must protect her children. It is an obsession that Gordon herself has voiced. In 1985, for example, immediately after the publication of *Men and Angels,* Gordon told an interviewer, "I think about it all the time. . . . If I were in Germany, what would I have done? . . . My husband thinks I'm insane to think about these things all day, but I've made him promise that if he's ever in the situation, he will save the children—never me or him" (Bolotin interview, 232). Yet Gordon and the narrator in "The Imagination of Disaster" know genuine nurture of a child precludes the child's being made aware of such dire possibilities; a mother, in other words, must give up one thing for another. This kind of essential sacrifice is the lesson another young mother learns in the story "Safe." After a frustrating afternoon get-together with her infant daughter and her sophisticated former lover, she returns home and comes to understand that any such liaison is dangerous, that safety is the fragile, single gift she can offer her husband and child; moving into her husband's embrace, she silently acknowledges, "I must live my life now knowing it is not my own . . . it must be the shape of my life to keep them at least from the danger I could bring them" (177).

In light of these two stories' emphases on mothers' awarenesses of danger, it is an interesting exercise to study Gordon's exploration of a child's perceptions of danger and violence in the story "The Murderer Guest" (1981). The ten-year-old Elizabeth is a child who measures everything and everyone against her already fierce coterie of absolutes, but these mask her fears of the Other, personified in her mind by German soldiers who haunt her dreams and by her half-German schoolmate, Judith Lowery. The threat of danger becomes more invasive when Mrs. Delehanty flies from Lincoln, Nebraska, to stay with Elizabeth's parents for a while. Elizabeth's mother's friend since childhood, Mrs. Delehanty had killed her drunken husband Stan, evidently in self-defense; now Stan's parents have her two children and she is being ostracized by her friends in Lincoln. Elizabeth sees that this murderer is a woman no different from her own mother; remembering her own murderous reaction to Judith Lowery, she also recognizes in herself the possibility of such an act. Still, her rational perceptions hold no sway against her irrational terrors when she is in Mrs. Delehanty's presence.

Gordon's prizewinning story "Separation" (1991)[10] explores the intersection of danger and motherly love in an entirely different and more devastating way. Gordon has explained that "the genesis for this story was watching mothers leave their children each morning in my son's nursery school class. One particularly extreme case suggested an even more extreme situation to me. But it was clear to me that the extremity was only another part of the story of all mothers and all sons."[11] In the story, JoAnn, whose obsessive devotion to their baby boy drove off her husband, moves from town to town, running away from every agency or attempt to socialize her young son Billy, to suggest that both mother and child need counseling, to separate him from a mother who knows, "But we are happiest alone. But never say it. She knew what people thought. Children need other children. They believe that, everyone believes it. Only I do not believe it. Only he and I" (187). Attempts to get Billy to stay in school without her end with his running out and back to his mother's car; they drive away "Happy, singing" toward yet another "better place to live in," and toward what the reader recognizes as a future in which young Billy (who might be compared with the male protagonist of the story "Billy") will never leave his mother, despite her final sentence disclaimer: "He will leave me soon enough" (193). A tomb of sorts for both of them has already been sealed.

An entirely different type of Mother—and a good one, at that—appears in the unlikely guise of a slovenly, "Ireland Irish" neighbor, Mrs.

Lynch, in the story "The Neighborhood" (1984). Mrs. Lynch's own family is an abusive chaos, and their home is a pigsty, both of which are embarrassments to the settled, second-generation Irish-American neighborhood. Nevertheless, her silent, nonegotistical ministrations to the young narrator (whose grief for her dead father has turned into a phobia) heal the child in a profound way—in sharp contrast to the absence of any such healing mediation in Gordon's 1977 story "The Thorn."

Gordon's interest in relationships within slovenly messes is something she also addressed in Isabel Moore's own housekeeping and in her later professional housecalls to invalids in *Final Payments,* each visit of which forms a memorable vignette. Another example is the 1990 story "At the Kirks',"[12] which, like "The Murderer Guest," is narrated by a young girl whose perceptions are close enough to Gordon's autobiographical essays and comments to give one pause. Like the stories "The Murderer Guest" and "The Neighborhood," this story is full of a young person's observations (and severe judgments) of class and ethnic differences, of the Kirks' daughters' sexuality. Mrs. Kirk, like Mrs. Lynch in "The Neighborhood," is a slattern at home but presentable outside the home; both stories' husbands, likewise, are inarticulate nonentities, in the young protagonists' minds. However, in "At the Kirks'," Gordon makes us far more attentive to the child's own sexuality, to her obsessions with her and her parents "not" being like the Kirks, to her own secret understanding that she is a child who is not a child. Gordon also includes a very funny but painfully revealing exercise in differentiation through words when the young girl finds a love letter the Kirks' daughter Monica had written: "'Dear Darling,' it began. . . . It was the final proof I needed that I was a creature so different from Monica that I would never have a chance at an experience resembling hers. I knew that you said 'dear,' or you said 'darling.' I knew that you did not say both. No feeling I would ever have for any man would cause me to make that error. And I felt that, knowing that, I would not be chosen . . ." (52)—an awareness that adds a particularly ironic twist to the final paragraph of the story.

"At the Kirks'" and "The Murderer Guest" include characters' prejudices against Germans and non-Catholics. "The Neighborhood," on the other hand, is one of several stories that cluster around dualities and complications within first- and second-generation Irish-American families and neighborhoods, all of which come together in Gordon's complex fourth novel, *The Other Side.* Three of these stories ("Delia," "Agnes," and "Eileen"[13]) form what Carolyn See has described as the "most elegant set" of the collection. In the stories, the character Nora (crippled, we note, like Gordon's mother) learns incrementally, as a child, as a youth, and then as a working adult, about the rewards of love: death in varying degrees. First, her beautiful aunt Delia, who also loves beautifully (unlike the rest of the family), but whose husband is a Protestant, dies in childbirth; then, Nora's bootlegger uncle's faithful, self-effacing mistress, Agnes, hangs herself when he breaks off all communication with her; finally, Nora herself faces a living death. Because of being crippled, the highly intelligent young woman is not allowed to teach, as she has planned, nor will she find a love, as she has dreamed of so long. Like the broken immigrant Eileen, who leaves to return to Ireland like "one of the dead," Nora recognizes the life ahead of her: it has "no real prospects that could lead to pleasure" (119). She must endure what she had come to understand long before, after Agnes's suicide, "if you had a girl child growing up like that you'd be best drowning it straight off, . . . so you'd save it all the pain and trouble later on" (75)—words we recognize from the narrator's comment about the son's plight in the story "Billy." Gordon's decision to scatter the three "Nora" episodes throughout the collection is astute, for we only gradually put together the whole story, at which point our recognition, like Nora's, is intensely painful.

Not all the story clusters are so *deadly* serious. Written some six years before the seven monologues that conclude Gordon's novel, *The Company of Women,* the five first-person narrations in "Now I Am Married" introduce us to the tenuous and highly distinctive shelter-constructs of five women characters. The story begins with the first-person narration of an American who has just become the second wife of an Englishman who is bringing her to visit his family for the first time. The narration then shifts to four women she visits: Marjorie, Doris, Elizabeth, and Susan, in the order of their first-person monologues. Although it is not conspicuously marked, the narration returns to the American in the last three pages of the story.

Gordon has dismissed this five-part story, her first published work of fiction, as an early, very romantic take on marriage. But the reasons it was chosen for the Balch Award (and for her including it in the collection) are obvious. The story, which was written only about a year and a half after Gordon had shifted from poetry to prose, embroiders the patterns of the women's minds and lives in rather astonishing detail. What's more, Gordon juxtaposes these details with stylistic finesse and, occasionally, with adroit humor. An instance of the latter is the narrator's describing the visit to her husband's family: "We do not make love here as we do at my mother's. She thinks sex is wicked, which is, of course, highly aphrodisiac, but here it is considered merely in bad taste" (120). It is the same droll mastery that, some eight years later in the story "Safe," Gordon employs to describe the narrator's former English lover: "Only centuries of careful marriages could have produced, for example, his nose. There are no noses like it in America. . . . He is the blondest man I have ever been with—this, in combination with his elegant, well-cut clothes, made him a disappointment naked. Really fair men always look foolish without their clothes, as if they ought to know better" (171).

Two typical examples of Gordon's early stylistic surprises might include, first, comments by Susan, an exhausted young wife and mother who has given up a scholarly career: "You shouldn't listen to me either," she tells the narrator. "I'm probably half-mad talking to babies all day. Only there's something sort of enormous and grey and cold about marriage. It's wonderful, isn't it, being a part of it? Or don't you feel that way?" (135); and second, the closing comments of the narrator who savors her husband, his body, their life together, like "a new exotic food. Does this mean everything or nothing? I stand with him in an ancient relationship, in a ruined age, listening beyond my understanding to the warning voices, to the promise of my own substantial heart" (139). A little vaulted, the latter, but there's no mistaking the art in it and the other "Gordonesques," just as there's no mistaking the mnemonic power in her placing side by side *ancient relationship* and *ruined age*.

While exploring any story in the collection or her more recent ones, we can recognize that one technical factor of her art is the way in which Gordon sets out a barrage of details, usually disparate, and then, without warning, parries the blow, the punch, of them; this device, of course, signals the next round and, at the same time, simultaneously delays and intensifies the plot's unfolding. When the time arrives for the final punch (or what one, more formally, might call the recognition scene), Gordon delivers it in an intense sequence in which she usually still manages to encapsulate disparate details.

All this is a part of what Gordon describes as "the craft of conceal-ment" (209) in "A Writing Lesson" (1978), the rather odd little story about writing a story with which she concludes *Temporary Shelter*. Gordon's decision to put this early didactic story at the end of the collec-tion is both calculated and risky. By considering the similarities and dif-ferences between a fairy tale and what she describes as "the kind of fic-tion we are more used to," she risks opening up for formulaic inspection the previous nineteen stories. But the risks are worth taking, for as

Christopher Lehmann-Haupt has pointed out, "'A Writing Lesson' . . . could just as well have been called 'A Reading Lesson'" ("Temporary," 25). His point is well taken; the story *is* more valuable to Gordon's readers than to those who want to write well. The most valuable instructions have to do with our learning to follow Gordon's craft of fictional cues, understatement, delaying mechanisms, control of paired and triadic characters, and, of course, details. The final instructions of the story suggest a methodology for fiction writing and reading as well as for fictional explication and analysis: "Once you have decided upon the path of your narrative and have understood its implications, go back to the beginning of the story. Describe the house" (213).

"The gift of . . . conjuring"

The blurred demarcation zones that Gordon opens up within the genres of fairy tale and short story serve as reminders of how Gordon blurs an even more important demarcation: the boundary between fiction and nonfiction. Occasionally, when asked specifically about her use of autobiographical material, Gordon has approached the blurring; for example, in 1980, she said, "I feel more free to be autobiographical in short stories than in novels. Somehow talking about yourself for ten pages is okay, but talking about yourself for three hundred pages is a bit much" (Cooper-Clark interview, 272).

Still, as I mentioned earlier, Gordon resists this sort of inquiry. On the most apparent level, we can understand her avoidance of the subject: writers use what and who they know best for their subjects, characters, language, imagery, and foci. Gordon's blazing debut as a novelist is a case in point, one that attests to her mastery of the American Catholic world view, manners, and mores she had absorbed in her life up to that point. When she began to enlarge and complicate that arena as she matured, the newly absorbed perspectives and subjects of her third and fourth novels, *Men and Angels* and *The Other Side,* included those of art, fundamentalism, secular worldviews, motherhood, and immigration, the latter of which is her heritage from all four of her grandparents as well as her father. Thus, one naturally expects that her essays, stories, novels, novellas will share, to a certain degree, her evolving interests and views. But when one opens up *The Shadow Man,* Gordon's memoir-biography of her father as well as her mother and their respective families, certain alarm bells start to go off. We already know much of this "real," factual material; we recognize it; we've read it in her stories; we've met these characters in her novels. We know the young narrator of the story "The Thorn," the child grieving for her dead father, is young Gordon herself after her father's death. We remember that the narrator repeats to herself the father's almost identical words—"I love you more than anyone will ever love you. I love you more than God loves you" (103)—that Gordon includes in the memoir. And all the details of Mary's childhood are a part of the short story. We also recognize the details, family life, work, dress habits, skin, wit, crippled leg, and candor of Mary's mother in Nora, the narrator of "Delia," "Agnes," and "Eileen," and in the narrator's mother in "The Neighborhood" and in "The Murderer Guest." Gordon has confirmed biographical details of the "Nora" stories in a 1988 interview, "Well, actually my mother is a polio victim and a lot of that stuff is family stories. Some of them are my family and some the other. That's *the* thing that was good about my family. They were good storytellers." Then she moves to more specifics, "That little girl [Nora] is really a version of my mother. She grows to be an adult in "Delia," where the husband comes back. That actually happened to my mother. And the episode of being turned down at normal school actually happened to her. And I did have this uncle who was a bootlegger that did have this extremely plain mistress who supported him, whom he then left for somebody else" (Keyishian interview, 75).

Gordon adds more, but these comments are enough to introduce the factual resonances that occur in these and other stories. For example, by the time we read the memoir, we already know from the story "The Neighborhood" that Mary's mother moved out of her family's home after sixty years, just as we know about her broken friendships and difficult filial relationships from the "Nora" stories, *The Other Side,* and the 1991 article "Snapshot: A Parting of Friends."

And there's more: we already know the memoir's streets, boroughs, and houses, its neighbors, sounds, crucifixes, kitchen tables, bedrooms, arguments, class distinctions, priests, nuns, and women's retreat groups. Gordon's fiction has already introduced us to them. And other interviews have clarified additional crossovers between fact and fiction. For instance, Gordon has confirmed being raped in Wales during the summer after she graduated from Barnard, a trauma that eventually surfaced in the story "Violation" and in the essay "George Eliot, Dorothea and Me: Rereading (and rereading) 'Middlemarch.'" Similarly when asked about the description of a first husband in the story "Safe," Gordon has said simply, "That's Jim [Brain, Gordon's first husband]. . . . He is an impressive man, but he was totally wrong for me" (Bennett interview,

18). In light of this and other comments about her first husband, their divorce, and her second husband, one pays special attention, for example, to such episodes as a lovemaking scene in the story "Safe," during which the narrator-wife muses about her second husband, "Because of this, because of what I feel for him, what he feels for me, of what we do, can do, have done together in this bed, I left another husband. Broke all sorts of laws: the state's, the church's. Caused a good man pain. And yet it has turned out well. Everyone is happier than ever. I do not understand this" (171).

If such genre crossovers sometimes become confusing to Gordon's readers, we're not alone in our confusion—and our fascination. For instance, an autobiographical essay, "The Important Houses," published first in the *New Yorker* in 1992, was included, despite Gordon's protests, in *Best American Short Stories 1993*. In the contributors' notes at the end of the volume, Gordon is forthright about it: "The story of this 'story' is that it is not a story. It is part of a project I am working on, a sort of biography, a sort of memoir—a history of my father." After describing the work's oblique angle, which her father's "fantastical character" seemed to mandate, she continues, "I have to suppose that it read like 'fiction' because I am primarily a fiction writer, and I create a character using the techniques of fiction: an accretion of detail, a penetration to the inner life, a series of scenes" (*Best American,* 367). When asked about this genre confusion in an interview, Gordon added to the saga, "I told Louise Erdrich, 'I can't take this!' But she told me I'd won it." Then Gordon began laughing and admitted, "Well, I was not going to turn down being in the *Best American Short Stories*. And I *did* tell her—if you noticed my author's comments in the back" (Bennett interview, 19).

For her part, Erdrich's introduction to the volume discusses and praises Gordon's "eidetic and detailed" work which, because of its having "the most devastating last line in the collection," she placed at the edition's conclusion. But Erdrich continues, and her perspective on Gordon's "story that is not a story" is intriguing. Erdrich proposes, "The description here is so meticulous and compelling that it verges on memoir, *and yet the line blurs* [my italics], for Gordon's powers to recreate are so profound. 'The Important Houses' has the gift of deeply imagined conjuring and presents the presiding genius of a place or person in every sentence" (*Best American,* xviii). I agree. It is not simply a case of what Gordon has explained away as "If you use the real names it's nonfiction. If you change the names it's fiction. The rest of that is total crap" (Bennett interview, 19).

It is not simply that Gordon's mother, Anna Gagliano Gordon, becomes, for example, Nora in the stories "Delia," "Agnes," and "Eileen"; then Charlotte Taylor in *The Company of Women;* then the young narrator's mother in "The Thorn" and "The Neighborhood"; then her now elderly, invalided self in Gordon's stunning 1995 essay, "My Mother Is Speaking from the Desert." In Gordon's hands, her mother and all other nonfictional materials are transformed. They become as much a conjured and a conjurer's art as her fiction. And so, if we ask of Gordon's writing: who or which is her mother, really? or her father?, we must answer: they are the mother and father of her life and, equally important, of her artist's mind. In other words, hers is a conjurer's mind that gives her permission to cross back and forth between worlds without a passport, to bring back whomever and whatever she chooses to transform. In explaining about a single descriptive sentence a friend relayed to her that led to her story "Out of the Fray," Gordon has inadvertently sketched out the transformative process: "that absolutely grabbed me. But I made up the central people. I had no interest in what they were in real life actually. . . . But, you know, this is a sort of terrible thing because I don't actually want their story. I want to use parts of their story and retell it in my own way. I might even need a couple of their lines, but then, you know, they can just go off" (Keyishian interview, 75–76). It is in such transformations, her seemingly instinctive breaking down of the traditional differentiations between the genres, that Gordon continues to make some of her most innovative contributions to contemporary fiction. These blurred, arbitrary boundaries are her real "writing lessons," her most intriguing instructions in artistic imagination and freedoms.

An Epilogue on Shelters

In a dizzyingly truthful sequence readers come to expect from Gordon, the narrator of "Now I Am Married" (discussing the precarious nature of contemporary marriages) offers a kind of manifesto-in-miniature for the *Temporary Shelter* collection: "It is the satisfaction of a dying civilization: one perfects the form, knowing it has the thrill of doom upon it. . . . It is harder than art and more dangerous" (137–38). It is just this sort of sequence that lingers on in one's mind after reading Gordon's stories and that probably leads critics, such as Christopher Lehmann-Haupt, to suggest, "What one remembers most acutely is the voice of the narrator—by turns warm, knowing, angry, ironic, self-lacerating, cynical, but ultimately healing and forgiving. Most of all, what this voice conveys is a moral commitment to seek the shelter of civilization and decent behavior, no matter how temporary it may prove" ("Temporary," C25). Knowing that Gordon was grouping together the twenty versions of this narrative voice at the same time she was writing her fourth novel, *The Other Side* (with its complex narrators and commitments and its illusory happinesses), gives added weight to the "temporary shelter" and fictional considerations of her stories. What's more, we learn much from Gordon's work in the short-story genre, with its inherent concentrated vulnerability, about how she has attempted to perfect this form and the novel's as well. In a technologically driven world, her work and that of other fiction writers stubbornly reflect both the headaches and (like the narrator's comments on marriage in "Now I Am Married") "the satisfaction of a dying civilization . . . knowing it has the thrill of doom upon it" (138).

Chapter Six

"Respice, Adspice, Prospice": *The Other Side*

The 1989 publication of *The Other Side* marks the beginning of a hiatus in Gordon's association with Random House. When asked in 1995 about the switch to Viking Penguin for *The Other Side, Good Boys and Dead Girls and Other Essays,* and *The Rest of Life,* Gordon (who, by that time, was back with Random House) explained, "Well, my editor [Anne Freedgood] was fired. . . . So I did an act of loyalty which didn't quite work out" (Bennett interview, 22). As we discover, Gordon's characteristic sense of loyalty plays a central role in her fourth novel. The trait shows up in other ways; for example, *The Other Side* is dedicated to Richard Gilman, who, in Gordon's words, "helped me a lot" as a reader for this novel, as did Jan Schmidt, to whom Gordon dedicated *Temporary Shelter* (Bennett interview, 22).

"homage to the ghosts"

The Other Side explores four generations of an Irish-American family, the MacNamaras, as well as the generation in Ireland from whom they descended. The backward and forward motions of the exploration are complex and ambitious, so much so that they bring to mind the kind of heraldic goals reflected in the Latin motto of the City College of New York: "Respice, Adspice, Prospice." Such a directive—examine the past, examine the present, examine the future—might be an appropriate summary of the novelistic strategies within any multigenerational family saga. Gordon, however, adds several distinctive directives to the agenda for her fourth novel.

The first of these, as we learn from a number of 1985 interviews, is driven by her attention to both national and personal history. For example, during the early gestation period of the novel that was, at the time, tentatively entitled *The Rose Tree*[1] but would be published four years later as *The Other Side,* Gordon commented to Walter Clemons, "I think I'm probably of the last generation to feel itself slightly apart from the

American mainstream. If I take my children to Ellis Island . . . they won't feel quite the way I do when I see it. I want to write about that before it entirely disappears" ("Ah," 75). Elsewhere, Gordon described the novel in progress as being "about how the experience of immigration affects different generations, and how it still has an effect on my generation, but how I think we'll really be the last. It's been done for the Jews, but I don't think anybody's talked about the experiences of Irish immigration—except for schlock novelists. . . . I think it's too good a subject for them to have" (Bolotin interview, 234). In yet another 1985 interview, Gordon was more specific about the autobiographical motivations behind her project when she suddenly asked Herbert Mitgang, "Have you ever been to Ellis Island? My grandmother arrived there at the age of 17 [in 1896]. It is a chilling, moving place today" ("Cabin," 30).

Gordon's maternal grandmother was not her only familial motivation. All four of her grandparents (one from Ireland, one from Sicily, and two from Lithuania) were immigrants. In a 1985 *New York Times Magazine* essay, Gordon wrote, "And so I made a journey there [Ellis Island] to find my history, like any Rotarian traveling in his Winnebago to Antietam to find his. . . . The monument I traveled to was not, however, a tribute to some old glory. The minute I set foot upon the island I could feel all that it stood for: insecurity, obedience, anxiety, dehumanization, the terrified and careful deference of the displaced. I hadn't traveled to the Battery and boarded a ferry across from the Statue of Liberty to raise flags or breathe a richer, more triumphant air. I wanted to do homage to the ghosts."[2] What Gordon did not know until 1994 was that her father also arrived at Baltimore as a Yiddish-speaking six-year-old immigrant from Vilna, Lithuania. In other words, the novelist who wrote *The Other Side* was more closely related to the immigrant experience than she believed at the time. She is, in fact, both a second- and a third-generation American, a shifting that adds poignancy to her subject choice for a fourth novel and to a critic's comment in 1990 about *The Other Side:* "I don't know that this novel is semi-autobiographical, but it does have the feel of someone trying to understand her own ancestry."[3]

That Mary Gordon's deceased father, David, had felt the need to pose as a *second*-generation American authenticates, in hindsight, her second goal for this novel, a goal she has addressed with fierce intensity in the memoir, in several essays and stories, and in one novella: "I want to undo that lie about immigration: that all our parents came over and they were instant and flourishing successes. Maybe people were crushed by the experience of immigration, really crushed" (Bennett interview, 8). In the novel, Vincent MacNamara's granddaughter had raised the possibility when, for a night-school oral report project, she was taping his descriptions of his experiences and work: "If you came here, Granddaddy, as a skilled machinist, why did it take so many years to get a job commensurate with your skills? Was it your Irish heritage that held you back? Statistics show the Irish don't achieve as they could be expected to. As a nationality, they don't live up to their potential" (304). Vincent's answers to Sheilah (and his musings on all that he does not tell her) address the first of these questions and the complicated path of his career. He thinks about his first grueling job as a digger for the Whitehall Street-Montague Street Tunnel between Brooklyn and Manhattan, his unhappy work for Acme Tool and Die in Long Island City, his proud work for the IRT (Broadway Line) between 103rd and 125th Streets, at which point he joined the company's union. Then he remembered starting the work "he had been trained to all along, machinist's work, at the Kent Avenue Power Plant" (287); his heart attack at the age of forty in 1935; then his work for Patent Scaffolding in Queens, from which he retired in 1961. Vincent certainly was no "instant and flourishing success," to use Gordon's words. But he is not a crushed immigrant, nor is he is interested in Sheilah's later questions about the Irish, which the novel itself is designed to answer partially: "He wanted to tell her: You're asking the wrong questions. Questions like that are not the kind I like to answer. He wanted to describe how the place looked" (288), the sounds of it, the blueprints, the machinery, the orders: "'Vincent, we want fifty-three fittings pronto, hole 73/8,' and you'd have to make them. You thought at first you couldn't; then you realized you could" (289), details that reflect one immigrant's immovable delight in his work.

When we come to know the matriarch of *The Other Side,* Ellen Costelloe MacNamara, we face another possibility that Gordon raises: maybe people were crushed, "really crushed," even before they boarded the ships, and such damage was the invisible, immigrant cargo stowed away in the ships' holds and then unloaded on "the other side." John B. Breslin has pointed out that "The blight they [Ellen and Vincent MacNamara] carried with them from the other side infects in one form or another all three of their children and most of the next two generations."[4] In discussing the traumatic damage both Ellen and Vincent experienced separately in their Irish homes, Breslin does not track "the blight in their baggage" far enough. He makes us understand why Ellen will be marked for life by the damage; as her granddaughter Camille observes, "Ellen MacNamara made a happy marriage. But it was not enough. She came into it from a life already scalded by shame, stiffened by disappointment, judgment, fear" (37). Thus, her immigration in 1911 is shadowed by damage that she hides behind an angry facade. But Breslin does not pursue an important contradiction: Vincent MacNamara's approach to America in 1916 and his subsequent life are much more resilient, gentle, and hopeful. One would hardly expect this from a young child who was brutalized continually by an older brother, a brother who, knowing how Vincent and their mother loved an orphaned lamb they were raising, had slit its throat. Going over the scene in his mind, the elderly Vincent remembers his reaction: "The first thing he took in with calm; it was simple: the animal was dead. The second made him frightened: he could see the remnants of life still within the animal. . . . The third thing he knew made fear and anger grow inside his brain, like trees that grow from the same root beside each other, harmful and competitive, yet bound. His brother had done this to harm him. It was Vincent's throat, not the poor animal's, he would have liked to cut" (227). From then on, the studious, mechanical whiz of a boy had known he would have to leave his family's farm and this brother who "would always be happy only at his [Vincent's] harm" (228). Still, he leaves home at the age of fifteen and, eventually, he sails from Ireland with buoyant hope and a strong faith, and without anger.

The differences between these responses are another of the possibilities Gordon addresses in the novel. We recognize that, at their core, the differences continue the inquiry she raised at the conclusion of *Men and Angels.* There, in an interior monologue, the character Anne Foster muses about the unpredictableness of children's responses to trauma: they "throve or starved, and no one knew why, or what killed or saved." The same is true for adults as well, Anne realizes: "there was no guarantee. Some grew in the face of sorrow, and some were undone. Some opened and enlarged, and some were ground to dust" (238). As *The Other Side* makes clear, the immigration experience itself can either augment or assuage children's and adults' traumas. The novel also shows that when damage hardens into the core of an individual's world view, an immigrant such as Ellen will project that damage on the widening circles of her own children, grandchildren, and great-grandchildren.

At this level, the novel's familial preoccupations become universal: radical damage can affect generations of *any* family. Who is incapable or capable of breaking up or resisting such patterns and how and why they can or cannot do so are, of course, parts of the novel's larger psychological inquiry, an inquiry that one critic wryly attempts to deflate when she insists, "other people's awful families do tend, in fiction at least, to have a bracing effect."[5] Nevertheless, Gordon's primary goal for *The Other Side* is to debunk the myths we (especially those of us who are either long established, outsiders, or newcomers to the U.S.A.) prefer to cloak around immigrant experiences and opportunities in the United States. This is not a new goal for Gordon; almost a decade before the publication of *The Other Side,* she was addressing and undermining myths about Catholic immigrants: "What is touching and moving is the loneliness of the immigrant experience, always feeling an outsider, always defining yourself as 'not Protestant,' and even later on as 'not Jewish,' knowing that you somehow never had access to the real power, and kind of looking in with your nose pressed against the window" (Cooper-Clark interview, 271). At other times, Gordon has done her debunking in a rather mischievous high style; in a 1985 essay, for instance, she recounts trying to get away from a Russian linguist's keen interest in her being, as he describes it, "really somebody who comes from what is called the boiling pot of America." Making her exit, Gordon muses, "I thought it would be too hard to explain to him the relation of the boiling potters to the main course." But what follows in her explanation seems prescient of the serious debunking she would bring together, four years later, in *The Other Side:* "I told him that the only thing I could think of that united people whose backgrounds, histories and points of view were utterly diverse was that their people had landed at a place called Ellis Island" ("More Than Just," 65).

In her fourth novel, Gordon is searingly unsentimental about immigration and about the Irish themselves; this is no "rags to riches" story, no "Kiss Me I'm Irish" button, no St. Patrick's Day Parade down Fifth Avenue. Moreover, as we have come to expect in her earlier novels, Gordon does not stop at expected parameters of explication. She always adds surprises to her agendas, and the novel's most surprising premise is one that debunks a myth that few Americans address with any degree of comfort. Demonstrated by the characters Ellen and Vincent MacNamara and by their marriage, which is the only successful one in the story, Gordon's premise is that the immigrants themselves (damage notwithstanding) are much stronger, more vital, more significant, than their American-born progeny. On both national and personal levels, this is a threatening premise, one that inevitably attracts critical attention. For example, while puzzling over "whether it is a failure in Gordon's art or a mark of it, and of her keen sociological insight," David Toolan observes, "the farther we get from Ellen's moon and Vincent's sun along the line of descent, the more that energy dissipates."[6] Alice Bloom, on the other hand, has no such reservations; in the midst of praising Gordon's expertise in creating a twenty-character, family-portrait gallery, Bloom suggests, "for each life, a whole America is painted in, beginning with immigrant life in New York, early union organizing, two world wars, the Depression, holding the family together despite all, up to a new slacker America of divorce, scattered households, weaker characters, more money but far less sense, much less beauty" ("Why the Novel," 163). All this is to introduce the fact that *The Other Side* reflects a novelist's acute sense of responsibility to the past, the present, and the future (and to the novel genre itself) that is as personal, historic, and surprising as it is multivalent.

"see the line of it"

The novel's structure and language reflect both the expansive ambitions and innovative reining-ins that differentiate this novel from its predecessors. Unlike the triadic emphases she has deployed in earlier novels, Gordon divides *The Other Side* into five parts. The lengths of the five parts and each of the thirty-four chapters are markedly irregular. The chapters themselves continually vary in length, sometimes only three paragraphs long, sometimes eighty-eight pages. Likewise, the narrative voices shift from chapter to chapter. Yet, there are two definite gravitational centers within the narratives: Gordon anchors the multigenerational, alternating voices in Parts One, Three, and Five around Part Two (three long chapters given to the voice of Ellen MacNamara, the matriarch of the family) and Part Four (one long chapter narrated by Vincent MacNamara, the patriarch of the family). And in prioritizing the voices of Ellen and Vincent and, subsequently, two of their grandchildren, the cousins Camille and Dan, Gordon is also directing the reader toward the only functional duos within the family. This direction, nevertheless, heightens an awareness of their and the others' dysfunction within the family.

The result of Gordon's technical strategies and descriptive details is an unsettling, transatlantic family portrait in which few of the five generations of an Irish-American family are smiling. The MacNamara family is, according to Judith Thurman, "the kind about which a cynical voice from a Philip Larkin poem whispers, 'Get out as early as you can.'"[7] Thurman even suggests Larkin's poem "This Be the Verse" as an appropriate epigraph for the novel.[8] Gordon's nonchronological, multigenerational approach to her less cynical but equally harrowing family portrait suggests a technical and thematic construct very much like that used in montage. Only gradually does she fit together the individual immigrations of Ellen Costelloe and her future husband Vincent MacNamara, their Irish childhoods and families, their initial experiences in America and subsequent work, marriage, friends, politics, religion, and progeny.

The emerging faces and facts within the portrait are framed within two static devices. First of all, the family's evolution across the seven decades since Ellen's and Vincent's arrivals is examined within the Aristotelian unities of time and place. The story unfolds within a single day, August 14, 1985, at 128 Linden Street in Queens Village, New York, which has been Ellen and Vincent's home for some sixty-three years. Our sense of the unity of place is intensified by the story's quietly informing us that "Almost all of them [four generations of MacNamaras] live within forty-five minutes of Queens Village . . . an oddity in mobile, shifting America" (7).

Another "oddity" within the novel, one that is not at all arbitrary, is Gordon's choosing August 14 for the gathering of four MacNamara generations around the dying, ninety-year-old Ellen. The date, which represents the novel's second static device, is the most delicious but painful irony of the story, one that only eighty-nine-year-old Vincent obliquely recalls but does not mention, as he reluctantly prepares to return home from a long convalescence to Ellen, whom he had promised years earlier that she could, as she begged him, die at home and with him beside her. The irony is that the fourteenth of August is marked in the Catholic Church calendar as the day of vigil. It is the day before the Feast of Assumption that celebrates the bodily ascension of the Virgin Mary into heaven after her death. Gordon, in effect, has set up an ironic contrast between the vigil in Queens and the vigil for the Queen of Heaven. The latter is just the sort of celebratory observance that Ellen, in her total repudiation of Catholicism, might have mocked savagely, if she had been coherent during the MacNamara family's private vigil for her. Moreover, the dying Ellen's foulmouthed ragings and her actions as a young woman and as a mother are fierce contradictions of the gentle, obedient, long-suffering Virgin's model, so much so that if any verbal attempt had been made among the MacNamaras to parallel the Virgin Mary's capacity for maternal love, a serene death, and heavenly rewards with Ellen's, such a suggestion would have been greeted by many of her progeny with an inarticulate savagery that equaled their matriarch's.

From the start, then, Gordon opens up a charged arena in which unarticulated and articulated repudiations of transatlantic, religious, and cultural traditions are linked to anger and death and, more importantly, to what one kills within oneself and others during life. In addition, the familial vigil around Ellen's deathbed intensifies the novel's structural and thematic purposes. Gordon, in essence, creates a circular context of grief, anger, and unrealized hopes within which she challenges a core of myths and assumptions that have grown up around immigrant assimilations into the American mainstream.

Nowhere is Gordon's repudiation of facile immigrations seen more clearly than in the character of Ellen MacNamara. In Ellen, Gordon explores an emigré, whose radical belligerence against homogeneity, whose strength, rage, intelligence, love, and damage cast long shadows across her life, her husband's and three generations of their family. What's more, Ellen's repudiation of her Irish heritage debunks all sorts of nostalgia-for-the home country myths; a typical example is Ellen's habit of insisting dramatically, "What would I go [back] for? Pigs and dirt and begging relatives. No thanks, none of that 'I'll Take You Home Again Kathleen' cod for me, thank you. That's my husband's department. Say the word 'bog' only and he's drowning in the water of his tears" (86–87). This dichotomy with emigré attitudes is clear to Ellen from the start. As the sixteen-year-old sets off alone for America, she regards herself as an outsider and refuses to be assimilated or comforted even within the homogeneity of the other Irish immigrants. "On the ship," the dying Ellen recalls, "she kept entirely to herself . . . the foolish buzzing around her, the ridiculous girls talking . . . a danger to herself, that thing she was by herself, apart from other people, that thing that people had to keep their distance from" (103).

A lifetime of such repudiations comes together at the vigil, which gradually assumes the nature of a wake for the living, for which, we notice, Gordon has prepared us by mentioning that the gathering before Vincent's departure from Ireland, years before, was called the "American Wake" (242). The Irish-American MacNamaras' vigil-wake is an act of mourning for a living legacy of profound damage that has survived and evolved since its transplanting from Ireland. It is, as Judith Thurman has mentioned, also "a wake for all those living parents who are dead to their children" ("Sad But," 100), a parental configuration we have encountered in such Gordon stories as "The Magician's Wife," "The Only Son of the Doctor," and "Mrs. Cassidy's Last Year," the last of which is the first fictional exploration of *The Other Side*'s story.

Unexpectedly, the vigil includes a strange but central act of mourning for an immigrant's strength, her high principles, and her remarkably successful marriage, none of which her progeny will ever match. Thus, the progeny gather and take their places in Ellen and Vincent's little home in Queens. In the midst of the gathering, one grandson telephones his mistress to report, "Nobody's killed anyone yet. Not bad for the house of Atreus" (185). Another grandchild, Marilyn (who must somehow, during the vigil, break the news that her third marriage has failed, notices, "The net of kinship spreads around them, spreads and draws. There is a place for everyone, she thinks, but not all places are equal and not everyone is happy with his place" (8).

Gordon's use of August 14 and the unities serves the novel well. It also enables her to escape the strictures of a chronological plot development, while it allows her full access to those techniques in which she excels: interior monologues, portraiture, and flashbacks, each of which she uses to delineate the characters and their complex relationships. As Madison Smartt Bell has emphasized, "There's plot enough in 'The Other Side' for several novels, but the main purpose of all the action is to illuminate individual character: what it is and how it comes to be. Ms. Gordon has set out to discover how each self is formed in relation to other selves, to learn to what extent identity is chosen and to what extent it is imposed."[9]

A Reined-In Virtuosity

The understatement and general restraint Gordon employs in the novel's language seem to mark a major shift in her style, a premise with which some critics, such as Anita Brookner, would disagree. Her review of *The Other Side* suggests that Gordon is "defeated by her style," which Brookner faults as "orotund" and "portentous" ("Appeal" 37). Others, however, also have recognized the changes in Gordon's syntax. Writing for the *New Yorker,* Judith Thurman, for example, notes, "Gordon's sentences used to be better than her novels, like the kind of lavish hair which outrivals a woman's face. But the prose of 'The Other Side' is matter-of-fact . . . more precisely, its poetic lushness has been suppressed" ("Sad But," 99). Most habitual readers of Gordon's fiction would suggest, with some relief, that, well, not all of the "poetic lushness" has disappeared from this novel. It simply submerges and reemerges more irregularly in such passages as: "Ellen MacNamara lies in her white net of cloud and sees only glimpses. Lucid rhomboids of the past. She sees her mother rocking in the darkness, gibbering in the dark. She sees her cruel father and his mistress, and the mistress's ankles, and her cruel back. . . . In her bed now, more than seventy years later, weakened beyond action, beyond speech, beyond the power of coherent image-making, Ellen renews her vow. That she will not forgive" (63).

Still, it is apparent that Gordon has reined in her considerable lyrical talent, what she herself has described as her interest in "virtuoso prose" (Bennett interview, 35). In its place she sometimes employs the kind of ludic flashes we saw in her first novel. For instance, Camille, Ellen and Vincent's granddaughter, suddenly says to Ira Silverman, her Jewish lover, "I'm the only person in America who really understands Phil Donahue. He's just mimicking a particular kind of priest. There was always one of them, not the pastor, the assistant pastor, prematurely gray. The middle-aged women always went to him to confession. . . . They felt they could talk to him about birth control. . . . The women all said to their husbands: Why can't you be more like him? Eventually, he became a pastor and he stopped talking to the ladies. But while he lasted, they were in heaven" (59). The pithy third sentence in this passage is itself worth the price of the novel; the same is true in the softer and more revealing style Gordon fashions for Camille's private recollections of learning to read: "She was amazed from the moment that the letters of the alphabet unlocked themselves into a tray of meaning she could sample and re-combine, certain that others who read—who pretended to be reading—weren't experiencing what she did. Either it wasn't the same thing, or they were cleverly making their faces blank so that no one could guess the value of what was happening behind their eyes. . . . Dissimulation seemed a duty. She began then to frown when she was reading so that no one would suspect her joy" (15–16).

Another stylistic change in Gordon's monologues and dialogues is the accelerated pace of syntactical contrasts. Mary Flanagan, for instance, has noticed that Gordon "has a lilting even rhapsodic style, punctuated with a stacatto [sic] of unattached phrases and clauses that links the contemporary with the past."[10] One of several hundred demonstrations of this combination is in the dying Ellen's clouded struggles to remember: "Now running through her mind past all the bodies she has been. The girl child running behind the easy body of her mother, mother's body like a ship, then older limbs, light, long, and painful in their joints, and the new arrivals: breasts, hair, blood, monthly pain. Grown used to that at last, the self lost, and herself a mother, who does not see herself a ship at ease in movement. . . . The lost body forever lost. But not the voices. No. Not lost. Bella. She hears Bella's voice, as she has always. Bella. My friend. She calls out" (121–22). Many other passages, on the other hand, are reined in until they set up a stylistic evenness that represents another innovation in Gordon's work; they serve an added purpose at the same time: the exposition of a great many details. A fairly typical example of this occurs in Ellen's silent, extended protest (italicized in the text) to other immigrants, which ends: "*So sing on. Choke yourselves with lies about what you never had, and weep now for not having.*" Ellen's recollections move directly to: "She felt her shame amidst the other greenhorns and held it up against their sorrow. *Come home and let me see your face before I die.* She was the criminal among them. Only Delia knew. Ellen would die grateful to her for that. . . . But among the weeping sons and daughters who'd been sent off with tears, with grieving, Ellen felt herself flayed. It made her credulous and grateful . . . to be told by first the housekeeper, then Mrs. Fitzpatrick herself, that she would do. She seemed a girl of promise, but she must work hard. The work was never hard. It was the nature of the life that killed her. All the lies that stopped her breath" (116–17). That it was lies, a different set of lies, that drove her away from Ireland in the first place brings up the issue of Ireland and the Irish.

Breaking the Silence: "the sickle-cell anemia of the Irish"

Gordon's approach to Ireland and to immigrants' origins and offspring is not without sentiment. There is sentiment aplenty in *The Other Side,* but her approach is determinedly *un*sentimental. Throughout her career, some critics have mistaken Gordon's intensity for sentimentality, especially if that intensity focuses on a subject with which the critic is seemingly uncomfortable or uninformed, or if the intensity is reflected in passionate lyricism. This is not to suggest that such criticism has always been misguided; any novelist who is as engaged as Gordon has been with her subject matter, and as verbally gifted, risks crossing certain boundaries of excess. Still, the probable target of most of these critical "sentimentality" missives was and is Gordon's novelistic intensity itself, a different subject altogether. Being cognizant of the different issues is essential if we are to appreciate Gordon's maturation in the handling of both sentiment and her hallmark intensity in *The Other Side,* a maturation that she demonstrates through a linguistic, subjective, and structural checks-and-balances system.

From the start of the novel, it is obvious that Gordon does not intend to address the Irish famine of 1845–52 or the broader economic and sociological forces that led to the massive influx of Irish immigrants into the United States during the eighty years following the famine years.[11] Moreover, unlike her pained nonfictional accounts of medical inspections and quarantines at Ellis Island, Gordon's fourth novel does not address the issues of diseases and the initial treatment of immigrants. Instead, as will be discussed, Gordon emphasizes the long-range results of psychological, familial, and national damage that immigrants have brought from Ireland. And her novel's overarching focus is on the immigrants' new lives and progeny in the United States; this is where she begins.

Gordon has done her homework on the issues surrounding those waves of immigrants who served as a cheap labor force for American capitalism, and the acknowledgments section of the book points us to the specific resources for her research on these issues. The results are impressive. Some of the stronger writing in the novel depicts the energy and products of that force (the building of the New York subway, for example); the national, local, and ecclesial (Catholic) political pressures on immigrant workers and servants; the wage- and power-rigging systems; and the resulting trade union movement.

An essential factor in the success of Gordon's presentation of these issues is that she keeps them tightly fused; for example, as the dying Ellen muses over the early years of her and Vincent's marriage, she remembers, "Excited as a boy and boyish in his ardor, he would come to her at night, home from a late [secret trade union organizing] meeting, now older, heavier in his body, and his rough cheek, cold from the outside, would arouse her. In the mornings, he would talk at the breakfast table to the children about starving workers, and the hope of the trade unions, about Sacco and Vanzetti, the tragedy of it, Al Smith, he's Irish, children, but he might yet be the President, about how the Pope himself would sooner or later endorse labor unions, he knew it on good authority, they needn't fear what the priests said. She'd get angry then: 'What do you care a damn for a priest's words, there's not a one of them who's not a liar or a thief. Or a pansy on the top of it'" (148).

The irascible, intelligent Ellen would never allow Vincent any free zone of comfort, any compartmentalizing of issues; she recalls "Arguing with Vincent against religion. 'You're a union man. They've [the Catholic Church] threatened every Irishman who has a union card with eternal damnation. They've held the labor unions back for fifty years.' Turning the radio up so he would have to hear the voice of Father

Coughlin, she says, "'This is the mouthpiece of the church you want
your children brought up bending the knee to. Filth. Poison. And you
want their veins opened up to that'" (148–49).

Such examples, which fill almost half of the novel's pages, also
demonstrate that Gordon's exploration of Irish-Americans and Ireland
is designed to undercut the whole stereotypical arsenal of glib or comforting clichés and of pejorative or condescending phrases that we have
come to expect in novels and films about our own or others' immigrant
origins, characteristics, and New World experiences, especially those
of the Irish. As Mary Flanagan has noticed, "There are no stereotypes,
no jokes, no stage Irishmen. The characters are complex and disturbingly real" ("Threnody," 34). Flanagan's comments and, especially,
her phrase "disturbingly real" seem closer to the mark than Judith
Thurman's suggestion that Gordon's earlier novels "repudiated the
pieties, fantasies, and clichés of Irish-American life or attempted to
transcend them. Here she simply discloses their mediocrity and sadness" ("Sad But," 99). Probably intended as a segue to later comments
about the MacNamaras' weaker progeny, Thurman's comments skirt
the fierce, risk-filled questions at the core of this novel: what about the
Irish? what *is* it about the Irish? what is it in *any* genetic, racial, or
national lineage that can lead to long-term, deadly familial dynamics?
Such questions are, to reborrow Flanagan's phrase, made "disturbingly
real" in this novel. As David Toolan has admitted, "Most readers, be
they of Irish extraction or not, will recognize the poisoned gene pool
and the family dysfunctions that Gordon anatomically dissects here,
and if they strike discomfortingly close to home (as they did for me), all
the better" ("Other," 15).

Gordon begins to offer some scathing answers to the questions in the
first chapter of Part III, which appears between Ellen's three long chapters in Part II and Vincent's long chapter that makes up Part IV. It is a
carefully placed vantage point between the voices of two disparate Irish
immigrants, and it is their grandson Dan who sees the larger context of
those voices' contradictions and their family's dysfunction, the same
grandson whom Ellen took away from his young, sleazy mother after
John, the child's father and Ellen's adored son, died in World War II.

Growing up in the home of his grandparents, Ellen and Vincent,
young Dan MacNamara could never form a focused picture of Ireland in
his mind. It was not only the news and pictures of Europe during World
War II that clouded his imagination. He could never put together the
two Irelands of the household. Dan often wondered, "Was it the green

country of his grandfather, or the hard, filthy place that she [Ellen] spoke of?" (160), the country she described as a "bog, a backwater, a filthy hole" (159). Throughout his and his first cousin Camille's childhood in their grandparents' home, Ellen had ridiculed first-generation immigrants who wanted to show their home country to their own children: "To see what? she would say. The cattle shitting in the streets, . . . the children with their teeth rotted out of their heads, the beautiful thatched cottages swept only once a year. . . . Oh, this beautiful thing, Ellen would say, through furious cruel teeth, we loved it so, that's why we couldn't wait to leave" (159). If, for the grandchildren's sake, the usually gentle, courtly Vincent would recall memories of the grass, milk, bread, songs, and peat fires of his own childhood, Ellen "would raise the hammer of her scorn" (160). But then in 1983, Dan, his two daughters, and his cousin Camille had visited Ireland. When they make pilgrimages to Dromnia, the rural farm country of his grandfather's youth, and to Tulla, Ellen's birthplace, which is, Dan recognizes, a town of "bleak, commercial greed" (163), he discovers that both accounts had been accurate; there *were* two Irelands.

Dan's recognitions go further, and in these Gordon's unsentimental approach shows itself to be as well-crafted as it is witheringly insightful. Despite the agricultural frustrations of the Irish land, Dan sees that the "real life [of the Irish] was in the countryside. . . . the country was miraculous" (162). The Irish towns, by contrast, reinforce his deciding that the Irish were a "people whose genius was rural" (162), rather than urban or commercial. The towns' stripped-down-for-commerce architecture reflects, in Dan's mind, a willed blindness, these towns with their "blunt disregard for beauty, a blank, punitive, ungenerous self-presentation, a reproach to ornament, to prideful style" (162). Likewise, he sees in their homes a colonized people who had learned from the English "the wrong half," the tacky half, of "their symbols of prosperity and of success," to which the Irish women added defensive, unnatural attempts at cleanliness and cleaning and an "obsession with concealment, or protection," by "dust-resistant covers on their furniture," and by the doilies with which everything was covered (161). These and other observations come together in Dan's mind as "the proof of the Irish temperament, the doomed service of the ideal, the blatant disregard of present pleasure" (160). Dan, in other words, has discovered the proof of his inheritance, the explanations of his family's dysfunctions; Ireland, for Dan (and for the novel), is the "sign: they could never be happy, any of them, coming from people like the Irish. Unhappiness was bred into the bone, a message in the blood, a code of weakness. The sickle-cell anemia of the Irish: they had to thwart joy in their lives" (160).

This assertion is both Dan's and Gordon's most startling and threatening presupposition, one demonstrated by each of the twenty-odd MacNamaras, in his or her unique way and respective generation. And some of them are able to articulate (silently, of course) the lineage of the MacNamaras' undermined happinesses. For instance, as Dan watches the adversarial jockeying within the gathering family at Ellen and Vincent's home, he thinks to himself, "He can see the line of it, starting with Ellen, hating herself, refusing to love her daughters, stealing him from his mother, taking Cam [Camille] from Magdalene; he sees John and Sheilah in their mother's blackened house. And he and Marilyn, always a little desperate: We'll fix it, wait a minute, we'll do something; it will be all right" (157–58).

Dan's summary exemplifies the ways in which Gordon accentuates habitual thwartings of happiness by constantly rearranging paired characters: husbands and wives, siblings, parents and children, grandparents and grandchildren, cousins, lovers, and friends. These shifting rearrangements, in turn, link individuals' reactions across generations whose lives are more often than not expressed in private anger, hate, guilt, fear, withdrawals, rejection, and broken ambitions. A typical example of this occurs when Camille and Dan temporarily escape from the family vigil to go on a walk after another of the habitual confrontations between Camille and her vicious, coldly pious Aunt Theresa; Cam "sees him [Dan] floundering, desperately trying to be interesting, to make her laugh so that she'll give it up, this anger that she treasures, that she doesn't want to give up, that she enjoys hoarding, fingering. . . . She can know who she is in the world if she is somebody's antagonist; to be Theresa's enemy, therefore *not Theresa* in the world, satisfies her, gives her certainty and hope. But Dan is drowning in his efforts to make her stop . . . She'll give it up for him, this anger, desirable to her, valuable as medicine or wealth" (158–59).

By the time we have reached this point of the novel (the opening chapter of Part III), we know all too well where she learned the art of anger: at Ellen's feet.[12] And we know Ellen's and her daughter Theresa's mutual fury at each other and the ways in which Camille's agoraphobic mother, Magdalene, has absorbed and repressed her own and her mother's fury. As Dan's daughter, the fourth-generational Darci, notices, "Secretly she liked her great-aunt Magdalene, but saw that Cam both did and didn't want her to. . . . She saw the way Magdalene used Cam;

she saw her beloved Cam grow into a hard stranger in her mother's presence. She saw, too, with the vision of the gifted young, that the adult world was a series of armed camps that demanded loyalties that she was glad to give because they must be absolute" (69–70).

In such ways, Gordon fashions the links of anger and thwarted happiness, the underminings of pleasure, that leap back and forth across the generations and, more alarmingly, will continue. Vincent and his grandson, Dan, are, to some extent, less-active participants in the damaging cycles, but their passivity wreaks its own tolls. It is interesting to notice, however, that these two and Ira Silverman, Cam's Jewish lover (who plays a minor, outsider role), demonstrate Gordon's maturation in depicting full-blown, male characters. Nevertheless, they are no match for the strength of the female characters, Ellen and her granddaughter Cam, who, though a professional success, is her grandmother's younger counterpart. Moreover, the focus of the novel's main questions and the "sickle-cell anemia" within the MacNamara family lead back to Ellen and, through her, back to Ireland itself.

To Ireland and Back

It is in Ireland that the complex metaphor for Ellen's lifelong damage and anger forms: the sound of a swarm of bees in the Knock James Church in Tulla, a swarm that none of the other "kind- and stupid-faced" parishioners fear and whose departure they greet with gratitude. For Ellen, the bees' "noise was the clamor of her fear, the drone of her entrapment. Their stain, their leavings were the family sin" (101); their buzzing becomes the "sound of all her terror" (87) and of all she is fleeing. It is the fused metaphor of her beautiful mother's descent into an obese, gibbering insanity and the buzzing swarm of mindless fools, like those in her village and parish, who could make you "easily forget who you were, that large acts were possible, that the world could change, you could change, could get away" (103). Likewise, such buzzing signals her own weakness, hopelessness, and what she naively perceives as her criminal exit from Ireland.

Thus, Ellen determines early on that she can mask her legacy by keeping herself from others. On the surface, this temerity seems to serve her purposes well during her first years in America and the early years of her marriage. From the start, however, the secrets define the parameters that eventually will yield the Irish-American MacNamaras' "House of Atreus." As a now elderly man, Vincent thinks about Ellen's working

formula for life: "You kept things to yourself. You kept them hidden. . . .
You did not show off. . . . Anger only was allowed" (250). Only after
years of marriage had he discovered the secrets Ellen had brought to
America. Those secrets included her mother's insanity, the result of eight
failed, bloody births and a husband's growing disgust; Ellen's adored
father's replacing the mother with a slut; and Ellen's plotting both her
revenge on her father and her escape by slowly stealing enough money
from him to buy her passage to America. Not for Ellen then were
Vincent's conversations enroute to America about how "the past was
past and everything in the world was theirs" (245).

For Ellen, the past is never past, and this, Gordon seems to suggest, is
a critical factor in the legacy of Irish immigrants. Even partially
repressed, Ellen's legacy fuels her belligerence; her keeping herself apart
from friends, community, and members of her family; her inability to
either forget or forgive any small or large failure, any sign of weakness in
herself and others. It is not that she is unaware. Gordon shows us that
Ellen is not only acutely aware of it all, but that the "sickle-cell anemia"
of her Irish mind willfully undermines opportunities for happiness or
healing for both herself and others. For example, although inarticulate
on her deathbed, Ellen still rails in her mind against her two daughters,
"one a coward and the other heartless" (108), but then she rails against
herself for resisting their infant softness and denying both her love.
Likewise, as her flickering memories savor the uninhibited sexuality she
shared with Vincent, she screams against the male sexual needs that
replaced her mother with a whore: "I know what they do. . . . I stiffen all
my life against them. I become a weapon. I become an eye, a glass, a fire
burning up their pleasure . . . I keep it all in my mind which . . . lets go
of nothing" (130). And even as she is soothed by the presence of her
grandson Dan beside her bed, Ellen cannot forgive herself for taking
Dan away from his mother, after the infant's father, Ellen's firstborn, is
killed in World War II. Nor can she forgive her son's widow, whom Ellen
considered a cheap slut, not unlike the one who replaced her own
mother.

These reflect something of the legacy of injury and will that Ellen has
carried to and continued in America. They first keep Ellen apart from
the other immigrants; from the moment she sets out, she has no dream
of going back, no tender sentiment. These same shames and resistances
also render her speechless in the great cause of her early immigrant life,
the Women's Trade Union. Although Bella, a Russian Jewish immigrant
who is Ellen's best friend, can speak up with force and ease at the

group's gatherings, "her huge lacks would be seen" (134). Thus, Ellen remains silent, and in so doing, closes the doors to the radical female leadership for which her temperament and intelligence ideally suit her. However, such ventures are impossible for her. For at the center of her mind, Ellen hears her mother's low, inarticulate gibberish, "the noise of her words that weren't words" that act on her life like the worst of all curses: "Forget your efforts. Nothing will prevail" (135).

Nevertheless, as a result of Ellen's painstaking nurture and goadings, Dan and Camille (the two grandchildren whom she took from their mothers) are fairly resilient individuals who have successful careers as attorneys. At least, then, in the third generation of this immigrant family, two of the MacNamaras have been strong enough to answer "that clear call from the outside" Ellen had thought about as she sailed toward America, but to which neither she nor her daughters could adequately respond. And the two great-granddaughters, especially Darci, evince enough inner confidence to create happier futures for themselves. These four, however, are the four possible exceptions within the family. The rest remain severely injured within themselves and in their relationships with their families, spouses, careers, and communities. Thus, the novel's New World characters continue to reenact Dan's Old World theory: the "proof of the Irish temperament . . . the blatant disregard of present pleasure" (160). As the eighty-nine-year-old Vincent reluctantly prepares to leave the convalescent home where he has been happier and more serene than at any time in his life, he realizes that "He wants to enjoy his life. No one he knew had ever lived like that. It was a thing the young had thought up, not his children or their generation, but the generation after that" (274). Later, he continues his musings: "He doesn't think they're wrong to be concerned about their happiness. Perhaps if he and Ellen had done more of it, more for the children, thought about their happiness, it would have done some good" (276). One of the primary lessons is that they either could not or would not. Another lesson of the novel is that Ellen would have thought him a fool for even suggesting it.

Alice Bloom has pointed out that "For so many years now, news has seemed more unbelievable than fiction. And so, as though to correct our balance, fiction has often taken on the job of making real life seem real" ("Why the Novel," 156). That certainly seems to be the task Mary Gordon assigned herself in *The Other Side,* and one of her nonfiction comments, written when she was finishing this novel, brings Bloom's premise about fiction full circle: "I want to say, of course, that not everything about Irish Catholics is harmful to a writer. For one thing, the Irish are always interesting. There is the wit, and the refinement of language that the sense of the necessity for constant ridicule engenders. And the very hiddenness of the lives of Irish-Americans makes them an irresistible subject for fiction. One has the sense of breaking into a private treasure, kept from the eyes of most, and therefore a real piece of news" ("Can't Stand," 37).

Most of Gordon's readers are well acquainted with her novels and stories that expose the sequestered "private treasures" and foibles of the Irish and the Irish-Americans. But, as the previous quote demonstrates, several of her essays do the same. Gordon's essay "'I Can't Stand Your Books': A Writer Goes Home" is particularly helpful. For instance, in her explication of the dearth of Irish-American writers, she points out that "The great linguistic facility of the Irish restricted itself in this country to two forms: journalism and political speeches." Equally interesting is her elaborate commentary on the literary and psychological effects of the double colonizations of Ireland by the English and by the Catholic Church. However, the most helpful features of the essay make it an essential resource for any study of *The Other Side,* because the essay illuminates many of the novel's most complex questions and issues, issues such as Irish fear of exposure, secrecy, silence and concealment, and sexual puritanism.

This is not the only nonfiction resource. In a 1987 interview with Annie Lally Milhaven for the book *The Inside Stories: 13 Valiant Women Challenging the Church,* Gordon talks about her work on the novel: "I've thought a lot about the Irish. I'm reading about their history and thinking a lot about them. I love and feel drawn to them. At the same time, I find them appalling at some levels, particularly in America. So I have a real love/hate for them. I think that there is an Irish attachment to both language and nature: the beauties of language and the beauties of nature that is quite extraordinary. And that makes them a very special and different situation from a lot of people."[13]

An earlier essay, which appeared in 1985 (the year in which she first talked publicly about the themes for her novel in progress that would become *The Other Side*), reflects the first stages of her research on immigration, in general, and Ellis Island and her family's entrances, in particular. In addition, "More Than Just a Shrine: Paying Homage to the Ghosts of Ellis Island" reinforces important clues about the formation of certain characters in *The Other Side:* for example, in summarizing her reasons for visiting Ellis Island, Gordon mentions, "I came to the island, too, so I could tell the ghosts that I was one of them, and that I honored them—their stoicism, and their innocence, the fear that turned them inward, and their pride" (104). This passage, with its "fear that turned them inward, and their pride" phrase, immediately brings the young Ellen Costelloe to mind, the fierce, terrified, and guilt-ridden emigré who "kept entirely to herself . . . that thing she was by herself, apart from other people, that thing that people had to keep their distance from" (103). As her future husband comes to realize during their long marriage, "that thing" becomes Ellen's mode of life: "You kept things to yourself. You kept them hidden. . . . Anger only was allowed" (250). Ellen's life and language, therefore, prove her to be one of the Irish who are, in the words of Gordon's 1988 essay, "masters at the language of concealment." Continuing to test Ellen by Gordon's astute phrases from that essay, we recognize the Irish heritage in the young, middle-aged, and elderly Ellen's concealments and silence. These are her "self-protection," her "balked expression[s] of love," her scarcely hidden "overt hostility," her "form[s] of protective coloration," her permanent disguise ("Can't Stand," (36). And we recognize our concealments in hers at the same time that we recognize, as Catherine Ward has pointed out, *The Other Side* breaks this code of silence; it is an antidote to [in Gordon's words] the Irish 'fear of exposure'" ("Wake Homes," 91).

Ellen's dying, like her immigration, like many of her offsprings' living, is one of inarticulate rage. Looking at the beautiful, translucent skin of her forehead, one of the family members gathered around her bed thinks, "you would expect the brain beneath this bone and skin to be serene. But it is not" (6). Ellen, true to form and to poet Dylan Thomas's suggestion, is not going "gentle into that good night." Nor is she going to take her leave without her spouse beside her. Vincent arrives. Recognizing his step, Ellen opens her eyes. The novel ends. Yet readers are left still questioning the immigrant "brain beneath this [novel's] bone and skin," which *is not* serene in America, which *was not* serene in Europe. As Ellen and Vincent's grandson had observed when visiting his grandmother's home town in Ireland, "He felt they were his people, the Irish, and he pitied and admired them. He enjoyed them, but he felt that, like him, they had no idea how to live" (163). While Gordon's multiplications of negativity in *The Other Side* may not result in a mathematical positive, they create, as do all her novels, essential questions. The novelist then leaves us to face this problematic legacy and to examine within ourselves and our cultures the buzzing sounds of individual, familial, racial, national, and international *dis*assimilations, our only partially realized "other sides."

Chapter Seven

"a great deal I wanted to say": Gordon as Essayist-Critic

That "Mary Gordon has views"[1] is the most succinct understatement in any review of Gordon's work as an essayist-critic. Not unexpectedly then, reviewers of her 1991 *Good Boys and Dead Girls and Other Essays,*[2] which collects twenty-eight essays, reviews, articles, and journal entries written between 1978 and 1991, address Gordon's intensity. For example, Wendy Martin's review in the *New York Times Book Review* includes such adjectives as "passionate," "bracing," and "provocative" to describe Gordon's nonfiction ("Passions," 9). Similarly, Paul Baumann suggests that Gordon's "passionate attachments and her willingness to declare her allegiances are among the most attractive things about her writing" ("Search," 327), a judgment echoed in Alison Lurie's noting that "Mary Gordon's essays on women, men, books, and the Catholic Church are intelligent, lively, original—and sure to be controversial. Even if you don't agree with all she says, you can't help admiring the way she says it."[3] Garry Wills, on the other hand, offers no such qualification: "Mary Gordon is so curious and honest that one almost wants to protect her from saying such outrageous things because they are true."[4]

To approach Gordon's nonfiction work in this chapter, I somewhat follow the collection's organizational scheme. The first and longest section addresses the collection's Part I: Gordon's writing about writers and writing. In an attempt to avoid duplicating discussions of essays and articles in other chapters, in my second section I pull from the collection's Part II ("The World, The Church, The Lives of Women") and Part III ("Parts of a Journal") as well as from some essays that appeared after the collection was published to examine Gordon's commentary on art, Catholicism, and a number of highly charged moral and spiritual issues. "An Aesthetic and Analytical Interchange," the chapter's third section, cites essays and articles that exemplify the distinctive freedom with which Gordon dispatches autobiographical materials.

A Writer on Writing

Of the fifteen essays, reviews, and introductions that Gordon selected for Part I, "On Writers and Writing," eleven address either women writers, women in fiction, or women as readers; two deal with novelistic depictions of the Irish; two deal with novelists' treatments of Catholicism; five study novelists' explorations of intimate familial and societal dynamics; and some six address writers' fictional preoccupations with strangely isolated children or adults. Her foci and each author's foci in these works are, of course, about much more. But it bears emphasizing that while Gordon explicates each author's language, technical and stylistic penchants, and vision, the selections reflect her own engagement with these thematic interests as well as with the novel and short-story genres. At the same time, a few of Gordon's essays reflect a critical timbre as "combative, adversarial, discriminating, and engaged" as her description of Mary McCarthy's voice.[5]

The first, and title, essay is a case in point. Gordon first presented "Good Boys and Dead Girls"[6] as a lecture at the New York Public Library in late March of 1991, making it the most recent of the twenty-eight selections, and thus also marking it not as an earlier contemporary, for example, of her similarly fiery articles about Pope John Paul II, but rather, as evidence that when subjects or events raise her ire, she has not grown more cautious, as happens often to successful authors.

What Gordon takes on in the title essay is the nineteenth- and twentieth-century literary tradition that embodies the conspicuously North American fantasy of the "innocent boy killers" who "must be able to move. . . . Move freely. Quickly" (3). Their real enemies, which they proceed to destroy, are those physical and societal fetterings represented by female sexuality and vulnerability, by civilization, and by Nature. Taking into account Leslie Fiedler's and R. W. B. Lewis's groundbreaking works on this American phenomenon as well as her own analysis of the differences between European and American literary depictions of innocence, Gordon begins with Melville's *Billy Budd*. She continues with characters such as Clyde Griffiths of Theodore Dreiser's *An American Tragedy,* Joe Christmas of William Faulkner's *Light in August,* and finally, Rabbit of John Updike's *Rabbit* novel series, the last author garnering Gordon's most scathing judgments (which have appeared in different contexts throughout her career).

Gordon adds two interesting emphases to scholars' long-standing discussions of this American phenomenon. First, she insists that contemporary American male authors, such as Updike, must be held accountable when they continue the tradition that Gordon summarizes as "the search for the unfettered self" (22), in which encumbrances of the Female must be eluded by the male protagonist, at all costs; second, women readers must recognize their responsibilities and rights in "reading gifted but distorting writers" (23).[7] Using the metaphor of "an arresting but undependable guide" who leads his reader to a waterfall, a river, and a fetid swamp, Gordon insists that, for the latter, women exercise the right to say: "I won't go with you there. I will stand at the edge of the swamp, but I won't hesitate to describe the smell." Then Gordon concludes with a withering suggestion: "Before, we [women readers] were afraid of what we would see, expecting that we would encounter the august patriarch, . . . Now we have learned that the face beneath the veil is not the bearded father's but the pimply boy's" (23), a suggestion that, as might be expected, has attracted criticism and praise.

As we notice from scholars' and critics' responses, Gordon's arresting phrases sometimes take on lives of their own. This is true of "the search for the unfettered self," since it makes us aware of an almost primal preoccupation with fettering (in personal, professional, and institutional contexts) that moves below the surfaces of her novels. In her essays and articles, however, Gordon frequently weights gendered facts of this preoccupation. An example is Gordon's essay on Virginia Woolf,[8] which first appeared in 1981 as an introduction to a reissue of *A Room of One's Own*. The introduction also appeared that same year in the *New York Times Book Review* and in abbreviated form as a 1994 playbill essay "Genius Needs Freedom" for Eileen Atkins's one-woman performances of *A Room of One's Own* at Arena Stage in Washington, D. C.

Gordon frames her essay's opening and closing with Woolf's private comments. These framing devices provide approachable vignettes of both women's literary marginalizations and Woolf herself. In between these points, Gordon constructs the historical context around which developed Woolf's elitism, her visionary yet pragmatic clarity regarding necessary equipment for a writer's vocation, her understanding that the creation of works of genius must take precedence over human happiness, and her recognizing that World War I's shattering of illusions and a way of life has intensified male projections of anger on women students and writers. Then Gordon discusses Woolf's respondent anger and follows her beyond anger and gender into her advocacy of an androgynous (and thus unfettered) mind for both male and female writers. Thus, the strategy of Gordon's explication is to emphasize Woolf's strategy.

In other essays, however, Gordon strikes out on far more original tacks to discuss attitudes that have adversely affected and limited the careers of contemporary women writers. She approaches these negative phenomena from both societal and individual directions. An example of the former is Gordon's important 1995 essay "The Angel of Malignity: The Cold Beauty of Katherine Anne Porter"[9] (also discussed later), in which Gordon insists that there is a direct relationship in Porter's not being read to the (male) literary dominance of Ernest Hemingway whose journalistic style and machismo fulfilled American fantasies, both male and female, of what contemporary writing (and a writer) should be. This point is a significant extension of Gordon's commentary in the essays "Good Boys and Dead Girls" and "Ford Madox Ford: A Man Who Loved Women, a Womanly Man."

Using highly individual examples, Gordon's essay "The Parable of a Cave; or, in Praise of Watercolors"[10] (in Part II of the collection) explores the kinds of restraints that male writers and critics frequently have imposed on women writers, in general, and herself, in particular. She begins with a scatological analogy for women writers that "a famous writer" (W. D. Snodgrass, in fact) told her, an analogy in which he compared writing by women to the released fecal matter that explodes from a female bear whose rectum has been corked during winter hibernation in a cave. Then, after mentioning male critics' praising her own work in such terms as "exquisite," "like a watercolor" (in other words, not the important oil paintings of male writers), she first examines the traditional game of dividing literature into "major" (male) and "minor" (female) categories; then, using her own literary and familial experiences, she attacks the literary tradition in which style plus detachment equals major work. Eventually, she shrugs off both encumbering traditions to insist: "I can say it now: I would rather own a Mary Cassatt watercolor than a Velázquez oil" (150), and, more important, "My subject as a writer has far more to do with family happiness than with the music of the spheres. . . . I have a good ear. What it hears best are daily rhythms, for that is what I value, what I would wish, as a writer to preserve. My father would have thought this a stubborn predilection for the minor. My mother knows better" (152).

Gordon's nonfiction attention to problems surrounding women in and of literature and art moves through her career. And it is interesting to notice that she begins and ends Part I of the 1991 collection with essays on the subject. If the title essay (1991) is the collection's opening *allegro con brio,* the final essay (1986) of Part I is its genial *adagio* rebuttal:

"Ford Madox Ford: A Man Who Loved Women, a Womanly Man."[11] As Gordon declares half way through the essay, "Ford is one of the few writers I can think of who does not punish his women characters for being sexual" (117). The essay's initial point (one of those charged Gordon aphorisms that elicit involuntary memorization: "we do not read as angels, without sex") is a pivot into an explication of women as readers in a literary world in which "most books, let us admit it, were written by men for men" (112). Gordon then sets up an imaginative inventory that begins: "When I read Milton, Melville, Conrad, I feel I am, quite daringly, having to impersonate a man; I must enter the Men's Club in drag, for clearly, as I am, I am not wanted. Some writers are more tactful. Blake and Fielding greet me with the message: 'Well, I hadn't thought of you, of course, but now you're here, come in, come in. Why not?'" (112–13). From this hypothetical exercise, Gordon turns to her theses, the first of which is: "No one makes a woman so welcome as Ford Madox Ford" (113).

His name is sprinkled across interviews and symposia comments Gordon has given throughout her career. For Gordon, Ford represents, not a literary influence, but rather a comfortable amalgam of artistic craftsmanship, intelligence, physicality, daily life, culinary passion, and relationships. Moreover, as Gordon's essay considers, for Ford, the exchange of ideas with a woman was as essential as sexuality, the culminating example of which Gordon selects from Ford's *A Man Could Stand Up:* "That was what a young woman was for. You seduced a young woman in order to be able to finish your talks with her. You could not do that without living with her. You could not live with her without seducing her; but that was the by-product. The point is that you can't otherwise talk" (116).

The resonant points of Gordon's essay (which, in many ways, can be considered a granddaughter's addendum to Woolf's *A Room of One's Own*) move beyond Ford and gender. As in the more aggressive title essay, this essay's final point has to do with Gordon's suggestion that writers can and will be held accountable for their implicit and explicit attitudes toward the reader. Such a premise suggests that any writer's most intimate of relationships is with the reader and the act of writing for, to, about the reader who, in the "best of all worlds," is made welcome and accepts the open invitation into discourse.

Gordon's interest in the difficulties of contemporary discourse, in writers' searches for and obsessions with language itself, is reflected in her reviews of works by Christa Wolf, Ingeborg Bachmann, and David

Plante, who evidence similar preoccupations in startlingly different ways. Noting Wolf's ability to ground "her most abstract notions in concrete life" in the language and methodology of her novel *Accident/A Day's News,*[12] Gordon pays close attention to the protagonist's obsession with language. Summarizing these sequences, Gordon catalogs a number of the protagonist's questions: "What, she wonders, is the connection between language and this taste for destruction that seems built into the species? . . . Devoting her life to language as she has, is she part of the murderous complicity whose end is the China syndrome? How does her desire for purity of speech tie in with the scientist's compulsion to follow whatever lead is offered him . . . ?" (55–56). Then Gordon quotes the protagonist's most essential question (directed to her brother, who is about to undergo brain surgery): "Is it worthwhile, brother, staking one's life on being able to express oneself ever more precisely, discernibly, unmistakably?" This question, in turn, provides the segue to Gordon's final point about Wolf: "These are exactly the things on which Christa Wolf stakes her life. She uses language as if her life depended upon finding the connections among the conflicting elements that make up the whole of life" (56).

Since for Gordon, Wolf's novel "is a model of passionate engagement," it is interesting to compare the 1989 Wolf review with Gordon's 1987 review of the reissued English translation of Ingeborg Bachmann's short story collection, *The Thirtieth Year,*[13] which might be considered as a model of passionate disengagement, or, at the very least, a redefined engagement. Created in the aftermath and rubble of Nazi Germany by a writer who would eventually die by self-immolation, the stories' characters, terrors, brutalities, and pessimism reflect Bachmann's attempt, in Gordon's account, to "create a new language, a pure speech: speech without desire, imagination, will. Speech beyond power" (104). Gordon's descriptions of the relationship of language and the children in Bachmann's story "Youth in an Austrian Town" offer a haunting answer to Christa Wolf's protagonist's questions: "The children's experience is shaped by their language, language that is dangerous and creative and generative of itself. The children's horrors and isolation, their passionate secret lives, mirror themselves in their words" (105). Even the children's gibberish fails them, at which point, as Gordon quotes Bachmann, "they invent a language that maddens them. . . . They push one another, go for each other with their fists and scuffle over a counter-word that doesn't exist" (105), one just as nonexistent as the kingdom longed for by the protagonist of Bachmann's story, "A Step Towards Gomorrah," a kingdom that is not that "of men and not that of women. Not this, not that" (107). The "not this, not that" offers a wrenching logo for Bachmann's efforts, which Gordon describes as "the strenuous, exhausting search for the new truthful language, the new set of saving images" (107).

Gordon's decision to follow the 1987 Bachmann review with her 1981 review of David Plante's novel *The Country*[14] is surely not arbitrary, since Plante's novel ultimately is concerned with lost and corrupted languages, lost and corrupted images and worlds of the male protagonist's family, his current struggles as a young writer, and his Indian, French, and French-Canadian ancestors. These losses are augmented by his broken, hardworking father's silences, and his insane mother's rambling patter, which Gordon captures memorably as "the exhausting scattershot that is the language of the mad" and "the effervescent, oddly energetic gas" of her insanity (109). In describing the conclusion of her close friend and literary confidant's novel, Gordon points out that for the protagonist Daniel, "Only his father's death teaches him the language of the large, dark Indian women; only through his father's death can he walk through the woods to the dark mother. It is a journey of language, through language; a journey and a last lament" (110). Gordon later underscores this passage with lines from Rainer Maria Rilke's Orpheus who, like the protagonists of Wolf, Bachmann, and Plante, also journeys in, through, and beyond language within lament.

If the laments within these works push their search for language beyond conventional boundaries, the eminently sophisticated laments Gordon examines in her 1987 introduction to Edith Wharton's *Ethan Frome and Other Short Fiction*[15] and in her 1979 review of Mary McCarthy's *Cannibals and Missionaries*[16] concern themselves with more traditional parameters that are nonetheless under threat. We recognize through Gordon's commentary that both of these writers, when it comes down to it, oppose anarchy, those untethered private and public actions that can shatter the foundations of society. Yet Wharton and McCarthy sensitize us to the individual costs as well as the societal mandates of such tethering. Gordon points out, for example, "the society that Wharton presents feeds on its young for its survival. And the alternative is— what? An anarchy she shrank from and condemned. We do not go to Edith Wharton to find a problem solver. Her view of life is tragic; her gods sit not on Olympus but on upholstered furniture" (26). As Gordon carefully explicates, Wharton's tragic view is one of intriguing tensions, in which her belief in innocence (and her obvious sympathy with her innocent characters) and in human yearnings for happiness are countered by her belief in "the impossibility of happiness" and in the inevitable (and sometimes, required) subjugation of innocents and individual dreams to "the machinery of the world." Wharton, in other words, acknowledges that individual desires are subservient to the larger societal forces of order and convention.

Likewise, the tension-filled exploration of subservience, values, order, and disorder in McCarthy's novel *Cannibals and Missionaries* is, as Gordon recognizes, an equally serious, albeit more contemporary and politicized, study of individual and societal counter-systems. These collide during what Gordon summarizes as "a kind of Canterbury pilgrimage with machine guns" (63), in which terrorists hijack an airplane carrying American art collectors on an archaeological tour and a liberal committee that is headed to Iran to explore atrocities. Gordon draws our attention to McCarthy's pitting her characters' individual and group value systems against one another at the same time she is revealing her "understanding of the psychology of terrorism" as well as her acknowledgment (like Wharton's, reluctant) of tragedy: in the contemporary world, "we have no recourse" against terrorism, which makes societal order and individual aspirations subservient to its mandates for disorder. In Gordon's conclusion of the McCarthy review, we recognize that, also like Wharton, McCarthy "does not imply that she does" have a new answer to what is replaceable and irreplaceable in society. What seems to characterize Gordon's respect for these two writers is that they both raise vexing questions (about individuality, morality, and societal order and values), and that the consummate linguistic mastery each employs (which Gordon explores in detail) for such questions never betrays its master.

The latter cause for respect certainly informs her 1994 explication of James Joyce's "The Dead," which she considers to be one of literature's most significant short stories, and which she includes each year in her teaching syllabi at Barnard College. In the introduction to the story Gordon wrote for *You've Got to Read This: Contemporary American Writers Introduce Stories That Held Them in Awe*, [17] Gordon ends the explication with one of her most freewheeling, nonfiction summaries: "Consider the daring of Joyce's final repetitions and reversals: 'falling faintly, faintly falling'—a triumph of pure sound, of language as music. No one has ever equaled it; it makes those who come after him pause for a minute, in awed gratitude, in discouragement. How can any of us come up to it? Only, perhaps, humbly, indifferently, in its honor and its name to try. And he did it all when he was twenty-five. The bastard" (*You've Got to Read*, 286).

Joyce needs no real advocacy; that his readership is vast is a given and thus does not concern Gordon. To study her overt skills in championing a writer, we can turn instead to two other recent essays, each of which is driven by a genuine *You've Got to Read This* mandate: first, the 1995 essay "The Angel of Malignity: The Cold Beauty of Katherine Anne Porter," which Gordon wrote for the *New York Times Book Review*'s continuing series of essays by, as they describe them, "distinguished writers about authors, books and literary work they passionately believe are ripe for rediscovery"; and second, Gordon's 1992 introduction to *Zelda Fitzgerald: The Collected Writings.*[18]

In the first, we watch Gordon's initial strategy in separating the Porter who "wrote like an angel" from Porter the anti-Semite, racist, drunk, betrayer of friends, and friend of Göring. Next, Gordon sets up a comparison between Porter and Ernest Hemingway, another "beauty, a poseur, a betrayer and a drunk—but certainly not unread." Admitting she enjoys attacking Hemingway ("On a bad day, I lay at his feet overpopulation, air pollution and harmful additives in foods"), Gordon summarizes his strengths and then builds up a context of those societal and literary forces that came together accidentally to set up Hemingway as the definitive voice for his and Porter's generation of American novelists, an elevation that ruined the readership prospects for such writers as F. Scott Fitzgerald and Porter, whose fiction combined lyricism and journalism. Gordon then points out that Porter's penchant for shorter forms and her relatively small productivity added to her being marginalized, just as her "cold realism and an unmistakably female point of view" excluded her even within the ranks of Southern writers ("Angel," 17).

In the midst of exploring the nontraditional greatness of Porter's highly successful novel *Ship of Fools,* Gordon suddenly gets down to the best of her critical business: stylistic analysis. Moving on to two of Porter's finest stories, "Holiday" and "Pale Horse, Pale Rider," Gordon demonstrates in paragraph after paragraph Porter's virtuosic genius with particulars, her "joy in nature and in simple living," her "ability to describe gesture and manners, to use them as a nest in which to enclose a statement of general, even metaphysical, significance" ("Angel," 18). Finally, Gordon connects Porter the writer and person in a remarkably convincing way: "Katherine Anne Porter was heroic in her commitment to looking properly to the art of the thing. This commitment allowed her to look in the face of such unimaginables as evil, death, the irreparable blows of fate, and force them to turn themselves beautiful. It was an exhausting and perilous enterprise, one that made it almost impossible to live" ("Angel," 19).

This final sentence could describe Zelda Fitzgerald's largely unknown work as a writer who also happened to be the wife of one of the greatest twentieth-century writers. In the first two pages of an introduction to *Zelda Fitzgerald: The Collected Writings,* Gordon gives a biographical sketch; as Gordon admits, "If this is not, in the words of Ford Madox Ford, the saddest story you have ever heard, it is certainly one of them" (*Collected,* xvi). She turns to a barrage of questions that challenge our discomfort in giving Zelda a writer's place beside Scott Fitzgerald, who felt that his wife's also using the material of their lives was a personal betrayal and an artistic threat to his own work. Gordon moves straight on to the core of her advocacy: an analysis of Zelda Fitzgerald's surrealistic method of "confusing and conjoining realms, types, categories to make up a rich atmosphere. Her use of *ands* and commas to create a strung together, litany effect accentuates the pileup of dissimilar elements. . . . an exhilarating ride that brings together glamour, terror, wit, and the seductive fog of the unconscious set loose" (*Collected,* xix). By the time Gordon has finished exploring the novel *Save Me the Waltz,* we have come to understand not only the differences between Zelda and Scott Fitzgerald's methods but that her fortes reflect little interest in private emotions; she is working instead across the dangerous borders between descriptions of surfaces and appearances, aphoristic generalizations, and abstract thought. As we have come to expect from Gordon, she inevitably makes a full circle; in this essay, she uses Zelda Fitzgerald's gifts for abstract thought as the segue back to biography, to Scott Fitzgerald's death, and to Zelda's subsequent and astute assessment of his work, a generosity that Gordon leaves as an unspoken mandate for Zelda Fitzgerald's readers.

In light of these two essays as well as others in the collection, it seems appropriate to puzzle over a key point in Gordon's explications of women writers and artists: her inclusion of biographical contexts—such things as class, privilege, physical beauty, accoutrements and clothing, personal experiences, and consciousnesses. For a writer who insists that she despises above all else personal interviews, the phenomenon is intriguing.[19] Certainly Gordon is not evincing a reclamation of pre-New Critical approaches to writers.[20] If not, then what? Four suggestions come to mind: On the most obvious level, Gordon is almost compulsively interested in the life models of other women artists. Second, these biographical contexts are part of Gordon's advocacy strategy for women artists: provide a human context as a sort of invitation to an underappreciated dance of genius. Third, she seems to have given herself a mandate to guide readers through the difficult tasks of separating biography from literary craft and contribution. It is an exercise in unfettering (or, at the least, a desire to unfetter) that is overt in her work on Porter and Zelda Fitzgerald. The same characterizes Gordon's 1979 review of Flannery O'Connor,[21] her 1985 essay "Mary Cassatt,"[22] the autobiographical 1988 essay "'I Can't Stand Your Books': A Writer Goes Home," and the first part of her 1991 essay "Some Things I Saw," all of which are in Parts II and III of the collection. Finally, and perhaps most habitually, Gordon uses biographical contexts as dramatic stage settings for the real work she is about to do and for the real work the writer has achieved. For example, Gordon suddenly reminds her readers after two long paragraphs about Porter's personal pilgrimage and shortcomings, "But none of this has to do, really, with why Katherine Anne Porter is not more widely read. Being read has not, thank God, rested on good behavior, loyalty to friends, sobriety or straight dealings with publishers" ("Angel," 17). As an elderly Porter herself had advised (a quote Gordon uses to conclude her Porter essay), "Practice an art for love and the happiness of your life—you will find it outlasts almost everything but breath" ("Angel," 19). The same, in a far less difficult context, might be applied to an assessment of Gordon's ongoing work as an essayist, novelist, and short-story writer. Borrowing from her words about Christa Wolf, we might speculate that "These are exactly the things on which [Mary Gordon] stakes her life. She uses language as if her life depended upon finding the connections among the conflicting elements that make up the whole of life" (56). At the same time, we see that Gordon uses language as if other writers' lives, male and female, depended on it; the time-consuming writing on their writing and art is, in other words, an intrinsic part of her professional commitment.

Activist Words, Journal Words

In an attempt to cover most of Gordon's other interests and nonfictional strategies, this section moves across Parts II and III of the collection as well as her uncollected nonfiction publications. However, many of these works are addressed in other chapters of my book. For example, Gordon's lecture-essay "Getting Here from There: A Writer's Reflections on a Religious Past" plays a major role in Chapters One, Two, and Three. And her autobiographical essays "David" (reissued as "My

Father's Daughter," 1985), "Childhood's End" (1987), "The Important Houses" (1992), "The Other Deaths" (1994), and "My Mother Is Speaking from the Desert" (1995) are absorbed directly and indirectly into the biographical Chapter One as well as into Chapter Nine on *The Shadow Man* (1996). In addition, the 1985 essay "More Than Just a Shrine: Paying Homage to the Ghosts of Ellis Island" and the 1988 essay "'I Can't Stand Your Books': A Writer Goes Home" are covered in Chapter Six. Therefore, to give her nonfiction publications equal coverage, I address other works that form rather natural groupings: Gordon's ongoing attention to art, to American Catholicism, and to difficult moral and spiritual issues.

Gordon's keen pleasure in art enlivens her 1985 novel *Men and Angels* through the research of the protagonist Anne Foster on the deceased *fin de siècle* artist Caroline Watson, whom Gordon fashioned from the letters, journals, lives, and careers of painters Cecilia Beaux, Mary Cassatt, Suzanne Valadon, and Paula Modersohn-Becker. A nonfiction spin-off from that effort is Gordon's essay "Mary Cassatt," which was published in *Art and Antiques* at the end of that same year. But Gordon's interest in Cassatt had been active long before her third novel emerged; we note, for example, that a Cassatt painting from a private collection was selected for the book jacket for her 1980 novel *The Company of Women.* Still, when we read both the essay and *Men and Angels,* we see how much Gordon has learned by 1985 about and from Cassatt, and we can recognize, especially in the essay, the reassurance provided Gordon in Cassatt's craft and in her unfashionable-for-her-times subjects. Acknowledging the significant contributions that feminist art critics have brought to American attitudes toward Cassatt, Gordon affirms the painter's "Balance, proportion, an instinct for the distant and the formal, an exuberance, a vividness, a clarity of line" (157)—the last three of which at least one literary critic has chosen to describe as Gordon's own achievement in this collection.[23] Gordon concludes with a powerful summary of Cassatt's achievement: "a master of line and color whose great achievement was to take the 'feminine' themes of mothers, children, women with their thoughts alone, to endow them with grandeur without withholding from them the tenderness that fits so easily alongside the rigor of her art" (159).

Still, Gordon did not choose a Cassatt painting for the book jacket for *Men and Angels,* but one by her favorite painter Vuillard, discussed in detail in Chapter Four. Two years later, Gordon's study of Vuillard's work and life, "The Silent Drama in Vuillard's Rooms,"[24] emerged in the *New York Times,* five days prior to her lecture "Emptiness and Fullness in

Vuillard" for the Brooklyn Museum's symposium "New Perspectives on Vuillard," which coincided with the opening of their major Vuillard exhibit. In the essay, we catch glimpses of unexpected facets of her interest in Vuillard. We know from a 1995 interview, for example, that his work offers her mental nourishment when, as she describes it, "I'm really stuck and despairing about my work" (Bennett interview, 29). But this is not so surprising as what we learn from her essay: in him she recognizes a colleague of the mind's eye who, like herself, has often been marginalized by critics. Gordon's essay starts off by examining the term *intimist,* which has been used to assign Vuillard to the minor echelon of painters. Then she gets more specific, and in the third sentence of the following quote, we see into her own propensities that run quietly through her earlier work and then emerge full-blown (as discussed in Chapter Eight) in her 1993 novellas *The Rest of Life:* "There are those, therefore, who think of him as enshrining an image of domestic tranquility. They should look again. Far from romanticizing domesticity, Vuillard reflects our intense ambivalence about life at home, where most of us continue, after all, to live" ("Silent Drama," 1).

There is little ambivalence in Gordon's acerbic four-part essay "Some Things I Saw" (1991), which begins and ends with intense essays on painters. The first entry, titled "The Case of Berthe Morisot," is aptly subtitled "Losing My Temper in the National Gallery, and Types of Feminist Shame." What angers her about the Morisot exhibit is that her appreciation of Morisot the Artist is preempted by "Le Repos," Manet's splendid painting of Morisot. Gordon, as she describes it, had "wanted to think of her as a painter, dislodged from her biography, from her physical beauty—separated from the admiring and powerful male gaze" (223).[25] Expanding upon her anger at the intrusive male gaze, Gordon moves to Georgia O'Keeffe's compliance in Stieglitz's famously intimate photographs of her, but then, circling back to Morisot, Gordon admits: "The truth is that for me—and I feel ashamed of it—Berthe Morisot's biography, as well as her physical beauty, is inseparable for me from her art" (224). Gordon's readers already know this from Parts I and II of the collected essays: her own writerly penchant to employ biographical and physical detail within advocacies of women writers. This runs counter to her feminist sensibilities, as evidenced, for example, throughout "Some Things I Saw." Yet, the autobiographical slants within her essays confirm that even such sensibilities cannot prevent her from pursuing the risky business of aesthetic drama, the same risky business that the curator of the Morisot exhibit knew all about.

Gordon's concern in the fourth part of this journal entry is something altogether different. Her response to Andy Warhol's art is pain, rather than anger. She recognizes his genius: "knowing what people were really like, what they were interested in" (239), but she also recognizes him as opposing everything Vuillard was, Warhol's nihilism being one that closed the nineteenth century and that violates everything he contemplates in the twentieth. Gordon sees Warhol as a negation that "says to everything I could possibly say: Bullshit. But he wouldn't say that; . . . what he says is worse, much worse. What he says is it doesn't matter. . . . The only thing that matters then; the only thing desirable: that the camera should always have something new to fix on. Should not stop" (239). Gordon's response to Warhol surely will continue to elicit responses that she misunderstood the premise of his art and its place in the evolution of contemporary art. But it is precisely in Gordon's taking Warhol's work at face value and in her holding him accountable for the philosophical import of his work that her comments are most refreshing.

Her 1992 essay "Born to Love,"[26] on the artist Gwen John (1876–1939), demonstrates how Gordon's critical surety about painters has continued to mature. The essay, accompanied by splendid selections from John's paintings, offers a carefully researched context for and advocacy of the painter's work that can hold their own in the rather formidable world of art criticism. Surely destined for Gordon's next essay collection, "Born to Love" also raises the possibility of an autonomous collection of Gordon's writing about art, a body of work that, in sheer volume alone, is quietly growing into almost a match for her much better-known essays and articles on religious issues.

A trust in the moral courage of Gordon's nonfiction voice has led to her emerging as a nationally recognized spokesperson-respondent regarding American Catholicism. At the beginning of her career, Gordon earned this trust with her first two novels, her early interviews and contributions to symposia, and her prominently placed essays, such as "More Catholic Than the Pope: Archbishop Lefebvre and the Romance of the One True Church" (*Harper's,* 1978) and "The Unexpected Things I Learned from the Woman Who Talked Back to the Pope" (*Ms.,* 1982).

Five years later, Gordon's highly autobiographical essay "The Irish Catholic Church"[27] appeared in a collection of essays by, as the editor described them, "Prominent Catholics and Ex-Catholics." That same year, after Pope John Paul II's visit to the United States was announced, Gordon was a part of several select groups of American Catholics (such as William F. Buckley, Jr., Bowie Kuhn, Father Andrew Greeley,

Kathleen Kennedy Townsend, and Joseph Califano, Jr.) asked to make comments or to offer issues that they would like the Pope to address. In her contribution to the *New York Times* symposium, "How Some American Catholics See John Paul II's Visit" (28), Gordon is unsparing: "I think a Pope could make a difference in the moral life of America but not this Pope." After citing the Pope's moral inconsistencies with such issues as nuclear weapons, abortion, and Kurt Waldheim, she then begins a stinging appraisal, in which she compares the Pope to Ronald Reagan's mediocrity as an actor and his media-driven presidency, comments that reconfirm the conclusion of her contribution to "From the Council to the Synod," in *Commonweal:* "At the beginning of the council [Vatican II] we had on the throne of St. Peter a genius and a saint; now we have a celebrity."[28] One day after her *New York Times* barrage, her contribution to a *Newsweek* symposium, "Chords of a Dissonant Choir,"[29] is expressed in a more measured voice, but it is equally forthright: "I don't think he [the Pope] can understand the American church. . . . The notion of a population where the laity has access to power is very foreign to him. The role of women in the American church must absolutely baffle him." Her most specific point—"I would like him to address the grievous insult he committed against Holocaust victims and the Jewish community calling [Austrian President Kurt] Waldheim a man of peace"—is one that she develops (along with her questioning the Pope's beatification of Janet Stein, a Jewish convert to Catholicism) in her essay "Offenses of the Pope,"[30] which Gordon contributed to the 1987 *Tikkun* symposium "The Pope and the Jews."

Two years later, Gordon, Don DeLillo, Andrew Greeley, Maureen Howard, John Guare, and some twelve other writers (all with Catholic backgrounds) wrote a remarkable letter to the editor[31] of the *New York Times,* in which they called down John Cardinal O'Connor for his criticism of Salman Rushdie and for his sympathetic response on behalf of the Muslim community. The group's letter ends with a two-punch knockout: "Mature Catholics do not believe that any dialogue with the non-Christian world can be conducted within a system that prejudges books. Mature Catholics do not believe that a death threat can be met with ambiguity."

On the other hand, Gordon's 1993 article for *New York Newsday,* "The Politics of Sexual Hysteria"[32] is a discussion of the destructive coercion tactics she sees in the New York Archdiocese's decision to disseminate information on school-board candidates provided by Pat Robertson's

Protestant fundamentalist organization. She concludes by suggesting that "the most grievous effect" of the decision "may be to reinforce the suspicion of some of the most loyal and ardent Catholics that the church is a univocal and draconian bureaucracy rather than the open table of the Gospel Christ" (104).

These contributions, like her 1993 "Government for the People: Memo to Bill [Clinton]—III,"[33] represent the acerbic personae of her voice, but her repertoire is highly mobile. Thus, in her 1982 essay "Coming to Terms with Mary: Meditations on Innocence, Grief, and Glory,"[34] we hear the quiet, fearless tone of her struggle to reconcile a feminist vision with religious faith, and particularly with the female model of Mary, as represented throughout the history of the church. In an extended meditation on three qualities of Mary—innocence, grief, and glory—Gordon turns to a number of artists' depictions that can assist the process. Finally, she concludes that "in the end, it is beyond reason, beyond argument," that "it is through poetry, through painting, sculpture, music, through those human works that are magnificently innocent of the terrible strain of sexual hatred by virtue of the labor, craft, and genius of their great creators, that one finds the surest way back to the Mother of God" (14). It is a daring struggle, one that is echoed in the collection's finale, "The Gospel According to Saint Mark,"[35] which is transformed by her acute writer's eye for details. What results is a hermeneutics, informed not only by her mind, faith, and skills, but also by the honesty with which she begins: "To write of this subject in this way is to acknowledge my place among the noninnocent" (240).

In broader considerations that are fundamentally linked, Gordon brings this same combination and thoughtfulness to her powerful 1993 essay on anger,[36] written for a *New York Times Book Review* series on the Deadly Sins, and to her 1992 essay, "Explaining Evil."[37] In "Anger," Gordon explores the seductive pleasures of anger: "This fascination begins in the mouth, then travels to the blood, thence to the mind, where it creates a connoisseur. One begins to note the intricate workmanship of one's own anger and soon to worship it, to devote oneself to its preservation, like any great work of art" ("Anger," 3). Part of the essay's power can be attributed to the candid personal example Gordon uses to illustrate this "corridor of pleasure" and sin. Somewhat similarly in the essay "Explaining Evil," Gordon uses her childhood and that of her children, especially her son, to approach one of the knottiest clusters of human questions and parental dilemmas: how to explain "the inexplicable, that dark part of the world that the light of reason seems unable to penetrate?" (30). Her suggestions (in this as well as the anger essay) are as wise as they are forthright.

Gordon is equally forthright about her liberal stance and bias as well as the intellectual and moral struggle of her vigorous arguments about abortion in the essays "Abortion: How Do We Think About It?"[38] and "Abortion: How Do We Really Choose?" and in the 1978 review of Linda Bird Francke's *The Ambivalence of Abortion* and James C. Mohr's *Abortion in America.*[39] The same is true of her 1987 article in *Ms.*: "'Baby M': New Questions About Biology and Destiny."[40] Her obvious goal in each of these is to raise as many important questions as is possible about these difficult issues. For example, in the latter essay, Gordon asks such things as: "why choose the altruism that serves a stranger at the price of never again laying eyes on the child of one's own womb? And the money?"; "Do I see these women [surrogate mothers], these others, really as kind of children, or lesser beings?"; "Even if these women say the experience of surrogacy won't be harmful to them, do I believe I and my kind know better?"; and "If it is 'natural' for women to bear children, is it 'unnatural' for them to choose not to?" ("'Baby M,'" 25–26). Like many of the writers who attract her attention, Gordon does not presume to offer definitive answers, but she is bent on asking the pivotal questions.

An Aesthetic and Analytical Interchange

Wendy Martin begins a review of *Good Boys and Dead Girls and Other Essays* by suggesting that "Novelists who write essays on politics, education, religion, art and literature participate in a venerable tradition." Citing some dozen nineteenth- and twentieth-century novelists who exemplify this tradition, Martin goes on to suggest "that creative and critical skills can enrich each other," and that Gordon's collection of essays "shows us once again that there need not be a schism between the esthetic and the analytical" ("Passions," 9). If such a schism ever existed in Gordon's mind, it was bridged by the time she published her first novel, *Final Payments,* with its narrative hallmarks articulated by the novel's protagonist, Isabel Moore: lyricism and an intense need for logical acuity. The same hallmarks—along with advocacy—distinguish her nonfiction work.

A particular benefit of the essay collection is that it provides more of the chronological routes of her interests, insights, and skills, as she shifts them across genres with the ease of a performer's rapid change of dramatic masks or personae. Occasionally, Gordon will employ an obvious shift-cue for dramatic purposes; for example, at the end of the painful familial and Irish-American disclosures in the 1988 essay "'I Can't Stand Your Books': A Writer Goes Home," Gordon muses, "I walked with my infant son to the car that would drive us to the cemetery, and I thought how perfectly the experience of Irish-American Catholicism had been captured in my uncle's death and burial. And I wondered how much of it I would want to pass on to my children. . . . But I knew one thing for certain: there was no doubt that I would write about it" (207). Readers of her first two novels, her short story collection, interviews, and essays such as "More Than Just a Shrine: Paying Homage to the Ghosts of Ellis Island" know that she had already been studying and writing about Irish Americans for a decade. And in 1990, two years after she published "'I Can't Stand Your Books,'" Gordon's culminating exploration emerged in her fourth novel *The Other Side,* with its five generations of an Irish-American family.

Gordon's cuing—"there was no doubt that I would write about it"—acts also as a directive regarding what seems to be a central creative frisson that energizes the interchanges between her more private and personal literary personae and her more public (formal and informal) literary personae, between her nonfiction and fiction. What is most unique in these interchanges is Gordon's unflinching imagination. If something—for example, her being raped as a twenty-two-year-old traveling in Wales and reading *Middlemarch*—can serve to show how one's reading of that work, any work, shifts throughout a lifetime, then the event may turn up as an essay, "George Eliot, Dorothea and Me: Rereading (and rereading) 'Middlemarch'" (1994),[41] some seven years after the experience emerged as the short story "Violation" (1987), without *Middlemarch* but with Yeats and Dylan Thomas.[42] The same experience probably informs a number of her moral inquiries and feminist stances. Whatever the case, her treatments of this one event typify the ways Gordon generates imaginative pivots within a single locus of interest.

One has the feeling that the generative core of such pivots is as intimate a zone as the "film of moisture [that] covers my flesh and my son's," which she describes in "Having a Baby, Finishing a Book," and it is as tension-filled as that quiet account's acknowledgment that "the thought of going back to work on it [her novel] makes me feel physically ill."[43] The end of that novel (*Men and Angels*), published like the earliest version of "Having a Baby, Finishing a Book" in 1985, concludes with another young mother, Anne Foster, thinking about returning to her writing as she holds her young son: "She kissed her son's damp head. She knew nothing about him, nothing of what he would become. Yet no one knew him better. He was hers, for now . . ." (238), and "This morning she could turn to the work of a woman forty-five years dead" (239). Thus, the trajectory of this second intimate example, like the first, moves across personal, psychological, gender, and literary personae, which, we need to keep in mind, Gordon wields with practiced control.

To suggest that her articles and essays, regardless of foci, reflect literary personae is not to suggest artifice or distance, but rather to emphasize that Gordon's writerly life of the mind shapes every sentence of her work as well as every decision in which she takes on a writer's mandate regarding contemporary issues. In both cases, the nonfictional personae within Gordon's literary agenda reflect the "venerable tradition" of multitalented novelists and a contemporary extension of the Romantic tradition best summarized by Shelley: "poets are the unacknowledged legislators of the world." Perhaps more important, those literary personae also suggest Gordon's unexpected extension of the modernist assertion, as Bob Perelman describes that of Pound and Joyce, of "a powerful sense of proprietary control over both language and society. The aim is to abolish the distinction between writing and the world and to fuse social and literary value."[44] It is not, however, as if Gordon harbors any naïveté about the sociological or political effects of her work. As she mentioned in 1991 in the *Economist,* "Today it is the private individual who is the reader, not society," to which she added: "I feel like a fresco painter in the age of oils." When asked why she goes on writing, Gordon suggested, "It's the only thing I'm good at, the thing that I love" (88).

Her readers should not be beguiled by the self-deprecating humor which, as her essay "The Parable of the Cave; or, In Praise of Watercolors" ("Parable," 27–32) makes stunningly clear, masks specific details of some of Gordon's most intense early struggles as a writer. Moreover, Gordon's trust in the voice and in the right to the writerly public voice is as fierce as her awareness and trust of her literary awareness. As Patricia Deleeuw has pointed out: "One never forgets that Mary Gordon is a woman who is reading, thinking, and writing in these essays" (Deleeuw, 275). The statement serves as advice. The reader's awareness of any author's authoring is especially crucial in Gordon's nonfictional and fictional treatments of personal information. It is not enough to say, as this same reviewer did, that "This collection of Mary

Gordon's essays paints a portrait of the novelist almost as complete as an autobiography might" (275). Gordon is consciously bringing much more than personal history to her most intimate of pages, a fact that another critic is moving toward in his response to Gordon's candid admission that her relationship to her faith and the Catholic Church "changes each day as I go along": "Gordon's formulation probably crosses some negotiable but necessary boundary into arbitrariness; it sounds more like fiction than Catholicism" ("Search," 327). The comments reflect the critic's defensive posture, but they inadvertently underscore the fact that Gordon's essays represent a writer's forum, one in which she applies the tools of her craft and imagination as intensely as others in the tradition of novelists-essayists, such as George Eliot, William Thackeray, Nathaniel Hawthorne, Henry James, Mark Twain, Salman Rushdie, Mary McCarthy, Margaret Atwood, and V. S. Naipaul (Martin, "Passions," 9). In other words, *Good Boys and Dead Girls and Other Essays* is (to borrow the title of her essay on Flannery O' Connor) as much about Gordon's "Habit of Genius" as it is about her opinions, arguments, tastes, and critical judgments.

Certainly, as Doris Earnshaw has emphasized, Gordon's essays "show the range possible to the modern woman writer,"[45] a range that she continues to expand. Her nonfiction work also teaches us much about Gordon's overriding literary purpose, a purpose she has commented on in other places but one found most succinctly in her description of another writer: "this pattern of traveling from the particular to the universal, from the familial to the political, this refusal to separate realms of thought" (54–55). And to date, Gordon's most singular nonfiction example of this purpose is found in the 1996 memoir-biography *The Shadow Man,* which is examined in Chapter Nine.

"neither night nor morning":
The Rest of Life: Three Novellas

From the start of her career, Gordon's works have attracted a wide range of readers, and if getting reviewed in *People* magazine is any sort of reliable indicator, that range has widened since August of 1993.[1] Still, for Gordon aficionados and her newer readers alike, the 1993 publication of Gordon's *The Rest of Life: Three Novellas*[2] marks the debut of a new genre interest that the author plans to continue from time to time. When asked about the genre shift, Gordon has explained, "I think that *The Other Side* [1989] was an enormous structural labor; it really kind of wore me out for a larger structure. So, I wanted something that was more compressed, more lyric in its impulse, and actually more poetic and not so dependent on author or structure." Then, responding to an observation that the novellas also suggest a major shift in her technical approach, she continued, "I'm probably more open to less linear, less thoroughly rational ways of structuring" (Bennett interview, 27). This is borne out in ways in which the nonchronological episodes of each protagonist's narrative move, like water currents, forward, backward, into self-interrupting eddies, around obstacle-constructs within the narrator's mind and life.

Not surprisingly then, each novella's plot is subservient to its episodic flow, which reflects, in turn, a meticulously controlled ambiguity, what Gordon describes as "permeability." An immediate demonstration of both the control and the ambiguity can be found in the novellas' conclusions. At the end of "Immaculate Man," the first unnamed female protagonist admits: "He holds me in his arms here on the street, the rue Jacob in Paris. 'I'll never leave you,' he says again. I believe him. But I don't know for how long" (76). In "Living at Home," the final musings of the second female protagonist (also unnamed) augment and move the ambiguity forward: "I worry about Lauro, alone, without me in that place. I am lying beside him now. . . . It is neither night nor morning. . . . But very soon he'll be awake. And then, I don't know what will happen" (164). Finally, in the third and title novella, "The Rest of Life," Paola, the seventy-eight-

year-old protagonist, with a lifetime of unresolved ambiguity suddenly
behind her, walks back toward her hotel in Turin, Italy: "The doorman
says, 'Your son, his friend, are waiting.' Yes, thank you, she says. *Sì, gra-
zie*" (257). The understated affirmation in the novella's final words represents not only Paola's first verbal reclamation of her life; the words also
suggest an unexpected, albeit still fragile, resolution to the ambiguity
underscored throughout the three novellas.

Gordon's close attention to the three conclusions exemplifies the resonances she creates between the novellas. In other words, the novellas are
not disparate; they form a deliberately crafted whole. Therefore, what is
left ambiguous and what is resolved in all three novellas (and how
Gordon achieves their connectedness) will be this chapter's larger consideration. But before approaching the connective tissues of the novellas,
perhaps brief summaries that pull together the episodic fragments
within each novella will serve as a helpful grounding.[3]

"Immaculate Man"

The collection's first novella is a first-person narrative by its unnamed
female protagonist, a forty-eight-year-old social worker and divorced
mother of two teenagers. Set in the early 1990s in New York State,
Manhattan, and Paris, the story focuses on her unexpected relationship
with Father Clement [Frank] Buckley, the last active priest of the dis-
banded Paracletist order, whose Motherhouse has been turned into a
battered-women's shelter that he keeps in repair and directs. The protagonist meets the boyishly handsome, forty-five-year-old priest when
she is called in as a consultant for his diocese's organization of the shelter. Clement, she observes, is a guileless man, both a poor judge of character and highly intuitive about human suffering.

An Illinois-born daughter of lackadaisical Congregationalists, the narrator initially has no guilt about their hidden relationship and little
knowledge of what the Catholic Church represents to priests of her and
earlier generations. She is not a believer, but she assumes that worship
should entail comprehensible rites that banish the dark mysteries to
which Clement is so devoted. Moreover, she equates the love of light
with women's sexuality and, conversely, the love of dark entrances into
mystery with men's desires to enter women's bodies.

Their relationship began three months after she started commuting
from Manhattan to the shelter, where, one day, she becomes ill. It is
then, in a former cell decorated with "I am the Resurrection and the

Life," that they first make love. The narrator feels that Clement has brought her back to faith, not in God, but in sexuality. Because he had never made love, never touched a woman, or looked at pornography, she knows his delight with her middle-aged body is rare and that he chose her when he found himself without a priestly order or work. She also understands why they will never marry. As the protagonist has gradually learned from Father Boniface Lally, Clement's Paracletist mentor and best friend, their marriage would strip Clement of everything he has loved since age thirteen. Moreover, Clement's harshness with her son and daughter would rupture her and her children's loving, healthily chaotic relationship. Even without marriage, she cannot imagine life without him. The elderly, seriously ill Boniface, who approves of their relationship, shares her feelings, and to her he confides his never-intimated sexual attraction to Clement. Her narrative ends when she and Clement are in Paris, a romantic trip he insists upon paying for with the first money he has ever earned. He vows again that he will never leave her; she remains unsure.

"Living at Home"

The middle novella is a first-person narration by an unnamed, British-born female protagonist, who, since the mid-80s, has lived with Lauro, a fifty-seven-year-old, Italian-born foreign correspondent who is compulsively interested in Third World trouble spots and revolutions. The narrator is a respected, forty-five-year-old psychiatrist who directs a London school for autistic children. An only child of Jewish parents who left Germany for London in 1935, the narrator—previously married three times (to a medical student, a doctor, and a half-Russian charmer) and a loving mother of two almost grown sons—has lived with Lauro for five years. A tactful, intuitive, and kind man (except to his mother and family), he frequently leaves on self-chosen, dangerous assignments. Seemingly impervious to a fear of death except when facing routine medical work, Lauro shares the narrator's need for "entrances and exits." Still, their relationship and London flat are their oases.

As her narration unfolds, she reveals an ability to enter autistic patients' obsessively closed worlds and to help them attempt openness with safety and without shame. Paradoxically, her medical speciality in dealing with children terrorized by change and fragmentation is intimately related to her personal life. Trying to cope with her widowed mother's decline, the psychiatrist is shamed and disoriented by the physical and mental changes in her mother. At the same time, the narrator reveals radical aversions to her mother's lifelong horror of change. Intellectually, the narrator had understood her mother's fixations on a home, fastidiousness, and objects brought from Germany; these were coping mechanisms after having to flee Germany and to leave London for ten years. Nevertheless, the protagonist, despite concern for her sons, leaves each of three marriages when her husband at the time settles into a fixed relationship with a place and objects. Not unexpectedly, then, the London flat that she and Lauro delight in is all-white, austere, with modern furniture and objects that carry no emotional attachments. And when she and Lauro go to Italy for his sister's wedding, the narrator recognizes in Lauro's petulance toward his mother his similar need "to be away from her [his mother] to feel he breathed air as a man."

The novella ends late at night, as the narrator expects Lauro to wake up momentarily. Like the children with whom she works, both she and Lauro fashion their life together around no future tense, no looking back; the present is all each claims, an open, permeable claim that admits her fear of his death and their mutual appreciation of being "mated, but in the way of our age, partial" (155).

"The Rest of Life"

The final novella is its protagonist's intensely private, third-person account, which she frequently interrupts by even more intense (italicized) passages, many of which are first-person, imaginary addresses to particular people. We recognize this technique as one Gordon tried out a few times with her character Ellen MacNamara in *The Other Side*. In "The Rest of Life," however, the self-interruptions are an integral part of the novella's structure, and one of the most pleasing aspects of this stylistic and rhetorical device is in studying Gordon's craft as she fashions each italicized section as an elaboration on a verbal cue from the preceding third-person narration.

The story opens and closes in 1991 in Italy, to which Paola, the seventy-eight-year-old, Turin-born protagonist, has returned after more than six decades. In 1928, after the suicide of her sixteen-year-old lover Leo Calvi, Paola's unnamed father, a widower and professor of entomology, had sent her away to live with relatives in America. Since then, she has mourned for the face of her father, who, despite his love, had failed to protect or defend her. Yet, she has sealed her mind against remembering Leo's face, blown away by his suicide. Since she had promised to join him in suicide, the fifteen-year-old Paola had left Italy with youthful perceptions of wrongdoing, betrayal, and shame, none of which were ameliorated by her father or shared, not even with her late husband, Joe Smaldone, a happy-spirited Sicilian-American whom she met during World War II. Still, she has tried to salvage a life that, at age fifteen, she was unwilling to give up. She recognizes that refusing to commit suicide was linked to her not wanting to leave her father and knowing that the brilliant, impetuous Leo did not, as he pretended, know it all; he was as ignorant about sex, life, and death, and even his idealized troubadours, as she. As in her youthful poem, which mistakenly had Eurydice rather than Orpheus look back, Paola had looked back at life, at her father, and Leo had died alone. But, like Orpheus, it is Paola whose life is torn apart by maenadic women, especially her vicious aunt, whom her father does not contradict in 1928. Conversely, seven decades later, when Carlo, the youngest of Paola's three sons, wants to marry his Nigerian-American supervisor, the granddaughter of an Igbo chief, Paola stands up for them, introducing Katherine to Joe's prejudiced family and defying them to injure the young couple's happiness. Their thanks is the trip back to Milan and Turin, where Paola finds that the accusing names, faces, and buildings have disappeared. Only when she makes a solitary trip to the nearby village of Bardonecchia, with its ancient, half-ruined tower where Leo committed suicide, does she weep for no one's having consoled either of them, especially Leo and all young men who died when others, like herself, lived. Finally, she understands that "the dead, being one and many, knew there was nothing to forgive" (257). Returning to the hotel, where the doorman tells her Carlo and Katherine are waiting, she (and the reader) knows that something essential has been salvaged.

"three [novellas] . . . in a first-class compartment"

For each novella, Gordon has created a singular female protagonist whose life and experiences address a different set of relational, physical, emotional, and spatial issues. On the most obvious level, the sets are linked in three ways, the first two of which are their intimate venues and the protagonists' mature stage of life (middle age and older). Gordon's comments during a 1993 telephone interview[4] relate directly to these. Prefacing her remarks with "I'm obsessed with how difficult it is to live an ordinary bourgeois life," Gordon described *The Rest of Life* as "meditations on the tricky navigation through daily life, which, in contrast to literature, is usually unmarked by high tragedy." In a 1994 interview,[5] she explained about her third novella, "The reason why I deliberately called it 'The Rest of Life' is that there is all that rest of life that is not tragic and high but takes even the moment of greatest tragedy and incorporates it in a way that is not perfect or heroic but more incarnational." In both interviews, she follows such contexts with specificity: for example, "I was interested in how a woman inhabits space, particularly domestic space, the world most women live in that is considered so unchallenging." While admitting that she "enjoyed writing about female desire," Gordon mentioned that in these novellas, she "was interested in the woman's body maturing" (Hunnewell interview, 25).

The most conspicuous and third link between the women protagonists is their present or past relationships with men. The ongoing intensity of these relationships in the minds and daily lives of the protagonists is the novellas' primary fuel, which is well described by Janette Turner Hospital in the *London Review of Books:* "Connection, the narrators intimate, . . . when it is passionately sexual, intellectual and emotional all at once, is like a supernova. It may burn you up. Afterwards there may be nothing but a black hole of loss and shame. And yet without these conflagrations, there would be nothing in the first place, no life, no meaning at all. And ordinary life—which requires gargantuan and exhausting effort—can only be achieved by the clear-sighted acceptance of this risk."[6]

As could be expected, Gordon's focus on such risks and conflagrations in her characters' lives has generated some feminist concern. For example, in her front-page review of the novellas in the *New York Times Book Review,* Alison Lurie is uneasy about each protagonist's involvement "in an obsessive, unequal sexual relationship." She goes on to query and then suggest: "What are we to make of this? Considering Mary Gordon's intelligence and her great gifts as a writer, I think we must read this book not as a post-feminist assertion of our essential emotional weakness but as a cautionary tale: a skilled and complex portrait of three strong, interesting and admirable women who have been deeply damaged by their dependence on men."[7] While understandable, such a reductive reading seems, in this case, myopic, even superficial. It causes Lurie to miss the mark on these novellas as well as the real risk-taking Gordon (a self-declared "red-alert feminist") sets out for herself in this venture, one that is just as risky as but yet more expansive than her novelistic and short story forays into Catholicism and motherhood and into women, parents, or couples who love too much or too little.

The risks for Gordon are in putting fictional pressure on the daily life, space, and intimacies of three women whose personhood *remains* porous, fluid, and ambiguous. The most singular metaphor that Gordon creates for the latter inquiry is her carefully researched information on autism, which she uses in the second novella. As the psychiatrist-protagonist of that novella observes, while thinking about her autistic children patients: "The children I treat have trouble understanding the idea of what makes up a person, a person consistently recognizable, consistently the same. The odd thing, to me, is how wholeheartedly the rest of us pretend to understand" (101).

Gordon's readers are accustomed to her creating fictional pressure within an enclosed group or relationship, but the novellas' exploratory pressure on personhood itself and the degree to which Gordon leaves that exploration unresolved, vulnerable, are something quite new. Moreover, the ease with which she combines the intimate pressures and ambiguities suggests a new stage of maturation; it is as if she broke through some invisible threshold in *The Other Side,* and now, on the other side of that, she has found new freedoms. Regardless of how and if Gordon continues this provocative combination in future work, *The Rest of Life* deploys it to posit three protagonists not as throwbacks to women who "don't seem to have heard the news" that their gender has "come a long way," as Lurie has suggested, but as convincing, mobile reflections of female (and male) contemporaneity, in general, and intimate, contemporary personhood, in particular.

The following exploration of the author's connective strategies for and details of such reflections will begin with overt similarities and then move to more subtle and important points. We can notice, first of all, that all three novellas are approximately the same length (73, 85, and 90 pages, respectively), and all have contemporary settings. The first, "Immaculate Man," and the third, "The Rest of Life," take place during the early 1990s; the second novella, "Living at Home," is set in 1989. Likewise, all three stories unfold in primary locations and a secondary location in another country; these locales are, in order: [1] Manhattan, New York State, and Paris; [2] London and Turin, Italy; and [3] Manhattan, Queens, and Milan and Turin, Italy. Gordon does weave a few mini-details through the novellas. For example, in "Living at Home," 1935 is the year in which the protagonist's parents flee Germany as well as the year in which the protagonist's father in "The Rest of Life" dies after being beaten by Fascist Blackshirts whom he defied. Likewise, Turin[8] appears in both "Living at Home" and "The Rest of Life" as, respectively, Lauro's birthplace and Paola's hometown. Another example is the Orpheus and Eurydice myth[9] that makes brief appearances, for varying purposes, in all three novellas. While these through lines add little to the novellas as a whole, the coincidences create tiny pleasures of recognition. More pleasure, however, comes from the crucial correspondences between the novellas.

Certainly, one of these (and one of the strongest achievements in the novellas) is in Gordon's having created three women protagonists whose personalities, daily lives, and loves are as distinctive as they are similar. At first, their personal and professional lives seem disparate. However, a closer scrutiny reveals a great number of similarities that converge into Gordon's larger agenda for the novellas.

The most fundamental similarity, other than the protagonists' gender, mature age, and their fixation on a present or past love, is the narrators' high consciousness of telling the story of their own most intimate life story, a venerable novelistic device that works extremely well in these novellas. For instance, in her first sentence, the protagonist of "Immaculate Man" announces the story she is about to tell ("What happened to me on the bus wasn't unusual"), then interrupts that story with an anecdote from a Russian novel, and finally, in the fifth paragraph, calls herself back to: "I don't know why I began talking about all that. I want to talk about what happened on the bus. But, after all, it's not so bad to start out with a story about a priest. This is a story about one. And, I suppose you could say, about adultery. I don't know yet how all this will turn out. I know that whatever will happen, everybody tried" (3–4). Likewise, on the third page of the second novella, "Living at Home," the protagonist stops her descriptions of her lover, Lauro, and her parents and their background to say: "I'm telling you this so you'll understand why, although I'm far from irresponsible, I've left so many men, and why with Lauro I have been so happy" (81). A few pages later, she abruptly interrupts a discussion of her autistic patients to check on her reader: "You may be wondering—since we're so different and we do such different things—how Lauro and I met. It was as you might suppose: through friends, at a dinner party" (89–90), a device she repeats much later in her account: "And so, you must be wondering, since Lauro can be so many people, how could I assume that he would be faithful to one person, me?" (134). Sometimes, however, that same protagonist will make us aware of her awareness of her storytelling and of us as her readers with subtler means: "I haven't really said enough about my mother, considering what a part she plays in all this. By 'all this' I guess I mean how I have shaped my life" (105).

Quite different but equally intriguing is the story of the delayed story that forms the core of the third novella, "The Rest of Life." Paola, its protagonist, has never divulged (not for sixty-three years) the central, informing story of her life. On the seventh page of the novella, Paola partially reconfirms to herself why not: "Words are too pliant, too elastic. It's another reason why she hasn't spoken. How can she trust words to tell her story so that it would be anything like the truth?" (173). Later along in the novella, Paola silently tries it out: "There is something she'd like to say, but she doesn't know how to begin. Or no, there are three ways she would like to begin, she doesn't know which is the right one. 'Let me tell you what I'm like.' 'Let me tell you about myself.' Or: 'Let me tell you who I am.' . . . She'd like a sentence that would be like music: three lines simultaneously woven. She wants to say three things at the same time, but they all mean something different. Yet she wants to say them all" (212). Not until the penultimate page of "The Rest of Life" can Paola feel free enough to broach sharing what she has kept hidden since she was fifteen (all of which the reader, of course, has already learned): "She is excited and expectant: she doesn't know for what. And yet she knows something has happened. Just a hint, a possibility: a suggestion of a face to whom she will tell her story. All the different stories. All the different ways it could have happened, each of them true. As all the faces were the face of Leo. As all the dead are one" (256).

In this collection, then, the protagonists' revealed stories about their lives come together as "three people . . . in a first-class compartment" (to borrow the first line of "The Rest of Life"), a sort of triad of confessions that, no matter how individually unique, add up to a whole that is larger than its parts. To describe the stories as confessional is not to suggest that they are so in any religious or self-indulgent sense. Although there is ruthless self-honesty and guilt in the novellas, there is no prurient cataloging, no sense of a public act of contrition or purgation. The motion of the words is toward the reader, that best of all confidants. This means that the narratives are not confessional in a diarist's sense of the word; the reader is engaged, even prompted, in these tellings. The syntactical and narrative resonances between the novellas are, of course, just the start, for within the distinctions that make up each story, there are myriad other similarities. Like Paola's recognition about the oneness of the dead, Gordon uses similarities to suggest the possibility that "all the [living] are one."

An irony is that the protagonists' lives have been constructed on a model that repudiates such oneness, and in this, Gordon teaches us how an undermining device can enhance the experience of the reader's recognizing its opposite, which in this case would be seeing a character (or oneself) as a part of "the other." All three of the women are conscious of trying to model their lives in stark contrast to another woman's or a parent's persona: The first protagonist's repudiation of her excessively moderate parents' life models surfaces in multiple ways: in her immoderate love of Clement, in the disorderly lives she chose to work with, in her wanting her own children "to have some sense of beauty and pleasure in their lives," to be more assertive, "to live fully, not to victimize" (53); at the same time, unlike her parents, she will not be shocked if they choose to be and do something other. In the second novella, the narrator, lying in Lauro's arms, tells him, "Everything I've just done is the part of me that's not my mother. As if I were a negative number whose name is Not My Mother" (93). Similarly, Paola, the protagonist of "The Rest of Life," had, from an early age, formed her sense of self around "I am not her," meaning her vicious, judgmental aunt (218).

We recognize this negative identification penchant, this mirroring, as a technique Gordon has given other, earlier female characters, such as Isabel (*Final Payments*), who identifies herself as "not Margaret"; Camille (*The Other Side*) who takes perverse comfort in not being Theresa; Theresa who embraces everything her mother, Ellen MacNamara, abhors; and, of course, Ellen, who crafts her adulthood in direct defiance of other Irish women immigrants as well as her heritage, her father, and his second wife. In both earlier novels, as well as in *The Rest of Life,* the women's negations are inextricably connected to rigidities rejected or embraced. And within those reactions to rigidities, Gordon uses abilities, inabilities, and refusals to change as a common ground to delineate and test the damage and health within her characters' private and public personae.

As mentioned earlier, the three protagonists' lives have been or are being transformed by singular love relationships, within which a complex set of similarities can be studied. First of all, both of the protagonists in their mid-forties (the first two novellas) savor their and their lovers' sexuality. That is as apparent as Gordon's hard-won ability to depict such sexuality convincingly. On first inspection, the much older Paola's attitude toward sexuality seems to be something altogether different. We know that her fledgling, naive, and anxious sexual experiences with Leo, at age fifteen, were left frozen, like the rest of her life, after his suicide and her being exiled to the United States. And it is not as if she has been celibate during all the subsequent years. As she remembers her deceased husband, Joe Smaldone, she makes a kind of catalog of those years: "She allowed Joe to marry her; she never felt that she had married him. She wants to turn to her son now and say, 'I never hurt your father. I never told him that I loved him. . . . I opened my legs for him. I denied him nothing. I gave him healthy sons. . . . I never returned his kindness with ingratitude'" (206). Her emotional and sexual detachments begin to take on a different resonance, however, when we notice that only Paola reveals her sexual fantasies and dreams; that, at age seventy-eight, she thinks more about sexuality than the younger protagonists; and that she is able to be pleased and amazed to think of her son and his fiancée's resilient happiness and "Carlo, sleeping happily in Katherine's arms . . . encircled by the girl who loves him freely, without fear, and whom he freely, fearlessly embraces, just as if this were an ordinary thing" (242). Because Paola has never known this "ordinary thing," her silent revelations are her only sexual freedoms, and their intensity matches, like a dark photographic negative, that of the younger protagonists.

A second corresponding feature of these protagonists' love relationships is one that simultaneously calls them into question: the man or men Gordon places at the center of each woman's life represents a fundamentally unknowable, unshareable other world: Father Clement [Frank] Buckley's closed world is the priesthood and what his lover, not knowing what to call it, refers to as "All that. . . . The Catholic Church. That way of thinking" (16). In the second novella, Lauro's is Third World trouble spots and his addiction to these dangerous journalistic assignments. In the third novella, Paola's father and young Leo Calvi represent, respectively, a closed double world of death (one by wartime politics, the second by suicide) that has sealed her off from the formative loves of her life and that came together to exile Paola permanently from her loving father, home, and country. It is obvious that, for the protagonists as well as the novellas themselves, the sealed-off worlds generate tension, in the same way that "No Trespassing," "Verboten," and "Pericoloso" signposts, or a wilting mound of flowers on any new grave do. However, Gordon's larger purpose in creating these "othernesses" seems to be precisely that: we can neither know fully nor be known fully. The partial, the flawed, are the given.

A working knowledge of this abstraction is heard, with regularity, in the voices of the women protagonists, each of whom is more troubled by what she does not know than what she knows. In fact, no one of them pretends to more knowledge than she has. The first protagonist, for instance, recognizes, "It's very possible I'll lose him, we [protagonist and Father Boniface] both will, and the church will, and the world. I know

just what the danger is. And almost who, and though who isn't important, it's a type of woman, what she represents. And maybe it would be
the best thing for him. To lose everything. To be lost. I just don't know"
(36). Then, while recalling her parents' embarrassment when her husband left her for another woman, she admits: "They thought I didn't
know what's what. I didn't know the score. Maybe my children don't
because I never have. . . . I've wanted them to enjoy their lives, to do
more good than harm. If, in the course of that, they occasionally tell me
to go get fucked, . . . I don't mind. Maybe that means that I don't know
the score" (53). The second protagonist would agree with that: "I wonder how we ever learn anything. Sometimes I think it's a trick or a miracle that we know anything at all. The problem: that we're often com-
pelled by our positions to act on this knowledge we only think we have.
This is true both for my work and for Lauro's. Damage or acts of hero-
ism, murder or crippling or rescues unbelievable in the light of day, are
all results of partial knowledge" (143).

The same partialness is confirmed in Gordon's depictions of the four
much-loved men in these novellas. Their personalities and daily behav-
iors are, in varying degrees and paired combinations, brave-weak, bril-
liant-ignorant, fearless-superstitious, kind-harsh, articulate-inarticulate,
and sensitive-insensitive. Parts of the women's more subtly defined com-
plexities (and flaws) are revealed in their recognitions and acceptances of
the men's foibles and strengths. Gordon herself has confirmed this
premise in pointing out, "I wanted to create men who women actually
love. We love flawed men and not heroes. I was trying to say that one of
the marks of mature love is learning that one is flawed and so is the
loved one, and we are not going to change" (Grossmann, 10E).

In light of the supposed maturity of the women protagonists, it is
interesting to notice that none of them—the first two, divorcees in their
mid-forties, and the third, a widow in her late seventies—want to
remarry or can envision themselves in another love relationship. As the
first protagonist realizes about Clement, "I know that I don't want
somebody else. Not after I've had him" (62). "His is to me the one desirable body, known, knowing, yearned-for, troubling, arousing, safe." (63)
Likewise, the second protagonist, thinking about the times when she
and Lauro "make love for hours," recalls that it is then "I understand
that this is the last body I will know in this way. I couldn't be interested
in another body again, having Lauro's as I have, so well, so thoroughly,
and having been so well known by him. So that if he should die it would
mark the end of a certain part of my bodily life too" (149).

Despite such typical, frequently proclaimed certainties, all three protagonists, at several points in each novella, articulate deep uncertainties
about pivotal relationships in their lives; these statements heighten both
the emotional tensions within each story and the reader's knowledge of
the ambiguities that form the core of the protagonists' sense of personhood. Three such statements are particularly good examples of this
uncertainty: In "Immaculate Man," the protagonist points out that
Clement is "a terrible judge of character. He makes mistakes with
women at the shelter all the time. . . . Well, he made a big mistake in
choosing me. He ought to have chosen someone simpler, like himself, or
more impermeable. Not like me" (14). When the second protagonist
meets Lauro's ex-wife, a research geneticist, her reaction is: "I understood why he had chosen her. . . . I was tempted to suggest that they get
back together: both Turinese, small, Christian, the same age. . . . Not
like Lauro and me. I'm younger, taller, English, but a Jew. . . . In taking
up with me, Lauro had taken on my displacement. Or my lack of place.
Within someone like him, he could have been placed, recognizable, and
so approved of on the street" (102). An example from "The Rest of Life"
captures one of Paola's impassioned, italicized, first-person, imaginary
addresses; in this case, she is speaking to her deceased husband, Joe: *You
could have had someone who was good as you were good, and open, and full of
faith in life. I'm sorry for you that you chose me, and that you were loyal to me.
I'm sorry you saw something in me that was valuable to you. I was dead already
when you met me*" (206).

Because of the intensity of the protagonists' relationships with men, it
is easy to overlook an entire cluster of additional similarities between the
three women. For example, none of the protagonists have or have had
close female friends; each is, with the possible exception of the first, a
very private person. All have children (Paola also has grandchildren)
with whom they have good relationships, although those of the second
and third protagonists are somewhat detached. All three women abhor
children's being damaged, shamed, or isolated; conversely, they take
delight in children's buoyant gestures of well-being. At the same time,
not one of them derives her sense of identity from her children.
Of course, Paola's self-defining secrets have made that impossible; she
recognizes that "she accepted maternity dumbly, as another price she
had to pay. Anesthetized for the births, she stayed that way for their
childhoods. . . . Sometimes, they charmed her. She knew they waited for
their father to come home to give them life" (210). Thus, her autonomy
springs from damage that distanced her from her sons. The other two

protagonists, however, take special pleasure in the autonomy that separates themselves and their children, an autonomy they both rightly recognize as healthy.

Another more prominent common denominator among the highly
intelligent protagonists is that all three have worked as professionals who
attempt to restore their constituents' lives, bodies, or minds; in other
words, they all are or have been professional nurturers, healers. The first
protagonist is a social worker, a recognized expert on shelters for abused
women; the second is a highly respected, highly skilled doctor and director of a school for autistic children; Paola, the third, was a rehabilitation
nurse during World War II, an experience she considered "the best time
of her life. . . . At night she read books on anatomy and the new knowledge made her happy. No more poetry: muscles, bones, ligaments,
joints, the flow of blood—not a metaphor but a real substance that
could cause movement, whose failure could prevent movement" (204).

Words and Personhood

Each of the protagonists has a stubborn penchant for living in the present, for avoiding histrionics, and for a certain candid modesty in her private musings. Of particular consequence is the protagonists' shared preoccupation with the meaning and implications of words in their and
others' lives. That Gordon is making consistent use of this preoccupation
is evidenced by the number of italicized words one sees when fanning the
pages of the collection. A careful examination of these occurrences shows
the variety of their usage. Sometimes, we notice, their occurrences are
rather normal, seemingly inevitable. For example, the first protagonist,
while describing the first time she met Father Clement Buckley, moves
forward in time to reflect, "That's the kind of thing Clement and I talk
about. The term *godforsaken*. How terrible it is. The meaning of *forsake*.
Or why it is that cyclone fences, especially the barbed-wire tops, always
make me think of the Rosenbergs. He can be so quick at understanding
things like that and so infuriatingly slow at understanding something
obvious" (14–15). Later, she muses that "*Faith* and *deceit* aren't words
Clement can place together in a sentence, keep in his mind at one time"
(19). Likewise, while thinking about the early years after her father had
exiled her to a cousin's home in America, the third protagonist, Paola,
recalls, "Her cousin was a doctor; his wife was the daughter of a man
who owned factories. They had no children. This rich American woman
had brought him to her home from Italy convinced that he would pros-

per. And he did. Prosperity: a choking word. Now, sixty years later, her throat is thick with it. *Prosperous*" (199).

Sometimes the word emphases occur in surprising contexts, such as the first protagonist's musings about those post-lovemaking "quiet times of grooming or of tending. 'Let me wash your hair.' 'Your shoulders are so tense.' And sleep. Holding, moving apart from. Waking. 'There you are.' Waking perhaps to penetration. The surprise. 'There you are. And here I am with you.' *With*. The beautiful and rare word. *With*" (63). In the third novella, a somewhat similar emphasis on a single word is handled like a swelling crescendo and sudden diminuendo in music: while trying to write a letter, "For my son, to be read after my death," Paola begins: "'It happened when I was fifteen years old,' she writes. But what was *it?* She sees the small word—*it*—the enemy, hard as a bullet. Was it the death, their history, the history of Italy, the history of poetry, the history of men and women? Whose name should be included: Goethe, Leopardi, his parents, her aunt, Mussolini, a host of female martyrs, the Virgin Mary, her dead mother, her father whom she loved above all things? *It*. She puts the pencil down. She rips up the paper" (252). An equally haunting, three-word examination surfaces as the second protagonist agonizes about the difficulties in explaining menstruation to her pubescent autistic girl patients and the harrowing realities of their sexuality: "We don't say to them. 'Don't worry, we'll see to it that you're barren.' Certain words terrify me: I'd rather not hear them coming from my mouth, entering the air, which after all I have to breathe again and would prefer not to have filled with terror. The terrible emptiness of the word *barren*. A dry pebble in a huge rusted bin, silent, unliving, jostled accidentally by who knows what. . . . *Barren:* the aftermath of an evisceration, the inhuman blank. A word we don't use for a man or boy. The word *sterile* holds nothing like the same terror. *Infertile:* just an accident, an oversight, a small inessential minus, a mistake. There is nothing curable or scientific that the word *barren* suggests. *Barren* is ancient, irreversible: a curse, a fate" (89).

Occasionally, the protagonists' attention to words is not italicized, an omission that can create an unexpected emphasis. An example of this is one of Gordon's most memorable and characteristically logical sequences: "Why should we call anything about sex love? I've loved some of the people I've had sex with. I haven't had sex with most of the people I have loved" (49). A more intriguing example occurs almost at the end of the third novella, when Paola, half-asleep, half-dreaming, decides that "If she could describe the woman [herself] lying on the bed, then she could believe herself free. She begins with a single sentence. 'A woman is lying on the bed.' The simplicity of the sentence relaxes her. What it describes hurts nobody. She feels a little safer, and she wants to make herself feel safer still. She tells herself to describe the woman on the bed. 'The woman on the bed is old and small, but youthful for her age.' The breathing around her is quieter now. Because she has made herself into something she can describe. Something that language fits. Something that language can explain" (241).

The decision to call so much attention to the protagonists' attention to words is not arbitrary. First of all, the passages show how Gordon puts her own obsession with words to remarkable use in and for the development of her characters as well as the issues she wants to rethink (and that she wants us to rethink) with particular patience and care. At the same time, such passages are an unusual aperture into Gordon's craft and logic: they reveal something of the most private dynamics within her love affair with language and craft, and in them, we hear her hearing, savoring, considering, weighing, discarding, and rearranging them word by word by phrase by sentence. Then we watch her broaden that inquiry into the daily ways in which the inherent splendors, limitations, and dangers within language reveal themselves. Examples of the first two have been given; two characteristically linked examples of the latter are found in the second protagonist's private musings: "What happens to language frightens me, and what happens to truthfulness when words seem to signify the opposite of what is intended, when what seems to be candor is an elaborate screen to keep people from what really is the case" (129–30). Then, the protagonist zeros in on the primary questions about death and life that "no one could ask . . . of the person they live beside because the answers would be too unbearable to live with" (130). But Gordon moves still further into a questioning of language itself and its arbitrary connections with perceived realities and selfhood; although this is addressed in all three novellas, its most careful exploration is in the second novella, where the protagonist discusses autism and her children patients. One of her most intriguing illustrations in this discussion includes these quiet, haunting sentences: "They speak only the present tense. . . . Not believing in the future, they often find it difficult to express desire. When you ask them what they want, they may answer with any word at all. Today, when we asked a little boy what he wanted to eat, he answered, 'Pandemonium'" (89), a riveting metaphor if one begins to reconsider language itself as well as personhood.

When we study the word- and language-focused passages as they occur throughout the novellas, we can see how the individual examinations of words and language accrete and merge; they lay the quiet, almost transparent groundwork, the gesso coat (to use a painter's strategy), of Gordon's larger inquiry into personhood and its daily revelations in the words and silences (and the recollections of words and silences) of pivotal relationships. With Gordon's skill, five words can be enough to summarize all three protagonists' "tricky navigation[s] through daily life" (Hunnewell interview, 25). For the first protagonist, all that has formed the life of her lover, Father Clement Buckley, and that now dictates their life together comes down to two words: "all that" (16). For the second protagonist, the entire conscious and unconscious shaping of her adult life was simply: "all this" (105). And for Paola, the whole shape of sixty-three years of her life was determined by the tragedy, the "It" (252).

Thus, one word, a few words, are how and what and as much as we know about who we are, who another is, what a thing, an event, is. And the stories of the stories that come together in *The Rest of Life* are Gordon's reminders that both personhood and language are inherently porous and ambiguous, that personhood *is* the spoken and unspoken language of our lives and loves, that they are "mated, but in the way of our age [and species], partial" (155). But one further suggestion, a kind of cryptic affirmation, lurks under the recognitions of and abstracted words for human and linguistic flaws and limitations. This, perhaps, can be best summarized by altering one of Lauro's slippery answers to an interviewer's question about why he liked being in the midst of dangerous, chaotic revolutions: "I've never felt as comfortable in [words and relationships] that are truly impermeable" (131).

Chapter Nine
"a local habitation and a name": *The Shadow Man*

My father had one of the greatest minds I have ever known. It was his inquiring mind added to his gift of faith that led him to Catholicism. He gave me an invaluable gift, good example which I will try to follow for my whole life.

Mary Gordon, age 10
Preface to unfinished biography of her father[1]

Thirty-seven years after her first attempt to write a biography of her father, who had died three years earlier, Gordon completed the task in a memoir-biography that is as unusual as it is brave. *The Shadow Man* (1996)[2] coincidentally created my book's full circle: an introduction and conclusion of auto/biography and judgment. The memoir-biography reflects a similar circle.

Gordon ends the book's preface by acknowledging about her father, "Having lost him, once, twice, I will have him forever. He is always with me, always mine" (xxiv). She concludes the book with a discovery: "What I have taken from the cemetery is a sentence that keeps running through my mind like music: Love is stronger than death" (274). Between these reaffirmations, Gordon engages in a sort of struggle to the death. The results are a book that suggests, if not a turning point in Gordon's career, then a distinctive, circular moment in which her life and family and her parents' lives and families come together under the full scrutiny of Gordon's critical, aesthetic, moral, and emotional judgment.

Gordon recognizes her first nonfiction book as being somehow "pivotal" in her career. In a 1995 interview, she explained, "I think it brings a lot of preoccupations together. 'Traces them' is the word—'tracks them,'" yet in the book's preface Gordon admits uncertainty about its genre, which she describes as "biography, or memoir, or some nonfiction genre whose proper name hasn't yet been found" (xiv). Soon after she gave the completed manuscript to her editor at Random House, she

affirmed the "memoir-biography" tag as being close enough.[3] Still, as
The Shadow Man demonstrates and as I discuss at the end of this chapter,
a term such as *trans-genre* may more accurately describe Gordon's habitual fusions of genres.

"To the Reader," Gordon's extended preface for *The Shadow Man,* provides an overview of her family and of the book that she summarizes as,
"This is what I've tried to do. To place or re-place both my father and
myself in the book of life. The book of the living" (xxiv). From the first
sentence of the preface, Gordon's dramatic strategy is in motion: by
plunging into recent biographical discoveries about her father as well as
her central dilemmas—how to reconcile a man whose writing was
"either wicked or mad" with her adored and adoring father and with
herself as a writer, scholar, and adult daughter—she immediately
involves the reader with the tensions and issues she will address in the
chapters that follow.

The tone of the entire preface is that of invocation, but, at one point,
Gordon is quite specific: "So I approach you, the reader, in a way I
wouldn't ordinarily, asking indulgence and attention. But is it you, really,
whose indulgence I ask? Or is it my father, whom I lost, and found again,
whom I both metaphorically and literally unburied and reburied in the
course of writing this book?" (xxiii–iv). The preface also includes a partial
provenance of the work. However, Gordon's listing only hints at the
essays, short stories, novels, articles, and interviews in which she has previously addressed themes and events now found within *The Shadow Man.*

The book's goal is similar to that found in the lines of a W. H. Auden
poem Gordon used in 1980 as the epigraph for *The Company of Women.*
Like Auden, Gordon sets herself the task of weighing truth against love
in the midst of human complexity. "Knowing My Father," the first chapter of *The Shadow Man,* begins the process by reexamining facts and
memories surrounding her father's heart attack and death in 1957,
which split her life "into the part when my father was alive and the part
when he was not" (5). The split, Gordon recognizes, redirected her childhood toward two self-appointed tasks: remembering her father and following the laws and teachings of the Catholic Church. As she points
out—and as her unfinished 1959 biography of her father confirms—she
also discovered a comforting fusion of those tasks in the model of the
Catholic Church's belief in transubstantiation (the transformation of
bread and wine into the body and blood of Christ): the young Gordon
wanted to transform her deceased father's life into a living story, into
"one of the Lives of the Saints" (10).

The review of her childhood brings Gordon to a knot of questions she cannot answer: "Who was my father, really? How as a child, a grieving child, did I construct the story that I have lived by? The story by which I named and knew myself, and in which I cloaked myself . . ." (11–2). Turning away from these, she searches through details of others' and her own memories of her father. Gordon puzzles at length over her earliest perceptions of her father's (and thus her) being both Jewish and Catholic as well as outsider. She then moves through four memory vignettes that she has held on to and replayed as extended, silent films: "I am watching my father and myself. I am feeding the machine. I am standing in the darkness, seeing a living man, a living child. I'm trying to know them" (21).

These memories offer no solace; the "invention and interpretation" within memory cannot be trusted (38). Nor can she trust kept and lost objects that had belonged to her father; the objects are surrounded by "a sea of stories," by narrative that "corrodes objects' inherent truthfulness" (27). The objects serve instead as reminders of her ongoing habits of losing prized objects, of getting lost, and of "lostness" as her "most true, most fixed, most natural home" (31–3). Gordon once again admits the "impossibility of knowing what happened to or with the dead." Nonetheless, the chapter concludes with the challenge she sets for herself in the book's subsequent chapters: "The task's impossibility doesn't mean I'm spared the obligation to take it on" (40).

"Reading My Father," the second chapter of *The Shadow Man,* follows Gordon's methodical search for her father "as a public man," as a writer, editor, and publisher. Before describing her father's publications now in collections of Columbia University, the New York Public Library, and Brown University, as well as in private collections, Gordon establishes the private context in which books and libraries formed the most protected territory of her early years with her father: "Reading with my father, I am always safe and he is always handsome" (47). Gordon reviews her father's teaching her to read at three, her early books, his writing translations over the words of a French coloring book, his taking her to the library to check out five books, all of which she finished on that same day. These details lead her to one thing she did not lose when she was carried to her grandmother's home on the night of her father's heart attack: a library book that eventually had to be taken back, after his death.

From this book, *Minty's Magic Garden,* Gordon segues to books her father had left behind, books full of marks and marginalia (including one note to "Mary, read at 18"). The marginalia suggest that David Gordon was probably steering his daughter toward a life as a nun; even clearer is the evidence that her father wanted to die, that he felt like a failure about not being able to provide for his wife and daughter, and, as his one-line translation of Virgil indicates, that he was seeking some comfort about death: "Among the dead, there are so many thousands of the beautiful" (50).

With the private context of books established for herself and her father, Gordon moves to David Gordon's public life-in-print, which spans some thirty-six years (1918–54). Gordon approaches the long-avoided task with the persona of a scholar, artist, critic, detective, and daughter. What she fashions, in essence, is an improvisatory *pas de deux* of identities by two writers, a dance that includes the writers' disparate historical contexts, political views, and agendas. However, one of the writers remains immobile, and so the other, his daughter, performs a complicated solo around the still figure of David Gordon the writer and his words in print.

At Butler Library of Columbia University and at the New York Public Library on 42nd Street, she pores through the ambitious intellectualism of her father's first three publications, all written in Cleveland, Ohio: an 1918 article for the *Nation* on an obscure World War I poet; a sonnet published in March 1918 in the *New Republic;* and a rather incongruous essay, "My Two Pastors," which was published in 1920 in the *Hibbert Journal,* Oxford. Gordon then pivots into her father's "other life" and his one publishing success, *Hot Dog,* a soft-porn girlie magazine for which David Gordon used the pseudonym Jack Dinnsmore. Larger collections of *Hot Dog* will lead her to Brown University and to New Haven, but Gordon first reexamines copies of *The Children's Hour,* her father's children's magazine of 1953 and 1954. She moves through the formative impact the magazine's pictures and stories had on her childhood; reading them now, she also recalls her early terror of her father's anti-Communism, of his support of Joe McCarthy and of the Rosenbergs' executions. Even as a child, she had recognized Joe McCarthy and Roy Cohn as "masters in the game of accusation and exposure . . . I know I am the hunted: I see no possibility of anything else. And I know my father is the hunted too, but he doesn't understand this, and it makes me feel doubly unsafe" (67).

Gordon makes the trip to the Hay Library, Brown University, with her closest writer friend, David Plante, who was born in Provincetown. At Brown, she finds some dozen copies of *Hot Dog: A Monthly For Regular Fellows* and one bound volume, *The Hot Dog Annual: The Funniest Book in the World.* Later in New Haven, she visits David Sloane, a university professor who has a collection of *Hot Dog* and who also edited the scholarly book *American Humor Magazines and Comic Periodicals,* which mentions *Hot Dog* and its editor. In the 1930s issues of *Hot Dog,* Gordon discovers a new stridency, a more explicit sexuality, and even more disturbing, a conspicuous anti-Semitism. For example, one of her father's articles about Albert Einstein begins: "This genius of a Jew-boy is the most likely of anyone living today to achieve immortality" and moves to: "Another ham-hater, Max Baer, licked Schmeling. But Einstein licked the old astronomer, Newton. Newton is dead and Schmeling isn't so strong these days, either" (75).

At the same time that Gordon recognizes all the reasons for her father's wanting to pass as a "regular fellow" in America, she knows that her father's killing himself as a "Jew-boy" is a kind of murder that "was the end of the only father I could love without difficulty" (77). She carries this knowledge into her study of the anti-Semitic vitriol and bizarre slants of his 1930s essays and to Father Coughlin and the "extreme, even mad" archconservatism of Father Leonard Feeney, both of whom strongly influenced her father. Because Feeney, the literary editor of the Jesuit magazine *America,* had been David Gordon's mentor and had published many of his works, Mary Gordon visits the Manhattan headquarters of *America* to copy her father's articles and poems.

Gordon's pleasure in his radiant meditations in the *Catholic International* and in his best poems which take the form of prayers (including one for his mother shortly after her death), is shattered by his virulent letters published in *America* that support Mussolini and Franco, revile the Lincoln Brigade, and worse still, show that he saw "no difference between the Nazis and the English and (was he insane?) defined the worst work of Hitler as closing Catholic schools in Bavaria" (84).

After fully considering her father's attempts to create a safe harbor for himself in a goyim world and in Catholicism, she admits, "I can't silence the voice that is hateful to me. My father's voice saying: 'Perfidei Judei . . . our Yiddisher democracy.' It isn't that I wouldn't like to. But I can't" (93). Gordon next delivers an equally difficult and forthright writer-critic's judgment of her father: "Everything he wrote or edited was patched together, cobbled together, not very smoothly, not very well. I'm not even left with the pride of the daughter of a fine stylist. He was far from great; he wasn't even very good" (95).

As a last bastion of comfort, Gordon turns back to the final month of her father's life and to her rediscovery of an envelope marked "Daddy's letters from the hospital." To read them, she returns to the New York Public Library, the site of his heart attack on 14 January 1956. The charming letters prove what she has always known: she was an adored daughter whose intelligence and faith gave him enormous joy. Still, in light of "everything else he wrote," hers is also an excruciating inheritance because of three immovable specters trapped in the amber of his words. First of all, his words inform what Gordon describes as "the making of ME" (92). Second, to read his words, all his words, carefully is to permanently alter the way in which an adored father can be perceived: "But I won't domesticate it. What's at stake isn't my personal history. I am someone alive after the Holocaust. It's essential that we, those living now, name ourselves as people who know what went before. That we mark our understanding of the effects of hatred of Jews. That we say that the hatred is not forgivable, even if it emanates from one who is a Jew himself" (94). This is further conflicted by Gordon's knowing that she is "a writer because he was one" and that "he does not allow me, the reading daughter, the writing daughter, a place of rest" (105). That restlessness fuels the next stage (and chapter) of her task.

Gordon approaches the end of the chapter in acute pain about her father's contradictions that leave her drowning in "the sea of the impossible love of a child for her father, the sea of oblivion, the sea of a daughter's shame" (105). She concludes the chapter quietly: "This is the story of my father I must simultaneously read and write. This is what it is to be his daughter" (105).

To review such a passage after having read the entire book is to recognize that Gordon forces us to slow down at the end of each chapter. She tethers us not only to the dogged, risk-filled logic of each closing but also to another level of vulnerability, which we then carry forward. Moreover, the final sentence of Chapter II—"This is what it is to be his daughter"—prepares a resonance we later find in the three stories entitled "This is What It Is Like," with which she concludes Chapter IV.

The third chapter, "Tracking My Father: In the Archives," follows Gordon's research, first, in the census records of the National Archives in lower Manhattan, and later, in Lorain and Cleveland, Ohio, in libraries, city directories, necrology files, and synagogue records, in a mental institution's files, and in personal interviews. The man who emerges is someone she scarcely recognizes. Certainly, the discovered facts create a haunting rebuttal to the little biography of 1959 in which a ten-year-old Mary Gordon asserts, for example, "So genius, sportsman, and imp, that, most likely is how my father spent the first twelve years of his life" and

"Most of Daddy's family is a mystery to me, but little by little the pieces of the puzzle fit into place."

Not until 1994, in fact, did the extant "pieces of the puzzle fit into place" in front of his stunned daughter, who discovered in the 1900 census not a David Gordon who had been born on March 25, 1899, in Lorain, Ohio, but an Israel Gordon born on March 25, 1894, in Vilna, Lithuania and who arrived in Baltimore in 1900 as a Yiddish-speaking six year old with his parents Joseph and Bessie Gordon and three sisters, Hattie, Rosa, and Annie. A decade later, the 1910 census still lists the Lorain, Ohio, family's language as Yiddish, but it also confirms that Joseph and Bessie Gordon's son Israel has become David, just as their daughter Rosa has become Rose, and their daughter Annie, Dorothy. What is so stinging to Gordon about these discoveries is not her father's having lied. She and her mother had learned a good bit about that habit earlier. For example, that he was not, as he claimed, an only child became clear immediately after his death when his sister Hattie phoned asking that his body be returned to Lorain. And years later, Gordon's mother had told Mary about finding out that he had been married before to a woman with a son when that stepson (who actually lived with his mother five miles from Valley Stream) showed up at their door. What *is* shocking, however, is Gordon's discovery of her father's hidden language, Yiddish, and the secret world it represents: his real childhood.

To find that, Gordon goes to Lorain and Cleveland, a journey documented in almost furious detail. In the Lorain Public Library, the city directories of 1905, 1907, and 1910 tell no success story: the immigrant family lives in Joseph Gordon's dry-goods store. But the 1912 directory tells the untellable, as far as Mary Gordon is concerned: by 1912, a six-teen-year-old David Gordon, still living at home, had dropped out of high school and was employed as a stenographer for the Baltimore and Ohio Railroad. Gordon reels out of the library, only slowly realizing: "My father, my intellectual father. Not in the classrooms of George Lyman Kittredge, of Irving Babbitt, of Alfred North Whitehead, study-ing alongside T. S. Eliot and the nephew of Henry James. Nothing like that. He's an autodidact. Stealing time from his office job to read at the public library" (127). When she pursues other traces of information about the Joseph Gordon family, one of only forty Jewish families in Lorain at the time, the response is always the same: "Nothing rings a bell," to which Gordon comments, "Instead of that chime, . . . there's silence. Instead of a mark made, a blank. Instead of Harvard, the B & O Railroad, which I never even wanted in Monopoly" (133)—the last phrase of which demonstrates Gordon's penchant for heightening pain by juxtaposing it to genuinely funny sentence spins. The search is dead-ending not just at her father and his family but at herself. Gordon sees that "he has become someone to whom I can feel no connection. And if I am not connected with him, who am I?" Her next logical step and sentence are inevitable: "If he's not a person I can recognize, I can no longer recognize myself" (135).

After Gordon returns to Manhattan, other partial traces continue to show up. With her father's stepson's help, she talks to a cousin of her father's first wife Miriam (a Protestant, Jazz Age free spirit who had attended Brown University). The cousin remembers Gordon's father only as being handsome and obviously Jewish. Then passport researchers indicate that he never had a passport; thus his stories of Oxford and the Left Bank of Paris join the other lies. However, the research of Arlene Rich, an indefatigable Ohioan expert on Jewish genealogy, begins to produce results. She finds a death notice for Dorothy Gordon, Mary's aunt, who died in 1914 of scarlet fever. And another sister Rose is traced to the State Mental Hospital, where she was admitted in 1922 and later transferred to Cleveland State Hospital in 1946, where she lived until her death in 1959. Her aunt's mental illness does not frighten Gordon for herself, she realizes, but in many ways for her father. Other papers indicate that Gordon's grandfather died in 1927 and her grandmother Bessie entered a Jewish charity home in 1932 (evidently the year David Gordon took off for New York) and died a year later. In 1966, the third sister Hattie died incompetent in a nursing home. In her personal effects were pictures of her niece Mary from infancy to age five and a hauntingly unattractive picture of Hattie made when she was naturalized in 1937. Gordon also contacts someone who remembered Hattie as a strange woman whose visits and disheveled hair had frightened the children in the family.

Meeting distant cousins from other, more prosperous, branches of the Lithuanian Gordons of Lorain and Cleveland does little to help Gordon understand her father and his family and her father's distancing himself from his aging mother and his sisters. What is certain in the Ohio information is that no traces of achievement or happiness remain. Equally certain are the telltale signs of immigrants who were crushed somehow, who were never able to reap any benefits from the boom years of Ohio, and who had nothing to buffer them during the Depression. Thus, along with vague glimpses of his family's individual struggles, David Gordon's self-fabrications create a profoundly sad portrait of his own immigrant struggle, of a desperate, self-taught intellectualism, of a young, intelligent Jewish boy who was determined to "pass" somehow in a world of Gentile power, even if it meant breaking away from his needy family.

In reviewing her efforts, Gordon sees herself as "the detective who is also the judge" of her father's publications and of the factual evidence of his life. Then admitting that "the detective in love with her client usually ends up murdering or murdered," she admits: "Both have happened to me. . . . I would have avoided both if I could. But I can't, because I am no longer capable of that love that silences questions with a kiss or a sigh" (162). She does not stop there because during her research she has seen all those others like herself desperate for glimpses of information, of happiness, of success, of "a past that belongs to us. To assure ourselves that we are not alone" (163). After a barrage about the futility of such quests, Gordon suddenly stops and then moves into a place beyond memory and quest: "I no longer remember why I was looking or what I thought I'd find" (164)—a state of lostness that will gather itself up into an interrogative fury in Chapter IV.

Gordon divides the fourth chapter into two parts, the first of which has no precedent in her writing. It is the most risk-filled section of the memoir-biography, one in which Gordon moves beyond memory to create a polyphonic interrogation and defense of her father in the only voices that can enter that space, her own.

In the chapter's much longer first part, "Placing My Father: A Police Investigation," further subdivided into fourteen sections, Gordon attempts to test her father—an anti-Semitic Jew and Catholic—within the context of his generation, more specifically, within a generation influenced by the anti-Semitic rhetoric of Henry Roth, H. L. Mencken, Bernard Berenson, and Ezra Pound. Beginning abruptly with "Scraps of Evidence" (anti-Semitic statements by Roth, Mencken, Berenson, and Pound), she equally abruptly moves to Section II: "The Facts of the Case"—a litany of thirteen cold facts that begins: "My Father was a Jew. My father was not born in America. My father was a Jew who hated Jews. My father was a Jew who became a Catholic." It moves to: "My father is dead. My father is a dead Jew, like the six million Jews killed in Europe, by European hands." She then places herself within his context and concludes: "I was born American, and baptized Catholic. I am, in some sense, a Jew. My father is dead. I am trying to understand these things" (168–9).

The final line provides the segue to Section III: "Procedure," in which she summarizes methodologies she has used. These have failed, so she

turns to the profession of police artist. But it soon becomes clear that
Gordon intends to invent a composite face, not of her father ("I will not
allow my father to be the villain of his own life"), but of those forces that
have murdered "the father I could, without difficulty, love" (169–70).

In Section IV, "To Catch the Criminal, I Decide to Impersonate My
Father," she talks her way toward the courage to take the last step, one
she recognizes as bordering on madness: "I must become my father. I
must, finally, begin to understand what it is to be a Jew." It is, she recognizes, probably not possible, for as an Hungarian historian[4] of the
Holocaust has explained to Gordon, "You must realize that for most Jews
throughout the history of the world it was impossible to be a Jew" (170).

In Section V, Gordon tests that impossibility by writing a first-person
narrative in her father's voice. The story begins in Lithuania, with his
constant terror of persecution and his father's equally constant insults,
then moves hopefully to America, where he ponders the differences
between the buoyant, hopeful, beautiful girls leaving churches on
Sunday morning and the unhopeful darkness of his family's carefully
unmarked synagogue in Lorain, which his mother and sisters leave without joy and with downcast heads and eyes. Haunted by his father's constant reminder that "It is all my fault" (like the self-negating buzz that
haunts Gordon's character Ellen MacNamara in *The Other Side*), he hears
"the buzz inside my skull" that "keeps saying, 'You will never live without this torment. Everything you are is wrong'" (174).

Gordon takes the narrative to her father's discovering in the Lorain
Public Library the Europe, not of his past, but of his dreams. Then she
moves to his work for the railroad, to his understanding: "My mother
and my father and my sisters will always be Jews" (177), and to his
dreams of escaping to a place "without reproach." But this is as far as she
can stand to go.

At this point in the memoir-biography, Gordon plunges into a deeper
zone of fantasy and dream (and risk-taking) that continues for the rest of
the fourteen sections. In Section VI, "I Am No Longer an Impersonator,
I Become a Witness," she studies her father in the context of "a 'he.'
That is to say one of many" boys all over America and in every socioeconomic circumstance who are dreaming of Europe. Her language is alter-
natingly Whitmanesque and Jamesian as she describes their fears of the
future, their swooning to be away from the "clamor and cheapness of
machines, of money" (179), and of cheap, fecund women in a ruined
America. Her father is among them, but suddenly afraid of "A Europe
that would never have him, that he has made himself forget as origin

and source," he moves toward "words that do not accuse but absorb accusation": *"Assisi. Provence. Languedoc, Toscana. Chartres."* But then the buzz begins: "Everything you do is wrong" (181).

In the six brusque sentences and phrases of Section VII, Gordon announces "A Plan for Procedure," in which she will act as witness, police artist, prosecutor, judge, and executioner. In the next section, "Choosing the Features," she selects (and then explains) the composite features of the face and words "that stalked my father," turning him into someone "I cannot easily love": "the skull of Bernard Berenson / the mouth of H. L. Mencken / the hair of Ezra Pound / the eyes of Henry Roth" (182). In Section IX, "The Lineup," she describes each and then accuses them all, to which each responds in protest and disdain. Her father too begins to protest against her; then the group turns to accuse her and orders her to "Testify about the dream."

In the next two sections—X: "The Final Evidence, the Dream" and XI: "My Turn in the Spotlight"—she tries to explain the dream and her not thinking of herself or her father as Jews. Then she moves to the ways in which, as a child, her mind and her masturbating were both blamed on her Jewishness, to her father's making a place for both of them in Catholicism, to his finding in the Church "the one place a Jew can go, not hide his Jewishness, and at the same time be free of it." Ignored by the accusers and told by the police artist (also herself), "Given this testimony, it is impossible to invent a face" (191), she ends up under the spotlight, alone and unsure. Her planned sequences of trials, dreams, and police sketches are breaking down.

In Section XII, "A Theory, and Its Residue," she speaks to her father, knowing that she is "alone in the darkness," knowing that the evidence, the files of her investigation cannot somehow be made to fit either a criminal or a victim. That uncontrollable element, she realizes, is "Something that partook of beauty and that was your own. . . . it was neither pitiable nor the stuff of shame. Perhaps it was the voice of God" (192). Then, in the quiet thirteenth section, "The Face the Police Artist Cannot Create," she approaches a faceless father knowing that she cannot join him in that place of illumination and peace.

In Section XIV, alone with facts that must be faced and written down, she begins a fifteen-line litany of facts: "My father is dead. We cannot know the dead. My father lied. . . . Too much time has passed. . . . David Gordon is a man I cannot know. . . . He is a Jew who hated Jews, condemned them even as millions of them were condemned to death. He is a Catholic who saw the face of God I cannot fathom and only partially believe in" (193–4). But as the desolation within this litany moves forward, it moves toward its contradiction: a daughter's words have replaced a father's, have given him a name and a place. Realizing that she has, in effect, given birth to her own father, the litany concludes, "His name is not David, or Israel. It is My Father. This man owes me his life, and he will live forever" (194).

For Part II of Chapter IV, Gordon turns away from the investigation that has driven the chapters up to this point. Instead, she employs the ritual that cemented her and her father's seven years together and that informed her professional life: she tells him stories "that will allow us to know who we are" (195). All three stories, each with an adult female protagonist and with a third-person narrator, are titled "This Is What It Is Like," and each of the three women moves through a painstaking quest to sort out the entire story of her private world's story. Each, in effect, is a miniature portrait of Gordon's entire project and her emotions during this quest. All end in partialness, in heightened vulnerability. At the end of the third story, Gordon adds a riveting summary in the first person: "Who is my father? The origin and my source. My shame and my delight. The figure behind every story. The stranger on the road. The double, feared and prized, approaching from the distance" (202). Any reader, by this time, might expect any writer to end with this painful, epiphanic moment. But Gordon is a writer who also recognized two pragmatic, public gestures standing in the wings of her project, gestures that enhance the memoir-biography's power in unexpected, even shocking ways.

Part I of the fifth and final chapter, "Transactions Made Among the Living," begins with unsparing candor to describe the ongoing decline of Gordon's mother, Anna Gagliano Gordon. This essay, "My Mother Is Speaking from the Desert," first appeared as a 1995 feature essay (accompanied by full-page and smaller photographs) in the *New York Times Magazine*. As Gordon confirms in the book's preface, "At the very time that I was engaging in this project of memory and discovery, my mother, in her late eighties, was losing her memory" (xxii). Gordon elsewhere has admitted that the essay in some ways "was an exposing act to my mother and to myself." Nevertheless, for the sake of others facing such painful realities, she decided, "it was important to speak truthfully about all the ambivalence—to me, the wild ambivalence—that one feels about this kind of degeneration" (Bennett interview, 34).

For *The Shadow Man*, Gordon has added a poignant context to the beginning of the essay: "My father is dead, but I do not live among the dead. . . . There is, for example, my mother. . . . When I speak about my father, people often ask me, 'But where was your mother in all this?' I don't know what to say. She was there, of course. And yet she wasn't with us. I don't know where she was." Nor does Gordon know "where she is now. She seems to be speaking from the desert" (205).

This image suggests an ancient prophet, but if so, Anna Gordon's loss of memory and hope and that part of her physical and mental degeneration that was willed (a long-standing desire for "rot," as her daughter stingingly describes it) are dire warnings. Now in her late eighties and in a first-rate Catholic nursing home on the West Side of Manhattan, Anna Gordon speaks in mechanical words, with an awareness of the present that disappears within an hour, with an awareness that everything in the past is lost and thus of no comfort. She is, in other words, a prophet of degeneration, whose only peace is in prayer and whose memory holds only sacred words, popular song lyrics from the past, and a vague sense of love for her daughter. She retains memories of neither current pleasures nor terrifying medical treatments, yet she retains the thing anyone would hope to lose first, the capacity for anticipatory dread and fear.

In this chapter and in real life, her daughter is involved in a double bereavement, a double search and remembrance, in which attempts to give her father a place and a name are paired with her simultaneous attempts to bring her mother back to her own life and her daughter's life. As the final half of the chapter shows, Gordon succeeds on behalf of her father. Yet nothing can fundamentally affect her mother; neither antidepressants nor personal interventions can help. As Gordon explains, "If I come upon her now and she isn't expecting me, I find her sitting with her head buried in her hands. . . . Yet I don't think she wants to die. She will not, I believe, die soon," an image and reality that would lend itself to a Giotto-like painting Gordon would entitle "The Death of Hope" (207).

Not surprisingly then, Gordon's daily frustrations about her mother often create complex combinations of responsibility, anger, and shame (241). Knowing that so many adult children of elderly parents struggle with the same, Gordon uses the public forum of the memoir-biography to address such realities. What emerges, however, goes far beyond this mandate and is as startling as the Manhattan and Ohio research on her father: Gordon fills in the rest of the autobiographical context of her life and her life with her mother.

Gordon sets up a series of contrasting portraits between her mother's life now and Gordon's early memories of her highly capable, working mother; her mother's robust, earthy zest and wit; her mother, the life of the party; her professional clothes and accoutrements; and her beautiful skin. Within these, the daughter begins to hammer out the most unsparing premise in her autobiographical accounts: for her mother "there must always have been a secret devotion to rot," which probably was connected to her polio and "her grief and shame about her body" (206–7). From her earliest childhood, Gordon's life and her relationship with her mother were impacted by that "damaged female body" (221): "It shaped the way we lived" (222).

In other words, at the age of seven, Gordon's childhood was ruptured by her father's death, but, from that time on, her life also was increasingly shadowed by her mother's being crippled, by her own guilt at being whole, by being shamed by many of the physical ways in which her mother compensated for her weakness, by Gordon's shame of her shame, and by losing what was left of her childhood in being her mother's able and ever-vigilant caretaker.

The young girl needed a mother; the mother, in turn, needed her mother and the gathered Gagliano family. When the grandmother died and the family shattered into divisive camps, Mary Gordon also began to lose her mother to evenings of alcohol, self-neglect, and neglect of their home. Except for her work, all that had been Anna Gordon's was gone, and, as she had known soon after Mary's birth, her daughter always had been "her father's daughter."

Gordon tracks her mother's self-neglect through her own years at Barnard and Syracuse and her marriages. Then she switches into an italicized first-person address to her mother, one that is almost a howl of pain, and one almost identical in its use and tone to Paola's similar passages in the novella "The Rest of Life."

Gordon concludes the essay with daily vignettes of her mother now, but in the midst of these, she weaves in a number of recognition scenes. First of all, she learned from her father "the sovereignty of the mind and the imagination; from my mother that there is nothing so important as piss and shit and flesh that can rot or be kept from rot"—both lessons of intense importance (241–2). Second, she acknowledges, "despite the wreckage of my parents' lives, I have been, I still am, greatly beloved" (243). Gordon then moves to the conclusion with the realization, "I can imagine a life for my father. . . . In death, he is more vibrant for me than she is in what is called her life. A life I cannot understand or recognize. . . . I cannot make her any different. This, of course, is the problem" (243–4).

"Unburying and Burying My Father: A Journal," the second part of the chapter and the memoir-biography's conclusion, is, like Gordon's description of Christa Wolf's work, "a model of passionate engagement." The same is true of Gordon's decision to have her father's body disinterred from its unmarked place in the Gagliano family plot.

She begins with an epigraph from Shakespeare's *The Tempest*. Then, after describing her invalid mother's response to Gordon's decision—"That's the thing about you, you always had wacky ideas"—she describes the occupants of the Gagliano plot and her father lying anonymously "among people who at best tolerated or patronized him, at worst despised him" (245). Suddenly absorbed again with the famous *Tempest* lines, "Those are pearls that were his eyes; /Nothing of him that doth fade/ But doth suffer a sea change/ Into something rich and strange," she turns first to those inevitable questions that come to mind about body decomposition. She then recalls her father in his coffin at the funeral parlor and the one quick moment she, feverish and covered with chicken pox, was allowed to see him and touch his cold hand before she was whisked back to an upstairs bedroom in her grandmother's home. Thus, his death and funeral have remained a broken film in her mind that, she finally decides after years of thinking about it, can be repaired only by a disinterment of his body—a rather formidable task that involves all kinds of "transactions that need to be made among the living" (250). Gary, a very close friend and a Jesuit priest in Manhattan, directs her to an undertaker who finds that the task is possible, but it will require signed affidavits from Anna Gordon and each of her siblings and a new cemetery plot for the Gordon-Cash family and her father.

The journal entries become more detailed with each further step: First comes the purchase of a cemetery plot, one in a different cemetery, Calvary, in Queens, which, because it is in "Our Town" (New York City), pleases Gordon very much and which, when she visits it, seems like "The Central Park West of the no-longer-alive" (263). Then she details the intricate negotiations for permissions from a family that had split in two after her grandmother's death; from there she segues to ordering a headstone and to the stories people begin to tell her about moving bodies from one place to another.

While some friends support her, others question her effort as "crazy," "fanatical," "fetishistic" (260). While admitting to herself the madness in her unstoppable obsessiveness, Gordon defends herself to friends with Shakespeare and a passage from *A Midsummer Night's Dream* that begins: "The lunatic, the lover and the poet" (whom Gordon identifies as herself) and ends with the results of the poet's pen: "A local habitation and a name" (for her father and for her mourning).

Gordon next struggles with herself about the money (which she will have to earn by writing) she is willing to pay for her father's headstone. In this, despite the allure of a ruinous extravagance, she is her mother's, not her father's, daughter, who gives her children's education precedence over her father's marker. Suddenly informed that the disinterment and reburial can be done almost immediately, Gordon begins to doubt the entire idea. The journal entries move more briskly after she and Gary plan the reburial service. Vignettes of emotions alternate with transportation plans for her invalid mother and the rest of the family, selections of clothes she and her mother will wear, flowers for the burial service, and food for when she, Arthur, and close friends will gather at their apartment after the service. All this accelerates toward everyone's meeting at her mother's nursing home, the trip to the cemetery, and Gordon's franticness at their temporarily not being able to find the grave site. But she describes the service in quiet, measured tones: the words, her breaking down when she tries to read "For consolation at the death of my father, David," the rose petals and two stones placed on his coffin, the lowering of the coffin, and the sudden "exhilaration in the air" (272).

The "habitation and a name" have been given. Obviously, in the course of this chapter, Gordon has given these to both of her parents. However, David Gordon's reburial, along with its documentation in the memoir-biography, is clearly a daughter's extravagant gesture, the like of which is rarely seen outside myth, opera, or scripture. Yet Gordon wisely concludes the book in quiet dailiness. At breakfast, she shares with her son, David, her hard-won certainty: "Love is stronger than death" (282).

David's response—"You should write that down before you forget"— is, as Gordon intended, a richly ironic final sentence for *The Shadow Man*. The sentence invites a retrograde review of Gordon's intrinsically bonded life and work. Such a review might move first to 1988 and her essay "'I Can't Stand Your Books': A Writer Goes Home," which concludes with her holding her infant son David and determining (after an uncle's funeral and after enduring a barrage of familial insults about her novels): "one thing's for sure I would write about it"; second, to 1977 and her short story "The Thorn," in which a young daughter tries desperately to retain a sharp memory of her dead father; third, to 1959 and Gordon as a ten year old trying to bring words and her father to life on the pages of a lined notebook: "My father had one of the greatest minds I have ever known"; then finally, to 1955 and the copy of Robert Louis Stevenson's

A Child's Garden of Verses, inscribed in seven languages that remind Gordon, "To my daughter, Mary Catherine, with love from her father. I love you."

That daughter has become a respected and successful writer, critic, and professor, whose first important female protagonist, Isabel Moore (*Final Payments,* 1978), also learned that her beloved's words were written on her body, mind, and life. As Isabel and now *The Shadow Man* affirm, it is a risk-filled business to respond to that metaphorical reality. Nonetheless, Gordon's multigenred obsession with language and its profound implications in people's lives forms the core of her first two decades of writing.

Gordon's habitual manipulation of autobiographical material across traditional genres may prove to be one of her most radical innovations, an innovation that suggests the coining of a term such as *trans-genre.* One of many interesting examples of such genre ambivalence is, as mentioned earlier, Gordon's autobiographical essay "The Important Houses" (1992), which was included in *Best American Short Stories 1993* despite Gordon's forthright explanation of its genre (reaffirmed in the collection's contributors' notes).

In those notes, Gordon speculates that the essay probably "read like 'fiction' because I am primarily a fiction writer, and I create a character using the techniques of fiction: an accretion of detail, a penetration to the inner life, a series of scenes" (367). Nevertheless, Gordon has no interest in discussing demarcations between fact and fiction or life and art. She has laughingly quipped, "If you use the real names it's non-fiction. If you change the names it's fiction. The rest of that is total crap" (Bennett interview, 19). Elsewhere, she has insisted that "the question of whether there is a different method for fiction and nonfiction . . . is the kind of thing that makes me want to take to my bed with the vapors" *(Best American,* 367).

Vapors are, in truth, anathema to Mary Gordon's personality and work habits. In 1994, some eleven months before completing *The Shadow Man,* she already had sketched out characters and plots for a fifth novel, *Pearl,* and three more novellas. By August of 1995, she also had begun to work out comic-erotic agenda for a sixth novel, *Her Muse,* about a woman artist and her male patron. If, as Gordon has suggested, *The Shadow Man* marks a pivot in her career, these next works warrant particular attention. Such a cue to her diverse readers seems unnecessary. To have followed Mary Gordon through the first two decades of her career is to be certain that "the rest of [her] life" and work will be as important as her past.

Notes and References

Chapter One

1. Alma Bennett, "Conversations with Mary Gordon," *South Carolina Review* 28, no. 1 (Fall 1995): 3; hereafter cited in the text as Bennett interview.

2. Margaret Drabble, "The Limits of Mother Love," *New York Times Book Review*, 31 March 1985, 31; hereafter cited in the text as "Limits."

3. Ralph B. Sipper, "Five women . . . and a priest," *Los Angeles Times Book Review*, 22 February 1981, 1.

4. Wendy Martin, "Passions and Provocations," *New York Times Book Review*, 28 April 1991, 9; hereafter cited in the text as "Passions."

5. William Zinsser, editor and introduction for *Spiritual Quests: The Art and Craft of Religious Writing* (Boston: Houghton Mifflin, 1988), 14. Gordon's lecture-essay "Getting Here From There" is cited in the text as "Getting Here."

6. Mary Ann Grossmann, "Mary Gordon wants to be known as more than a 'Catholic writer,'" *St. Paul Pioneer Press*, 27 October 1993, E10; hereafter cited in the text as "Gordon wants." Review (which includes details from a telephone interview) of *The Rest of Life* was picked up by Knight-Ridder.

7. Le Anne Schreiber, "A Talk with Mary Gordon," *New York Times Book Review*, 15 February 1981, 27; hereafter cited in the text as Schreiber interview.

8. Mary Gordon, "My Father's Daughter," *Mademoiselle* (May 1985): 184; hereafter cited in the text as "My Father's." The essay was first published as "David" in *Fathers: Reflections by Daughters* (New York: Pantheon, 1985).

9. Nan Robertson, "A Young Author Probes Old Themes," *New York Times*, 31 May 1978, C8. Because the brief essay contains important interview material, it will be cited in the text hereafter as Robertson interview. It was subsequently reprinted as "Mary Gordon! Mary Gordon!" in *Critic*, 2 September 1978, 4–5, 8.

10. See Chapter Nine, note 1.

11. Mary Gordon, "Looking for Seymour Glass" for "How the City Shapes Its Writers" symposium, *New York Times Book Review*, 28 April 1985, 33; hereafter cited in the text as "Looking."

12. Mary Gordon for "The Hum Inside the Skull" symposium, *New York Times Book Review*, 13 May 1984, 28; hereafter cited in the text as "Hum."

13. Mary Gordon, "Coming Home," *USAir Magazine* (November 1994): 136.

14. Trisha Gorman, "CA Interview," interview included in "Mary Gordon" entry, *Contemporary Authors* 102 (Detroit, MI: Gale Research Company, 1981): 225; hereafter cited in the text as Gorman interview.

Chapter Two

1. See, for example, brief annual summaries in *A Reader's Guide to the Twentieth-Century Novel,* edited by Peter Parker with consultant editor Frank Kermode (New York: Oxford UP, 1995). For in-depth annual contexts, see *The Timetables of History: a Horizontal Linkage of People and Events,* Bernard Grun, based on Werner Stein's *Kulturfahrplan,* updated edition (New York: Simon & Schuster, 1982).

2. Mary Gordon, *Final Payments* (New York: Random House, 1978).

3. Michiko Kakutani, "Portrait of the Artist as a First Novelist," *New York Times Book Review,* 8 June 1980, 7.

4. Maureen Howard, "Salvation in Queens," *New York Times Book Review,* 16 April 1978, 1.

5. Wilfrid Sheed, "The Defector's Secrets," *New York Review of Books,* 1 June 1978, 14–5. Later reprinted in Sheed's collection, *The Good Word and Other Words* (New York: Dutton, 1978), 259–65; hereafter cited in the text as "Defector's." Gordon has acknowledged that Sheed's was the only review of her first novel that proved to be helpful to her.

6. John Leonard, "The Saint as Kill-Joy," *New York Times,* 4 April 1978, 31; hereafter cited in the text as "Kill-Joy."

7. Edmund White, "Sex, Death, and Duty," *Washington Post Book World,* 9 April 1978, E1.

8. Frances Taliaferro, "Final Payments," *Harper's* (April 1978): 84–5; his review will hereafter be cited in the text as "Final."

9. Bruce Allen, *Sewanee Review* (Fall 1978): 616.

10. John Auchard, "Mary Gordon" entry, *American Novelists Since World War II,* Second Series (Detroit, MI: Gale Research Company, 1980), 109.

11. Paul Ableman, "Last Things," *Spectator,* 13 January 1979, 24.

12. James M. Rawley and Robert F. Moss, "The Pulp of the Matter," *Commonweal,* 27 October 1978, 686; hereafter cited in the text as "Pulp."

13. Benjamin DeMott, *Atlantic Monthly* (May 1978): 94. This review is incorrectly attributed to Amanda Heller in *Contemporary Literary Criticism,* vol. 13 (Detroit, MI: Gale Research Co., 1980), 249–50.

14. David Lodge, "The Arms of the Church," *Times Literary Supplement,* 1 September 1978, 985.

15. James Wolcott, "More Catholic Than the Pope," *Esquire* (March 1981): 21.

16. Mary Gordon, "Work in Progress," *New York Times Book Review,* 15 July 1979, 14; hereafter cited in the text as "Work in Progress."

17. Diana Cooper-Clark, "An Interview with Mary Gordon," *Commonweal,* 9 May 1980, 270, 272; hereafter cited in the text as Cooper-Clark interview.

18. Gordon explicates and praises similar devices in James Joyce's "The Dead," from *You've Got to Read This: Contemporary American Writers Introduce*

Stories that Held Them in Awe (New York: Harper Perennial, 1994), 284–6; hereafter cited in the text as *"You've Got."* See, in particular, Gordon's last four paragraphs.

19. Mary Gordon, "Growing up Catholic and Creative," *U. S. News & World Report,* 5 October 1987, 74; hereafter cited in the text as "Growing up Catholic." This three-section, first-person monologue is difficult to classify since the magazine indicates a "Conversations" heading and concludes with "conversations with Alvin P. Sanoff." However, Gordon has suggested that this not be placed with interviews; her private bibliography includes this as one of her articles.

20. Robert M. Polhemus, *Comic Faith: The Great Tradition from Austen to Joyce* (Chicago: U. of Chicago Press, 1980), 5.

21. W. H. Auden, "D. H. Lawrence," *The Dyer's Hand and Other Essays* (New York: Random House, 1963), 278.

22. Barbara A. Bannon, "Mary Gordon," *Publishers Weekly,* 6 February 1981, 274; hereafter cited in the text as Bannon interview.

23. M. M. Bakhtin, *The Dialogic Imagination* [reprint of 1934 publication, translated by Caryl Emerson, edited and translated by Michael Holquist] (Austin: University of Texas Press, 1981), 368.

24. As I discovered, Anita Gandolfo has also cited this Bakhtin quote in precisely the same context in her excellent study, *Testing the Faith: The New Catholic Fiction in America* (Westport, CT: Greenwood Press, 1992), 19. Gandolfo citations hereafter, with the exception of note 26, will be cited in the text as *Testing the Faith.*

25. Susan Bolotin, "Moral Aerobics," *Vogue* (April 1985), 232; hereafter cited in the text as Bolotin interview.

26. See Anita Gandolfo's work on this in *Testing the Faith,* 168–9, and her citations of others' related studies, such as Madonna Kolbenschlag's *Kiss Sleeping Beauty Good-bye.*

27. See Mary Gordon's poem, "Poem for the End of the Year," *New York Review of Books,* 25 December, 1981, 46. The poem makes an interesting use of such phrases as *Don't hurt anybody.* Note also the phrase *the other side,* which, in a totally different context, becomes the title of Gordon's fourth novel.

28. Victor Turner, *From Ritual to Theatre: The Human Seriousness of Play* (New York: PAJ Publications, 1982), 14; hereafter referred to in the text as *FRT.* In the context of social dramas and community rituals, Turner goes on to examine the unique level of disclosure made available to a work of art's audience. He quotes the German philosopher and social critic Wilhelm Dilthey's description of the artistic process as being where "life discloses itself at a depth inaccessible to observation, reflection, and theory." Artists, in Turner's restatement, "strive to find the perfect expressive form for their experience" (15), their *Erlebnis* ["lived-through experience"]. Having done so, that effort is available to its audience's responses and understandings even of its artist's

unconscious purposes and goals. Thus, an anthropological exploration of the structural and metaphoric layers within Gordon's novel (which she may or may not have been aware of during the creative process, a period in which she was married to an anthropologist) is one more active response to her allowing the audience, as Turner phrases it, "free access to the depths where 'life grasps life'" (15). See also Sarah Gilead's astute essay, "Mary Gordon's *Final Payments* and the Nineteenth-century English Novel," *Critique: Studies in Modern Fiction,* vol. xxvii, no. 4 (Summer 1986): 213–27, as well as Helen McNeil's review, "Miraculous Births," *Times Literary Supplement,* 3 July 1981, 747.

29.   Victor W. Turner, *The Ritual Process: Structure and Anti-Structure* (New York: Aldine Publishing Co., 1969), 21; hereafter cited in the text as *RP.*

30.   See John M. Neary's "Mary Gordon's *Final Payments:* A Romance of the One True Language," *Essays in Literature* 17, no. 1 (Spring 1990): 94–110. Note, on page 109, his references to ringed imagery.

31.   Cited in Maud Ellmann, *The Hunger Artists: Starving, Writing, and Imprisonment* (Cambridge, MA: Harvard UP, 1993), 7; hereafter cited in the text as *Hunger Artists.*

32.   Roberto Calasso, *The Ruin of Kasch* (Cambridge, MA: Belknap Press of Harvard UP, 1994), 134.

33.   W. H. Auden, "Hic et Ille," *The Dyer's Hand and Other Essays,* 104; hereafter cited in the text as "Hic et Ille."

Chapter Three

1.   M. Deiter Keyishian, "Radical Damage: An Interview with Mary Gordon," *Literary Review* (Fall 1988): 74–5; hereafter cited in the text as Keyishian interview.

2.   Francine Du Plessix Gray, "A Religious Romance," *New York Times Book Review,* 15 February 1981, 1; hereafter cited in the text as "Religious Romance."

3.   Brigitte Weeks, "Group Portrait with Felicitas," *Washington Post Book World,* 22 February 1981, 3.

4.   Barbara Grizzuti Harrison, "Eccentrics in Love," *Saturday Review* (February 1981): 62; hereafter cited in the text as "Eccentrics."

5.   William O'Rourke, "A Father Father Figure," *The Nation,* 28 February 1981, 246; hereafter cited in the text as "Father Father."

6.   Christopher Lehmann-Haupt, "*The Company of Women,*" *New York Times,* 13 February 1981, C28; hereafter cited in the text as "Company."

7.   Robert Towers, "Reconciliations," *New York Review of Books,* 19 March 1981, 7.

8.   Madonna Kolbenschlag, "Man, Woman, Catholic I," *America,* 11 July 1981, 4–5.

9.   W. H. Auden, "The Common Life," *Collected Poems,* (New York: Random House, 1976), 537–9. Gordon uses twenty-one lines from the 1963

poem as the epigraph for *The Company of Women*. Auden remains Gordon's favorite poet. In addition to this epigraph and occasional comments in interviews and symposia, Gordon has written a haunting poem about Auden, "Reading Auden while nursing my daughter," *New Statesman* 103, 18 June 1982, 22. As in *Final Payments*, Gordon also makes conspicuous in-text references in *The Company of Women* to a variety of authors' names and works, a penchant that wanes in her next two novels.

10. Bill Greenwell, "Novels for Contortionists," *New Statesman*, 17 July 1981, 22.

11. Le Anne Schreiber's 1981 interview (*New York Times Book Review*, 15 February, 27), which follows the Du Plessix Gray's *Company of Women* review, is a rich source of comments by Gordon on her purposes and strategies for the novel. See chapter 1, note 7.

12. Peter S. Prescott, "Honor and Humiliation," *Newsweek*, 16 February 1981, 89.

13. Comments made in conversation with Alma Bennett, in New York, 29 October 1994. (Not part of published Bennett interview with Gordon.)

14. Eleanor Wachtel, "Mary Gordon," in *Writers & Company: In Conversation with CBC Radio's Eleanor Wachtel* (Toronto, Canada: Alfred A. Knopf, 1993), 267.

15. Sally Fitzgerald, "Harsh Love & Human Happiness," *Commonweal*, 19 June 1981, 377.

16. Cited by Joseph Berger, "Being Catholic in America," *New York Times Magazine*, 23 August 1987, 64; hereafter cited in the text as "Being Catholic."

17. Mary Gordon, "'I Can't Stand Your Books': A Writer Goes Home," *New York Times Book Review*, 11 December 1988, 36; hereafter cited in the text as "Can't Stand."

18. Doris Grumbach, "Two Catholic Firsts," *Saturday Review*, 4 March 1978, 32.

19. Mary Gordon, "How Some American Catholics See John Paul II's Visit" [contribution to symposium], *New York Times*, 20 September 1987, section 4, 28.

Chapter Four

1. Mary Gordon, *Men and Angels* (New York: Random House, 1985); hereafter cited in the text. Immediately prior to the novel's publication, a two-page excerpt appeared as "A Mother's Love" in *Ms.* magazine (April 1985): 78–9.

2. For a variety of examples, see essays by Susan Rubin Suleiman, Judie Newman, Ellen Macleod Mahon, and reviews by Alida Becker, John Costello, Rosellen Brown—all cited within this chapter's footnotes.

3. John Costello, "*Men and Angels*," *America*, 13 July 1985, 19.

4.   Florence King, in "Good King Herod," *Reflections in a Jaundiced Eye* (New York: St. Martin's, 1989), 36.

5.   Judie Newman, "Telling a Woman's Story: Fiction as Biography and Biography as Fiction in Mary Gordon's *Men and Angels* and Alison Lurie's *The Truth About Lorin Jones,*" in *Neo-Realism in Contemporary American Fiction* (Amsterdam and Atlanta, GA: Rodopi, 1992), 172; hereafter cited in the text as "Telling."

6.   Helen Dudar, "Portrait of the Novelist as Young Mom," *Wall Street Journal,* 1 April 1985, 20.

7.   Susan Rubin Suleiman, "On Maternal Splitting: A Propos of Mary Gordon's *Men and Angels,*" *Signs: Journal of Women in Culture and Society,* 14, no. 1 (Autumn 1988): 33.

8.   An excellent introduction to the resonances between Gordon's and Vuillard's work is her own essay "The Silent Drama in Vuillard's Rooms" in *New York Times,* 13 May 1990, 1, 38. Of additional interest, in this chapter's larger context, is Gordon's discussion of Vuillard's being called and denigrated as an "intimist," the kind of marginalization with which Gordon is well acquainted.

9.   Walter Clemons, "'Ah, They're On to Me,'" *Newsweek,* 1 April 1985, 75; hereafter cited in the text as "Ah." This tiny, cogent interview appears on the same page as Clemons' review of *Men and Angels:* "Let Charity and Love Prevail."

10.   See Gordon's acknowledgments page in *Men and Angels.*

11.   See Susan Rubin Suleiman, "On Maternal Splitting: A Propos of Mary Gordon's *Men and Angels,*" *Signs* 14, no. 1: 25–41. See also Ellen Macleod Mahon's essay, "The Displaced Balance: Mary Gordon's *Men and Angels,*" in *Mother Puzzles: Daughters and Mothers in Contemporary American Literature* (Westport, CT: Greenwood Press, 1989), 91–9. In chapter 19 of this latter volume, refer to Abby H. P. Werlock's extremely helpful selected bibliography on "Nonfiction about Mothers and Daughters." See also *Narrating Mothers: Theorizing Maternal Subjectivities,* edited by Brenda O. Daly and Maureen T. Reddy (Knoxville: University of Tennessee Press, 1991). Of particular interest in these collected essays is Ruth Perry's essay, "Mary Gordon's Mothers," 209–21—an interesting aside to which is Perry's acknowledgment (page 221) of the assistance of Janice Thaddeus, who was one of Gordon's mentors at Barnard College.

12.   Michiko Kakutani, *"Men and Angels"* ["Books of the Times"], *New York Times,* 20 March 1985, C21; hereafter cited in the text as "Men."

13.   Herbert Mitgang, "A Cabin of One's Own," *New York Times Book Review,* 31 March 1985, 32; hereafter cited in the text as Mitgang interview.

14.   Walter Clemons, "Let Charity and Love Prevail," *Newsweek,* 1 April 1985, 75; hereafter cited in the text as "Charity."

15.   Alida Becker, "The Arts of Love," *Book World,* 31 March 1985, 6; hereafter cited in the text as "Arts."

16. Note also Ellen Macleod Mahon's approach to bone imagery in her essay "The Displaced Balance: Mary Gordon's *Men and Angels*," in *Mother Puzzles: Daughters and Mothers in Contemporary American Literature,* 97–9.

17. Rosellen Brown, "The Wages of Love," *New Republic,* 29 April 1985, 36. Robert Phillips's review of the novel (*Commonweal,* 17 May 1985, 308, 312) also mentions the same point on page 312.

Chapter Five

1. Mary Gordon, *Temporary Shelter* (New York: Random House, 1987).

2. Paul Gray, *"Temporary Shelter," Time,* 20 April 1987, 74.

3. Rachel Billington, "Women at Bay," *New York Times Book Review,* 19 April 1987, 8; hereafter cited in the text as "At Bay."

4. See Gordon's comments for "Contributors' Notes" section in *Best American Short Stories 1993* (Boston: Houghton Mifflin, 1993), 367; hereafter cited in the text as *Best American.*

5. Christopher Lehmann-Haupt, *"Temporary Shelter"* ["Books of the Times"], *New York Times,* 9 April 1987, C25; hereafter cited in the text as "Temporary."

6. Gordon dedicated "Living at Home," the second novella in *The Rest of Life,* to Helen Wilson. See also Gordon's comments about Wilson in Bennett interview, pages 22, 28.

7. Mary Gordon, "Walt," *Fiction* XII, no. 1 (1994): 58–77; hereafter cited in the text as "Walt."

8. Carolyn See, *"Temporary Shelter," Los Angeles Times Book Review,* 12 July 1987, 10.

9. In late March of 1995, Gordon mentioned that her next novel, *Pearl,* would develop the adult lives of the two children in the story "Temporary Shelter." See page 36 of the Bennett interview. During an off-the-tape conversation, Gordon added that she planned to portray Maria as a single-parent mother of an illegitimate daughter, and Gordon laughed while pointing out its obvious echo of Hester and her daughter Pearl in *The Scarlet Letter.*

10. Mary Gordon, "Separation," *Antaeus,* nos. 64/65 (Spring–Autumn 1990): 208–17; hereafter cited in the text as "Separation." This story was included in *Best American Short Stories 1991,* selected by Alice Adams with Katrina Kenison (Boston: Houghton Mifflin, 1991), 184–93.

11. See *Best American Short Stories 1991,* the "Contributors' Notes" section, page 402, for Gordon's comments.

12. Mary Gordon, "At the Kirks'," *Grand Street* IX, 2 (Winter 1990): 41–53; hereafter cited in the text as "Kirks'."

13. Mary Gordon, "Eileen," first published in *Temporary Shelter.* The story was anthologized in *Imagining America: Stories from the Promised Land,* edited by Wesley Brown and Amy Ling (New York: Persea Books, 1992), 55–63.

Chapter Six

1. See Keyishian interview, 70: "The occasion for our talk was the publication of her collection of short stories, *Temporary Shelter,* and in anticipation of her fourth novel, tentatively entitled *The Rose Tree,* the story of an Irish immigrant family."

2. Mary Gordon, "More Than Just a Shrine: Paying Homage to the Ghosts of Ellis Island," *New York Times Magazine,* 3 November 1985, 65; hereafter cited in the text as "More Than Just."

3. Alice Bloom, "Why the Novel (Still) Matters," *Hudson Review* XLII, no. 1 (Spring 1990): 163; hereafter cited in the text as "Why the Novel."

4. John B. Breslin, "The Blight in Their Baggage," *Commonweal,* 9 February 1990, 87.

5. Anita Brookner, "The Appeal of Other People's Awful Families," *Spectator,* 27 January 1990, 37; hereafter cited in the text as "Appeal."

6. David Toolan, "The Other Side," *America,* 13 January 1990, 16.

7. Judith Thurman, "Sad But True," *New Yorker,* 12 March 1990, 98; hereafter cited in the text as "Sad But."

8. Philip Larkin, "This Be the Verse," *High Windows* (New York: Farrar, Straus, and Giroux, 1974), 30.

9. Madison Smartt Bell, "Terrible, the Way It Was In Families," *New York Times Book Review,* 15 October 1989, 9.

10. Mary Flanagan, "Threnody for Marriage," *New Statesman,* 2 February 1990, 34; hereafter cited in the text as "Threnody."

11. See Catherine Ward's excellent contextual introduction to a range of Irish immigrant issues (as well as her work on Gordon) in her essay, "Wake Homes: Four Modern Novels of the Irish-American Family," *Eire-Island: A Journey of Irish Studies* (Summer 1991): 78–91; hereafter cited in the text as "Wake Homes."

12. See Gordon's essay entitled "Anger," *New York Times Book Review,* 13 June 1993, 3, 31. The essay is reprinted as Part One of *Deadly Sins* (New York: Morrow, 1994), a collection of eight commissioned essays, each of which first appeared in a *New York Times Book Review* series.

13. Mary Gordon, *The Inside Stories: 13 Valiant Women Challenging the Church,* edited and interviewed by Annie Lally Milhaven (Mystic, CT: Twenty-Third Publications, 1987), 109.

Chapter Seven

1. Paul Baumann, "A search for the 'unfettered self,'" *Commonweal,* 17 May 1991, 327; hereafter cited in the text as "Search."

2. Mary Gordon, *Good Boys and Dead Girls and Other Essays* (New York: Viking Penguin, 1991); hereafter cited in the text as *GB&DG.* Pagination in this chapter reflects the Penguin 1992 paperback edition. All other chapters reflect hardbound editions.

3. Alison Lurie's quotation appears on the back cover of the paperback edition of *Good Boys and Dead Girls and Other Essays*. Its original source (perhaps prepublication release) was not located.

4. Garry Wills's quotation appears inside the front cover of the paperback edition of *Good Boys and Dead Girls and Other Essays*. Its original source was not located.

5. Mary Gordon, "When Beauty Is Truth, Truth Beauty," [review of Mary McCarthy's *Occasional Prose*], *Esquire* (November 1985): 248. Reprinted in *Good Boys and Dead Girls and Other Essays*.

6. "Good Boys and Dead Girls" was presented as a lecture on 29 March 1991 at the New York Public Library. Its first publication is as the first and title essay in *Good Boys and Dead Girls and Other Essays*.

7. An interesting demonstration of Gordon's also applying these premises to film is "Who's Not Singing in the Singing Detective," page 231 ff., the third of her four-part journal entries-essay titled "Some Things I Saw." First published in *Salmagundi*, nos. 88–9 (Fall 1990 /Winter 1991): 109–26. Reprinted in *Good Boys and Dead Girls and Other Essays*.

8. Introduction to Virginia Woolf's *A Room of One's Own* (New York and London: Harcourt Brace Jovanovich, 1989). Reissued as "On *A Room of One's Own:* The Fate of Women of Genius," *New York Times Book Review*, 13 September 1981, 7ff. Reprinted in *Good Boys and Dead Girls and Other Essays*.

9. Mary Gordon, "The Angel of Malignity: The Cold Beauty of Katherine Anne Porter," *New York Times Book Review*, 6 April 1995, 17–9; hereafter cited in the text as "Angel." Part of a *New York Times Book Review* series of essays by outstanding writers on neglected writers.

10. Mary Gordon, "The Parable of a Cave; or, In Praise of Watercolors," *The Writer on Her Work*, edited by Janet Sternburg (New York: W. W. Norton, 1980), 27–32; hereafter cited in the text as "Parable." Reprinted in *Good Boys and Dead Girls and Other Essays*.

11. Mary Gordon, "A Man Who Loved Women, a Womanly Man" [on Ford Madox Ford], *Antaeus* (Spring 1986): 206–14. Reprinted in *Good Boys and Dead Girls and Other Essays*.

12. Mary Gordon, "Living with Hellish Dangers" [review of Christa Wolf's *Accident/A Day's News*], *New York Times Book Review*, 23 April 1989, 3. Reprinted in *Good Boys and Dead Girls and Other Essays*.

13. Mary Gordon, "Children Were Only Allowed to Whisper" [review of Ingeborg Bachmann's *The Thirtieth Year*], *New York Times Book Review*, 29 November 1987, 14–5. Reprinted in *Good Boys and Dead Girls and Other Essays*.

14. Mary Gordon, "A World of Baffled Love" [review of David Plante's *The Country*], *New York Times Book Review*, 4 October 1981, 13. Reprinted in *Good Boys and Dead Girls and Other Essays*.

15. Mary Gordon, Introduction to Edith Wharton's *Ethan Frome and Other Short Fiction* (New York: Bantam Classics, 1987). Reprinted in *Good Boys and Dead Girls and Other Essays*.

16. Mary Gordon, "A Novel of Terrorism" [review of Mary McCarthy's *Cannibals and Missionaries*], *New York Times Review of Books,* 30 September 1979, 1ff. Gordon's review of Mary McCarthy's *Occasional Prose* was first published as "When Beauty is Truth, Truth Beauty," *Esquire* (November 1985): 248–51. Both reviews are reprinted in *Good Boys and Dead Girls and Other Essays.*

17. Mary Gordon, "'The Dead': Introduction by Mary Gordon," *You've Got to Read This: Contemporary American Writers Introduce Stories That Held Them in Awe,* edited by Ron Hansen and Jim Shepard (New York: Harper Perennial, 1994), 284–6.

18. Mary Gordon, Introduction to *Zelda Fitzgerald: The Collected Writings* (New York: Collier Books, Macmillan Pub. Co., 1992), xv–xxvii; hereafter cited in the text as *Collected.*

19. See Bennett interview, 32.

20. Term coined by poet John Crowe Ransom. New Criticism is a movement in literary criticism that dominated literary criticism from the 1930s to the late 1960s and that is still in use. Closely associated with Ransom, Robert Penn Warren, Kenneth Burke, T. S. Eliot, I. A. Richards, and Cleanth Brooks, this criticism focuses on explicating the text of the artistic work, a focus that excludes the earlier critical tradition that also considered biographical and historical information.

21. Mary Gordon, "The Habit of Genius" [review of Flannery O'Connor's *The Habit of Being*], *Saturday Review,* 14 April 1979, 42–5. Reprinted in *Good Boys and Dead Girls and Other Essays.*

22. Mary Gordon, "Mary Cassatt," *Art and Antiques* (December 1985): 46–53. Anthologized in *Prentice Hall: Literature, Platinum,* edited by Ellen Bowler et al. (1994), 498–504.

23. Patricia A. Deleeuw, "Good Boys and Dead Girls," *America,* 19 October 1991, 275.

24. Mary Gordon, "The Silent Drama in Vuillard's Rooms," *New York Times,* 13 May 1990, published prior to May 18 lecture "Emptiness and Fullness in Vuillard" for Brooklyn Museum symposium, "New Perspectives on Vuillard."

25. Feminist debates on "the intrusive male gaze" have moved beyond the important first and second rounds of inquiry. See, for example, Wendy Lesser's fascinating *His Other Half: Men Looking at Women Through Art* (Cambridge, MA: Harvard UP, 1991).

26. Mary Gordon, "Born to Love," *Art and Antiques* (April 1992): 60–5. In 1995, Gordon published an equally interesting essay on Cecilia Beaux: "Recording the Good News of the Gilded Age" (*New York Times,* 29 October, 1995, 43, 47).

27. Mary Gordon, "The Irish Catholic Church," *Once a Catholic: Prominent Catholics and Ex-Catholics Discuss the Influence of the Church on Their Lives and Work* (Boston: Houghton Mifflin, 1987), 65–78.

28. Mary Gordon, "From the Council to the Synod," *Commonweal*, 18 October 1985, 570.

29. Mary Gordon, "Chords of a Dissonant Choir: Leading American Catholics Critique John Paul" [contribution to symposium], *Newsweek*, 21 September 1987, 30.

30. Mary Gordon, "Offenses of the Pope" [contribution to a symposium, "The Pope and the Jews"], *Tikkun* (September/October 1987): 52–3. Reprinted in *Good Boys and Dead Girls and Other Essays*. See also her 1995 comments about the Pope in "A Word with the Pope," published in *Newsday*, 5 October, B5.

31. Don DeLillo, Mary Gordon, and others, "Answer to the Cardinal" [letter to the editor], *New York Times*, 26 February 1989, E22.

32. Mary Gordon, "The Politics of Sexual Hysteria," *New York Newsday*, 29 April 1993, 104.

33. Mary Gordon, "Government for the People" [in section "Memo III to Bill"], *Nation*, 1 February 1993, 120–2.

34. Mary Gordon, "Coming to Terms with Mary: Meditations on Innocence, Grief, and Glory," *Commonweal*, 15 January 1982, 11–4. Anthologized in *Border Regions of Faith: An Anthology of Religion and Social Change*, edited by Kenneth Aman (Maryknoll, NY: Orbis Books, 1987), 65–70.

35. Mary Gordon, "The Gospel According to Saint Mark: Parts of a Journal," first published (and anthologized) in *Incarnation: Contemporary Writers on the New Testament* (New York: Viking, 1990). Reprinted in *Good Boys and Dead Girls and Other Essays*.

36. Mary Gordon, "Anger," *New York Times Book Review*, 13 June 1993, 3, 13. Reprinted in *Deadly Sins* (New York: William Morrow, 1993), 24–39. In a *Publishers Weekly* review of the collected essays by Gordon, Oates, Updike, Trevor, and others, the unnamed reviewer suggests, "Although each reflection is engaging and thoughtful, Mary Gordon's description of the murderous nature of anger is especially powerful," 8 August 1994, 406.

37. Mary Gordon, "Explaining Evil," *Redbook* (April 1992): 30–1.

38. Mary Gordon, "Abortion: How Do We Think About It?," in *Good Boys and Dead Girls and Other Essays*, 128–37. First published as "A Moral Choice," *Atlantic Monthly* (April 1990): 78, 80–3.

39. Mary Gordon, "The Predicament" [review of Linda Bird Francke's *The Ambivalence of Abortion* and James C. Mohr's *Abortion in America: The Origins and Evolution of National Policy, 1800–1900*], *New York Review of Books*, 20 July 1978, 37–9. Anthologized in *People and Ideas: A Rhetoric Reader*, edited by Robert Baylor and James Moore, 1980.

40. Mary Gordon, "'Baby M': New Questions About Biology and Destiny," *Ms.* (June 1987): 25–6, 28; hereafter cited in the text as "'Baby M.'"

41. Mary Gordon, "George Eliot, Dorothea and Me: Rereading (and rereading) 'Middlemarch,'" *New York Times Book Review*, 8 May 1994, 3.

42. Mary Gordon, "Violation," *Antaeus* 62 (Spring 1989): 59–62. Reprinted in *Temporary Shelter,* her 1987 collection of short stories.

43. Mary Gordon, "On Mothership and Authorhood," *New York Times Book Review,* 10 February 1985, 1, 34–5. Reprinted as "Having a Baby, Finishing a Book" in *Good Boys and Dead Girls and Other Essays.*

44. Bob Perelman, *The Trouble with Genius: Reading Pound, Joyce, Stein, and Zukofsky* (Berkeley: University of California Press, 1994), 10–1.

45. Doris Earnshaw, "English: Essays" section, *World Literature Today* (Spring 1992): 350.

Chapter Eight

1. See Louisa Ermelino's review of *The Rest of Life* in "Picks & Pans," *People,* 30 August 1993, 30–1.

2. Mary Gordon, *The Rest of Life: Three Novellas* (New York: Viking, 1993).

3. See also Alma Bennett on Mary Gordon's *The Rest of Life,* in *Masterplots II: Women's Literature* (6 vols.), edited by Frank N. Magill (Pasadena, CA: Salem Press, 1995), 1950–4.

4. Susannah Hunnewell, "What It's Like to Live in a Female Body," *New York Times Book Review,* 8 August 1993, 25; hereafter cited in the text as Hunnewell interview. Note that the interview is on the final page of Alison Lurie's review of *The Rest of Life.*

5. Patrick H. Samway, "An Interview with Mary Gordon," *America,* 14 May 1994, 15. Note that in the questions and answers regarding the third novella, "The Rest of Life," the protagonist's name is misspelled: "Paula," rather than the correct "Paola."

6. Janette Turner Hospital, "Body Maps," *London Review of Books,* 7 April 1994, 23.

7. Alison Lurie, "Love Has Its Consequences," *New York Times Book Review,* 8 August 1993, 25.

8. Gordon's use of Turin may have been consciously or unconsciously suggested by her trip there to interview Natalia Ginzburg and Gordon's subsequent essay, "Surviving History," *New York Times Magazine,* 25 March 1990, 42–3, 46, 62.

9. Gordon uses these kinds of small resonances, such as references to the Orpheus myth, in various ways. In "Immaculate Man," Orpheus appears only in a serial list to symbolize a woman's need for solidity in any relationship with a man (19). In "Living at Home" Gordon briefly pairs Eurydice with Lot's wife to suggest how, after the death of a loved one or a relationship, we often fight the realization that "there is no going back" (164). In "The Rest of Life," Gordon's use of the myth is more important. See, for example, pages 189–90 in which Paola's poem about Orpheus and Eurydice confuses who breaks the for-

bidden injunction (do not look back) and comes to symbolize her naïveté, intelligence, and refusal to join Leo in suicide.

According to Greek mythology, we recall, the musician-poet Orpheus goes to the Underworld to try to retrieve his bride, Eurydice, who died of snakebite on their wedding day. Having charmed the denizens of the Underworld with his music, Orpheus is allowed to lead Eurydice out of the Underworld of death, but he is given an injunction that he must not look back at her until they reach the earth's surface. Just before reaching their destination, however, Orpheus looks back at Eurydice, and she disappears—permanently, this time—back into the Underworld. Inconsolable after this second loss, Orpheus is eventually torn to pieces by frenzied female religious devotees, but his lyre and head are salvaged, a salvaging that will be also echoed by Paola at the end of the novella.

Chapter Nine

1.   Mary Gordon allowed me to photocopy her twenty-eight page manuscript of an unfinished biography (1959) of her father. Written and paginated in a careful cursive script in a lined Manhattan Special notebook, the manuscript begins with a formal preface, a blank Index page, and two dedication pages—the first of which reads: "My Father David F. Gordon," the second: "To Mommy and Father Dermot. Thanks for everything." Each of the short chapters that follow has its own title page: "Chapter I Early Years," "Chapter II Family," "Chapter III Education," "Chapter IV Search," and finally, "Chapter V Refusal," which trails off in midsentence on page 28. In light of *The Shadow Man,* the brave little biography makes for painful reading. Yet to see her paragraphing, word choices, combinations of details and interior monologues, her careful work on chapter openings and closings, and her development of charming vignettes is to discover a delightful aperture into her future work. It is also interesting to notice that, in 1995, as in 1959, Gordon once again chose Roman numerals for the memoir-biography's chapters.

2.   Mary Gordon, *The Shadow Man* (New York: Random House, 1996). I was able to include the memoir-biography in my book *only* because Gordon provided typewritten manuscript copies of chapters of *The Shadow Man* from March 1995 through the manuscript's advance proofs. *Reading My Father* was the working title of the memoir-biography until July 1995, when Gordon, at her editor's insistence, changed the title to *The Shadow Man.*

3.   Confirmed in my telephone conversation with Mary Gordon on 28 July 1995.

4.   Although unnamed in the memoir-biography, the scholar is Dr. Zsuzsanna Ozsvath (University of Texas at Dallas), who talked at length to Gordon about, among other things, the history of anti-Semitism among Lithuanian Jews in America.

Selected Bibliography

PRIMARY WORKS

Books

The Company of Women. New York: Random House, 1980. Novel. Paperback reprint edition, Ballantine, 1981. London hardback edition, Jonathan Cape, 1981. London paperback edition, Corgi, 1982. London paperback reprint edition, Black Swan, 1987. Condensation in *Redbook* (March 1981): 145–67. Translated into Italian, French, Portuguese, Dutch, Danish, Norwegian, and Finnish.

Final Payments. New York: Random House, 1978. Novel. Paperback reprint edition, Ballantine, 1979. London hardback edition, Hamish Hamilton, 1978. London paperback edition, Corgi, 1979. London paperback reprint edition, Excerpted briefly in *Celebration: 60 Years of Good Reading from 60 Authors Chosen by the Literary Guild,* edited by Nancy Potter and Nancy Sullivan, 1988. Translated into Swedish, Italian, French, Spanish, German, Dutch, Norwegian, Finnish, and Polish.

Good Boys and Dead Girls and Other Essays. New York: Viking Penguin, 1991. Essays, reviews, and articles. Paperback reprint edition, Penguin, 1992.

Her Muse. Novel in progress.

Men and Angels. New York: Random House, 1985. Novel. London hardback edition, Jonathan Cape, 1985. Paperback reprint edition, Ballantine, 1986. Paperback reprint edition, G. K. Hall, 1986. London paperback reprint editions, Penguin, 1985, 1987. Excerpted briefly as "A Mother's Love." in *Ms.* (April 1985): 78–9. Translated into Swedish, Norwegian, Portuguese, German, and French.

The Other Side. New York: Viking Penguin, 1989. Novel. Paperback reprint edition, Penguin, 1990. London hardback edition, Bloomsbury, 1990. London paperback reprint edition, Bloomsbury, 1991. Translated into Dutch.

Pearl. Novel in progress.

The Rest of Life: Three Novellas. New York: Viking Penguin, 1993. Novellas: "Immaculate Man," "Living at Home," and "The Rest of Life." Paperback reprint edition, Penguin, 1994. London hardback edition, Bloomsbury, 1994. London paperback edition, Bloomsbury, 1994.

The Shadow Man. New York: Random House, 1996. Memoir-biography.

Temporary Shelter. New York: Random House, 1987. Short stories. London hardback edition, Bloomsbury, 1987. Paperback reprint edition, Ballantine, 1988. London paperback reprint edition, Penguin, 1988. Translated into Dutch, Japanese, and French.

Short Stories

"At the Kirks'." *Grand Street* IX, 2 (Winter 1990): 41–53.

"City Life." *Plowshares* (Spring 1996): 91–109.

"The Dancing Party." *Ms.* (August 1986): 64, 66, 93. Reprinted in *Temporary Shelter.*

"Delia." *Atlantic* (June 1978): 42–5. Reprinted in *Temporary Shelter.*

"Eileen." *Temporary Shelter.* New York: Random House, 1987, 3–24. Reprinted in *Imagining America: Stories from the Promised Land,* edited by Wesley Brown and Amy Ling. New York: Persea Books, 1991, 55–63.

"The Imagination of Disaster." *Granta* (Summer 1985): 163–6. Reprinted in *Temporary Shelter.*

"Kindness." *Mademoiselle* (October 1977): 224, 226.

"The Magician's Wife." *Woman's Day,* 27 September 1978, 52ff. Reprinted in *Temporary Shelter.*

"Moving." *Southern Review* XV, no. 2 (Spring 1979): 420–32.

"Mrs. Cassidy's Last Year." *Antaeus* (Winter 1983): 150–8. Reprinted in *Temporary Shelter.* Vignette later expanded into novel *The Other Side.*

"Murder." *Antioch Review* 37 (Winter 1979): 106–9.

"The Murderer Guest." *Redbook* (November 1981): 29, 170, 172, 175. Reprinted in *Temporary Shelter.*

"The Neighborhood." *Ms.* (July 1984): 70, 72, 74, 76. Reprinted in *Temporary Shelter.*

"Now I Am Married." *Virginia Quarterly Review* 51 (Summer 1975): 380–400. Anthologized in *Love Stories for the Time Being,* edited by Genie D. Chipps and Bill Henderson (New York: Pushcart Press, 1989). Reprinted in *Temporary Shelter.*

"The Only Son of the Doctor." *Redbook* (August 1982): 45–6, 51–2, 54. Winner of an O. Henry award and anthologized in *Prize Stories, 1983: The O. Henry Awards,* edited by William Abrahams (New York: Doubleday, 1983), 203–15. Reissued in *Fiction Magazine* (January 1985): 42–9 and in *Cosmopolitan* (London, August 1987): 187–98. Also reprinted in *Temporary Shelter.*

"The Other Woman." *Redbook* (August 1976): 59–60. Reprinted in *Temporary Shelter.*

"Safe." *Ms.* (June 1982): 50, 52, 94. Anthologized in *The Editors' Choice: New American Stories,* vol. I, compiled by George E. Murphy, Jr. (New York: Bantam, 1985). Also anthologized in *Words of Love,* edited by Anne Gerd Petersen (Holsted, Denmark: Forlaget Futurum, 1992). Reprinted in *Temporary Shelter.*

"Separation." *Antaeus* 64/65 (Spring–Autumn 1990): 208–17. Anthologized in *Best Short Stories of 1991*, edited by Alice Adams and Katrina Kenison. (Boston: Houghton Mifflin, 1991), 184–93.

"A Serious Person." *Redbook* (August 1977): 61–2.

"Sisters." *Ladies' Home Journal* (July 1977): 78–9, 150, 152.

"Temporary Shelter." *Temporary Shelter*. New York: Random House, 1987, 3–24. Reissued in *New American Short Stories 2*, edited by Gloria Norris (New York: New American Library) and (Markam, Ontario: Penguin, 1989). Also reissued in *Mothers and Sons*, edited by Hiroko Sato and Shizuko Kawamoto (Tokyo: Kenkyusha).

"The Thorn." *Ms.* (January 1977): 66, 68, 95. Anthologized in *Fine Lines: The Best of "Ms." Fiction*, edited by Ruth Sullivan (New York: Scribner's, 1981). Reprinted in *Temporary Shelter*.

"Violation." *Mademoiselle* (May 1987): 132, 135, 138, 140, 142, 155. Anthologized in *American Families: Twenty-eight Short Stories*, edited by Barbara H. Solomon (New York: New American Library, 1989). Reprinted in *Temporary Shelter*.

"Vision." *Antaeus* 62 (Spring 1989): 59–62.

"Walt." *Fiction* XII, no. 1 (1994): 58–77.

"A Writing Lesson." *Mademoiselle* (April 1978): 246–8. Reprinted in *Temporary Shelter*.

Essays and Articles

"The Angel of Malignity: The Cold Beauty of Katherine Anne Porter." *New York Times Book Review*, 6 April 1995, 17–9.

"Anger." *New York Times Book Review*, 13 June 1993, 3, 31. Part one of commissioned works by eight writers, all reprinted in *Deadly Sins* (New York: Morrow, 1994).

"Answer to the Cardinal" (Letter to Editor, with Don DeLillo, Andrew Greeley, John Guare, Maureen Howard, Garry Wills, and eleven other writers) *New York Times*, 26 February 1989, 22.

"Around the World in 80 Daze: Staying Put, but Dreaming of Travel." *Travel & Leisure* (February 1992): 98, 100–1.

"'Baby M': New Questions About Biology and Destiny." *Ms.* (June 1987): 25–6, 28.

"Books That Gave Me Pleasure" (with other writers). *New York Times Book Review*, 5 December 1982, 9, 62–4.

"Born to Love" (on Gwen John). *Art and Antiques* (April 1992): 60–5.

"Childhood's End." *Family Circle*, 16 June 1987, 62, 64–5,121.

"Chords of a Dissonant Choir: Leading American Catholics Critique John Paul" (with other writers). *Newsweek*, 21 September 1987, 30.

"Close to Home" (interview with Glenn Close). *Fame* (September 1989): 80–99.

"Coming Home." *USAir Magazine*, vol. 1, no. 11 (November 1994): 136.

"Coming to Terms with Mary: Meditations on Innocence, Grief, and Glory."
    Commonweal, 15 January 1982, 11–4. Anthologized in *Border Regions of
    Faith: An Anthology of Religion and Social Change,* edited by Kenneth
    Aman (Maryknoll, NY: Orbis Books, 1987), 65–70.

"David." In *Fathers: Reflections by Daughters,* edited by Ursula Owen (New
    York: Pantheon, 1985), 106–3. Reissued as "My Father's Daughter" in
    Mademoiselle (May 1985): 184–5, 250, 252. Much of the biographical
    information in this essay appears in *The Shadow Man* (1996).

"Explaining Evil." *Redbook* (April 1992): 30–1. Anthologized in *Essays from
    Contemporary Culture,* edited by Katherine Anne Achley (New York:
    Harcourt Brace, 1992), 46–7.

"Father Chuck: A Reading of *Going My Way* and *The Bells of St. Mary's* or, Why
    Priests Make Us Crazy." *Catholic Lives/Contemporary America* (Summer
    1994): 591–601.

"From the Council to the Synod" (with other writers). *Commonweal,* 18 October
    1985, 569–70.

"George Eliot, Dorothea and Me: Rereading (and rereading) 'Middlemarch.'"
    New York Times Book Review, 8 May 1994, 3, 26.

"Getting Here From There: A Writer's Reflections on a Religious Past." In
    Spiritual Quests: The Art and Craft of Religious Writing, edited and with an
    introduction by William Zinsser (Boston: Houghton Mifflin for Book-
    of-the-Month-Club, 1988), 27–53. Anthologized in *Catholic Girls,* edit-
    ed by Amber Coverdale Sumrall and Patrice Vecchione (New York:
    Plume Books, 1992). Reprinted in *Good Boys and Dead Girls and Other
    Essays.*

"The Good Books: Writer's Choices" (symposium organized by Karen
    Fitzgerald). *Ms.* (December 1985): 80.

"The Gospel According to Saint Mark: Parts of a Journal." In *Incarnation:
    Contemporary Writers on the New Testament,* edited by Alfred Corn (New
    York: Viking, 1990); reissued (New York: Penguin, 1991). Reprinted in
    Good Boys and Dead Girls and Other Essays.

"Government for the People." *Nation,* 1 February 1993, 120, 122.

"Growing up Catholic and creative," *U.S. News & World Report,* 5 October
    1987, 74. Classifying this is somewhat difficult since the first-person
    monologue indicates "conversations with Alvin P. Sanoff." I follow
    Gordon's insistence that it should be labeled an article, not an interview.

"How Some American Catholics See John Paul II's Visit" (contribution to sym-
    posium). *New York Times: Week in Review,* 20 September 1987, 28.

"The Hum Inside the Skull—A Symposium" (with 16 other writers under 40).
    New York Times Book Review, 13 May 1984, 1, 28, 32. Gordon's entry is
    on page 28.

"'I Can't Stand Your Books': A Writer Goes Home." *New York Times Book
    Review,* 11 December 1988, 1, 36–8. Reprinted in *Good Boys and Dead
    Girls and Other Essays.*

"I Married an Alien." *Vogue* (May 1985): 189, 192–3.

"I Would Have Liked to Have Written . . ." (with other writers). *New York Times Book Review,* 6 December, 1981, 7, 68, 70.

"The Important Houses." *The New Yorker,* 28 September 1992, 34–45. Reprinted in *The Best American Short Stories 1993,* edited by Louise Erdrich and Katrina Kenison (Boston: Houghton Mifflin, 1993), 335–58. As mentioned in several contexts in my book, Gordon insisted to Erdrich (and has since reconfirmed) that "The Important Houses" is an auto/bio-graphical essay, not a short story. See both Erdrich's comments in the Introduction (xvii–xviii) and Gordon's comments in the Contributors' Notes section (358) of the *Best American* collection. In the preface to *The Shadow Man,* Gordon mentions the role this essay played in the evolution of the memoir-biography project.

Introduction. In *Ethan Frome and Other Short Fiction,* by Edith Wharton (New York: Bantam Classics, 1987). Reprinted in *Good Boys and Dead Girls and Other Essays.*

Introduction. In *The House of Mirth,* by Edith Wharton (New York: Vintage Books/Library of America, 1990).

Introduction. In *Morte D'Urban,* by J. F. Powers (London: Hogarth, 1985).

Introduction. In *Mother of God,* by Lawrence Cunningham and Nicolas Sapieha (San Francisco: Harper and Row, 1982).

Introduction. In *Novel on Yellow Paper,* by Stevie Smith (New York: Pinnacle Books, 1982). Reprinted in *Good Boys and Dead Girls and Other Essays.*

Introduction. In *Prince of Darkness,* by J. F. Powers (London: Hogarth, 1985). See review "The Priestly Comedy of J. F. Powers." (*Morte D'Urban* and *The Prince of Darkness and Other Stories* by J. F. Powers) in *New York Review of Books,* 27 May 1982, 29–34. Reprinted in *Good Boys and Dead Girls and Other Essays.*

Introduction (Foreword). In *A Room of One's Own,* by Virginia Woolf (New York and London: Harcourt Brace Jovanovich, 1989). See same essay that first appeared as "On *A Room of One's Own:* The Fate of Women of Genius" in *New York Times Book Review,* 13 September 1981, 7, 26, 28. Also reprinted as "Virginia Woolf: *A Room of One's Own*" in *Good Boys and Dead Girls and Other Essays.*

Introduction to James Joyce's "The Dead." In *You've Got to Read This: Contemporary American Writers Introduce Stories That Held Them in Awe,* edited by Ron Hansen and Jim Shepard (New York: Harper Perennial, 1994), 284–6.

Introduction. In *Zelda Fitzgerald: The Collected Writings,* edited by Matthew J. Bruccoli (New York: Collier Books, Macmillan Pub. Co., 1992), xv–xxvii.

"The Irish Catholic Church." In *Once a Catholic: Prominent Catholics and Ex-Catholics Discuss the Influence of the Church on Their Lives and Work,* edited by Peter Occhiogrosso (Boston: Houghton Mifflin, 1987), 64–78.

"Isabella" (Gordon's essay-interview with Isabella Rossellini). *Mirabella* (May 1991): 119–26.

"Let Us Now Praise Unsung Writers" (symposium). *Mother Jones* (January 1986): 28.

"Looking for Seymour Glass" (with Avery Corman and other writers in "How the City Shapes Its Writers). *New York Times Book Review,* 28 April 1985, 32.

"A Man Who Loved Women, a Womanly Man" (on Ford Madox Ford). *Antaeus* (Spring 1986): 206–14. Reprinted in *Good Boys and Dead Girls and Other Essays.*

"Mary Cassatt." *Art and Antiques* (December 1985): 46–53. Anthologized in *Prentice Hall: Literature, Platinum,* edited by Ellen Bowler et al. (1994), 498–504. Reprinted in *Good Boys and Dead Girls and Other Essays.*

"A Moral Choice." *Atlantic* (April 1990): 78, 80–4. Reprinted as "Abortion: How Do We Really Choose?" in *Good Boys and Dead Girls and Other Essays.* Anthologized as "Abortion: How Does a Woman Choose?" in *Best Essays by American Women,* edited by Wendy Steiner (New York: Beacon, 1993).

"More Catholic Than the Pope: Archbishop Lefebvre and the Romance of the One True Church." *Harper's* (July 1978): 58–69. Reprinted in *Good Boys and Dead Girls and Other Essays.*

"More Than Just a Shrine: Paying Homage to the Ghosts of Ellis Island." *New York Times Magazine,* 3 November 1985, 65, 102, 104. Reprinted in *Good Boys and Dead Girls and Other Essays.* Also reprinted in *The Oxford Book of Women's Writing in the United States,* edited by Linda Wagner-Martin and Cathy N. Davidson (Oxford and New York: Oxford UP, 1995), 352–6.

"Mother's Little Helper: What Happens When a Girl Can't Look to Her Mother's Body to Define Herself." *Allure* (April 1996): 100–2. See also final chapter of *The Shadow Man* (1996).

"My Mother Is Speaking from the Desert." *New York Times Magazine,* 19 March 1995, 44–9, 60, 63, 69–70. With only slight alterations, the essay appears as Part I of the final chapter of *The Shadow Man* (1996).

"My Summer Reading" (contribution to symposium). *New York Times Book Review,* 4 June 1978, 36–7.

"The Myth of the Tough Dame." *Mirabella* (November 1992): 102–8.

"Notes from California." *Antaeus* (Autumn 1988): 196–8. Reprinted in *Good Boys and Dead Girls and Other Essays.*

"Offenses of the Pope" (for "The Pope and the Jews" symposium). *Tikkun* (September/October 1987): 52–3. Reprinted in *Good Boys and Dead Girls and Other Essays.*

"On 'A Room of One's Own': The Fate of Women of Genius." *New York Times Book Review,* 13 September 1981, 7, 26, 28. Reprinted as foreword to Harcourt Brace Jovanovich 1989 edition of *A Room of One's Own* by

Virginia Woolf. Also reprinted as "Virginia Woolf: *A Room of One's Own*" in *Good Boys and Dead Girls and Other Essays*.

"On Mothership and Authorhood." *New York Times Book Review*, 10 February 1985, 1, 34–5.

"The Other Deaths." *Salmagundi* (Summer 1994): 3–34. Excerpted in *Trafika: An International Literary Review* (Prague,1994):117–30. Also published as "Die anderen Tode" in (festschrift for Christa Wolf) *ein text für C. W.* (Berlin: Janus Press, 1994), 87–8. Much of the material is absorbed into *The Shadow Man*.

"The Parable of a Cave; or, In Praise of Watercolors." In *The Writer on Her Work*, edited by Janet Sternburg (New York: W. W. Norton, 1980), 27–32. Reprinted in *Good Boys and Dead Girls and Other Essays*.

"The Politics of Sexual Hysteria." *New York Newsday*, 29 April 1993, 58, 104.

"Raising Sons" (one of three essays on subject). *Ms.* (November/December 1993): 45–50.

"Recording the Good News of the Gilded Age" (on Cecilia Beaux). *New York Times*, 29 October 1995, 43, 37. The essay, accompanied by four of Beaux's paintings, is an interesting continuation of Gordon's research on Beaux, as seen in *Men and Angels*.

"Sharon Gless & Tyne Daly." *Ms.* (January 1987): 40–1, 86–8.

"The Silent Drama in Vuillard's Rooms." *New York Times* (13 May 1990): 1,38.

"The 60's." *Woman's Day*, 27 October 1987, 78–82.

"Snapshot: A Parting of Friends." *Life* (November 1991): 117.

"Some Things I Saw." *Salmagundi* 88/89 (Fall 1990/Winter 1991): 109–26. Reprinted in *Good Boys and Dead Girls and Other Essays*.

"Surviving History." *New York Times Magazine*, 25 March 1990, 42, 44, 46, 62.

"Tracking My Father in the Archives." *DoubleTake* (Spring 1996): 18–32. Prepublication excerpt (chapter) from memoir-biography *The Shadow Man* (1996).

"The Unexpected Things I Learned From the Woman Who Talked Back to the Pope." *Ms.* (July/August 1982): 65–7, 69.

"Walter Clemons" (Obituary). *PEN News Letter* (Winter 1995): 21.

"Why I Love to Read About Movie Stars." *Ms.* (May 1986): 22–3. Essay includes brief reviews of four celebrity books: two star biographies (Ingrid Bergman and Katharine Hepburn) and two autobiographies (Priscilla Beaulieu Presley and Jane Russell).

"Women's Friendships." *Redbook* (July 1979): 31, 203, 206, 210.

"A Word with the Pope," Part II. *Newsday*, 5 October 1995, B5. As the cover page explains, Gordon is one of several "Catholics from Mario Cuomo to Lou Carnesecca to Mary Gordon [who] talk about what they would like to tell the pontiff" if they "had three minutes with the Pope" during his 1995 visit to the United States.

"Work in Progress." *New York Times Book Review*, 15 July 1979, 14.

"The Writer and the University" (panel, chaired by Williams Phillips, included Cynthia Ozick, Czeslaw Milosz, Harold Brodkey, Christopher Ricks). *Partisan Review* (Spring 1991): 388–92 (Gordon's comments).

Reviews

"Abasement Was Irresistible." (*The Black Box*, by Amos Oz). *New York Times Book Review*, 24 April 1988, 7.

"*Alfie Gives a Hand*" (by Shirley Hughes). *New York Times Book Review*, 24 June 1984, 33.

"Bedeviling Satan." (*The Origin of Satan*, by Elaine Pagels). *The Nation*, 26 June 1995, 931–3.

"A Catholic Romance: Kate O'Brien's *Mary Lavelle*." *Threepenny Review* (Winter 1996): 17–8.

"Children Were Only Allowed to Whisper." (*The Thirtieth Year*, by Ingeborg Bachmann). *New York Times Book Review*, 29 November 1987, 14–5. Reprinted in *Good Boys and Dead Girls and Other Essays*.

"Confession, Terminable and Interminable." (*A Diving Rock on the Hudson*, by Henry Roth). *New York Times Book Review*, 26 February 1995, 5–6.

"The Country Husband." (*The Journals of John Cheever*, by John Cheever). *New York Times Book Review*, 6 October 1994, 1, 21–2.

"The Failure of True Love." (*A Fanatic Heart*, by Edna O'Brien). *New York Times Book Review*, 18 November 1984, 1, 38. Reprinted in *Good Boys and Dead Girls and Other Essays*.

"*Francis: The Poor Man of Assisi*." (by Tomie de Paola). *New York Times Book Review*, 22 August 1982, 33.

"General Deliverance." (*The Second Coming*, by Walker Percy). *New York*, 28 July 1980, 45–6.

"*The Giant at the Ford*." (by Ursula Synge). *New York Times Book Review*, 27 April 1980, 45, 67.

"Growing Old in the 90's." (*Old Friends*, by Tracy Kidder). *New York Times Book Review*, 3 October 1993, 1, 32–3.

"The Habit of Genius." (*The Habit of Being*, by Flannery O'Connor). *Saturday Review*, 14 April 1979, 42–5. Reprinted in *Good Boys and Dead Girls and Other Essays*.

"The Life and Hard Times of Cinderella." (*Marya*, by Joyce Carol Oates). *New York Times Book Review*, 2 March 1986, 7, 9.

"Living With Hellish Dangers." (*Accident/A Day's News*, by Christa Wolf). *New York Times Book Review*, 23 April 1989, 3. Reprinted in *Good Boys and Dead Girls and Other Essays*.

"Love in Heavy Armor." (*Half the Way Home*, by Adam Hochschild). *New York Times Book Review*, 15 June 1986, 7. Reprinted in *Good Boys and Dead Girls and Other Essays*.

"Mythic History." (*China Men*, by Maxine Hong Kingston). *New York Times Book Review*, 15 June 1980, 1, 24–7.

"A Novel of Terrorism." (*Cannibals and Missionaries*, by Mary McCarthy). *New York Times Book Review*, 30 September 1979, 1, 33–5. Reprinted in *Good Boys and Dead Girls and Other Essays*.

"One Isolated World Within Another." (*Felice*, by Angela Davis-Gardner). *New York Times Book Review*, 6 June 1982, 12, 57, 58.

"Pig Tales." (*More Tales of Amanda Pig*, by Jean Van Leeuwen). *New York Times Book Review*, 10 November 1985, 43.

"The Predicament." (*The Ambivalence of Abortion*, by Linda Byrd Francke, and *Abortion in America*, by James C. Mohr). *New York Review of Books*, 20 July 1978, 37–9. Anthologized in *People and Ideas: A Rhetoric Reader*, edited by Robert Baylor and James Moore, 1980.

"The Priestly Comedy of J. F. Powers." (*Morte D'Urban* and *The Prince of Darkness and Other Stories*, by J. F. Powers). *New York Review of Books*, 27 May 1982, 29–34. Reprinted in *Good Boys and Dead Girls and Other Essays*.

"The Quest of Sister Mary Pelagia." (*The Glassy Sea*, by Marian Engel). *New York Times Book Review*, 9 September 1979, 12, 42.

"Swim or Sink." (*Other Shores*, by Diana Nyad). *New York Review of Books*, 21 December 1978, 52–4.

"Vanities of the Hunting Class." (*The Rising Tide*, by Molly Keane, and *Devoted Ladies*, by Polly Devlin). *New York Times Book Review*, 29 September 1985, 43.

"What He Found, What He Lost." (*Faith, Sex, Mystery*, by Richard Gilman). *New York Times Book Review*, 18 January 1987, 1, 26–7.

"What Makes a Woman a Woman?" (*"Feminism Is Not the Story of My Life": How Today's Feminist Elite Has Lost Touch with the Real Concerns of Women*, by Elizabeth Fox-Genovese). *New York Times Book Review*, 14 January 1996, 9.

"What Mary Ann Knew." (*Only Children*, by Alison Lurie). *New York Review of Books*, 14 June 1979, 31–2.

"What They Think About God." (*The Spiritual Life of Children*, by Robert Coles). *New York Times Book Review*, 25 November 1990, 1, 28–9.

"When Beauty is Truth, Truth Beauty." (*Occasional Prose*, by Mary McCarthy). *Esquire* (November 1985): 248–52. Reprinted in *Good Boys and Dead Girls and Other Essays*.

"The Word for Children." (*The Book of Adam to Moses*, by Lore Segal, and *Adam and Eve*, by Warwick Hutton). *New York Times Book Review*, 8 November 1987, 29, 55.

"A World of Baffled Love." (*The Country*, by David Plante). *New York Times Book Review*, 4 October 1981, 13. Reprinted in *Good Boys and Dead Girls and Other Essays*.

Poetry

"On the Death of Laurence Sterne" (limited edition broadside) (Shandy Hall, Coxwold, York: Laurence Sterne Trust, 1984).

"Poem for the End of the Year." *New York Review of Books* 28, 17 December 1981, 46.

"Reading Auden while nursing my daughter." *New Statesman* 103, 18 June 1982, 22.

"A Reading Problem." *Global City Review* (Fall 1994): 69–70.

Selected poems in *New American Poetry*, edited by Richard Monaco (New York: McGraw-Hill, 1973), 74–80. Poems include "On Trying to Telephone California," "To a Doctor," "Nancy Creighton (1814–59)," "The Dead Ladies," and "Quite a Comedown."

"To a Cow." *American Review* 16 (February 1973): 106.

"The Wedding Photograph: June 1921." *Times Literary Supplement*, 25 December 1981, 1501.

Published Interviews

Bannon, Barbara A. "PW Interviews Mary Gordon." *Publishers Weekly*, 6 February 1981, 274–5.

Bennett, Alma. "Conversations with Mary Gordon." *South Carolina Review*, 28, no. 1 (Fall 1995): 3–36.

Bolotin, Susan. "Moral Aerobics." *Vogue* (April 1985): 232, 234.

Clemons, Walter. "'Ah, They're On to Me.'" *Newsweek*, 1 April 1985, 75.

Cooper-Clark, Diana. "An Interview with Mary Gordon." *Commonweal*, 9 May 1980, 270–3.

Dudar, Helen. "Portrait of the Novelist as Young Mom." *Wall Street Journal*, 1 April 1985, 20.

Gorman, Trisha. "CA Interview." (on Gordon). Follows David Versical's "Mary Gordon" in *Contemporary Authors*, vol. 102, edited by Frances C. Locher (Detroit, MI: Gale Research Co., 1981), 225.

Hunnewell, Susannah. "What It's Like to Live in a Female Body." *New York Times Book Review*, 8 August 1993, 25.

Keyishian, M. Deiter. "Radical Damage: An Interview with Mary Gordon." *Literary Review* 32 (Fall 1988): 69–82.

Milhaven, Annie Lally. "Mary Gordon." In *The Inside Stories: Thirteen Valiant Women Challenging the Church*, edited by Annie Lally Milhaven (Mystic, CT: Twenty-third Publications, 1987), 101–18.

Mitgang, Herbert. "A Cabin of One's Own." *New York Times Book Review*, 31 March 1985, 32.

Robertson, Nan. "A Young Author Probes Old Themes." *New York Times*, 31 May 1978, C1, C8. Reprinted as "Mary Gordon! Mary Gordon!" *Critic*, 2 September 1978, 4–5, 8.

Samway, Patrick H. "An Interview With Mary Gordon." *America*, 14 May 1994, 12–5.

Sanoff, Alvin P. "Growing up Catholic and creative." *U.S. News & World Report*, 5 October 1987, 74. See comments under same title in Gordon's essays.

Schreiber, Le Anne. "A Talk With Mary Gordon." *New York Times Book Review,* 15 February 1981, 26–8.

Wachtel, Eleanor. "Mary Gordon." In *Writers and Company: In Conversation with CBS Radio's Eleanor Wachtel* (Toronto: Alfred A. Knopf, 1993), 262–72.

White, Edmund. "Talking with Mary Gordon." *Washington Post Book World,* 9 April 1978, E1, 4.

Recorded Interviews

"All Things Considered," National Public Radio, 2 March 1986 (4:15 minutes). Discussion labeled "Abortion ad redux," with host Lynn Neary. Appearance and topic coincided with Gordon's having signed a 2 March 1986 *New York Times* ad that supports Catholics who differ with the Church on abortion and other issues.

"Charlie Rose," PBS, 24 September 1994 (20 minutes). Discussion of *The Rest of Life.* According to Gordon's comments to me in 1994, Rose "acted out the premise that men don't take women writers seriously. He hadn't read the novellas."

"Fresh Air," WHYY: Philadelphia, 1 March 1988 (10 minutes). Host Terry Gross and Gordon discuss *Temporary Shelter,* her recently published collection of short stories, and her previous novels.

"Fresh Air," WHYY: Philadelphia, 22 April 1991 (23:29 minutes). Gordon and host Terry Gross discuss her new collection of essays, *Good Boys and Dead Girls and Other Essays.* The interview also includes discussions about her views on American fiction by men, Catholicism, and abortion.

"Fresh Air," WHYY: Philadelphia, 11 October 1993 (23:29 minutes). Gordon talks to host Terry Gross about love and the female protagonists of her recent book *The Rest of Life: Three Novellas.* Other feminist issues are included.

"Morning Edition," National Public Radio, 19 April 1985 (5:45 minutes). Gordon discusses *Men and Angels* with host Bob Edwards.

"New York & Company," WNYC, 25 November 1993 (30 minutes). Host Leonard Lopate interviews Mary Gordon about her new book, *The Rest of Life: Three Novellas,* and about her career.

"The Talk of the Nation," National Public Radio, 14 March 1994 (59 minutes). After host Ray Swarez's introduction of the program's series on the Ten Commandments, Gordon reads an unpublished essay on lying (Commandment 9) and then makes spirited responses to call-in listeners.

"Weekend Edition, Saturdays," National Public Radio, 1 October 1989 (7:30 minutes). Gordon reads from *The Other Side* and then discusses with host Susan Stamberg immigrant experiences of "differentness" that affect first-, second-, and third-generation Americans. Gordon also makes interesting observations about women novelists now moving into broader historical explorations.

SECONDARY WORKS

Reference Works

Auchard, John. "Mary Gordon." In *Dictionary of Literary Biography: American Novelists Since World War II,* vol. 6, Second Series, edited by James E. Kibler, Jr. (Detroit: Gale Research Co., 1980), 109–12.

Bennett, Alma. "Selected Bibliography." Concludes Bennett's essay "Mary Gordon" in *American Writers: Supplement IV, Part One* (New York: Charles Scribner's Sons, 1996), 297–318.

Goldsworthy, Joan. "Mary Gordon." In *Contemporary Authors, New Revision Series* 44, edited by Susan M. Trosky (Detroit: Gale Research Co., 1994), 162–5.

"Mary Gordon." In *Contemporary Literary Criticism,* vol. 13, edited by Dedria Bryfonski (Detroit: Gale Research Co., 1980), 249–51.

"Mary Gordon." In *Contemporary Literary Criticism,* vol. 22, edited by Sharon R. Gunton and Jean C. Stine (Detroit: Gale Research Co.,1982), 184–8.

"Mary Gordon." In *Who's Who in America,* 49th edition, vol. A–K (New Providence, NJ: Reed Reference, 1995).

"Mary Gordon." In *World Authors 1975–1980,* edited by Vineta Colby (New York: H. W. Wilson Co., 1985), 275–7.

May, John R. "Mary Gordon." In *Dictionary of Literary Biography Yearbook,* edited by Karen L. Rood, Jean W. Ross, and Richard Ziegfeld (Detroit: Gale Research Co., 1981), 81–5.

Ragen, Brian Abel. "Mary Gordon." In *The Oxford Companion to Women's Writing in the United States,* editors-in-chief Cathy N. Davidson and Linda Wagner-Martin (New York and Oxford: Oxford UP, 1995), 358–9.

Versical, David. "Mary Gordon." In *Contemporary Authors,* vol. 102, edited by Frances C. Locher (Detroit: Gale Research Co., 1981), 223–5. Gordon entry followed by Trisha Gorman's "CA Interview" with Gordon.

Bibliographies

Bennett, Alma. "Selected Bibliography." In *Mary Gordon* (New York: Twayne Publishers, 1996), 197–214.

Bennett, Alma. "Selected Bibliography." Concludes Bennett's essay "Mary Gordon" in *American Writers: Supplement IV, Part One* (New York: Charles Scribner's Sons, 1996), 297–318.

Mahon, John W. "A Bibliography of Writings by Mary Gordon" and "A Bibliography of Writings about Mary Gordon." In *American Women Writing Fiction: Memory, Identity, Family, Space,* edited by Mickey Pearlman (Lexington: UP of Kentucky, 1989), 60–7.

Books, Chapters of Books, and Other Articles

Bennett, Alma. *Mary Gordon.* United States Authors Series (New York: Twayne Publishers, 1996).

Berger, Joseph. "Being Catholic in America." *New York Times Magazine,* 23 August 1987, 22–7, 64–5.

Feeney, Joseph J. "Imagining Religion in America: Three Contemporary Novelists." *Critic* 42 (Winter 1987): 58–74.

Gandolfo, Anita. *Testing the Faith: The New Catholic Fiction in America* (Westport, CT: Greenwood Press, 1992). The book provides invaluable sociological and literary contexts regarding American Catholicism and American "Catholic novelists." Although Gordon is cited throughout the book, Gandolfo pays particularly important attention to Gordon in Chapters Eight and Nine.

Gilead, Sarah. "Mary Gordon's *Final Payments* and the Nineteenth-century English Novel." *Critique: Studies in Modern Fiction* XXVII, no. 4 (Summer 1986): 213–27.

Iannone, Carol. "The Secret of Mary Gordon's Success." *Commentary* 79 (June 1985): 62–6.

Johnston, Eileen Tess. "The Biblical Matrix of Mary Gordon's *Final Payments.*" *Christianity and Literature,* vol. 44, no. 2 (Winter 1995): 144–67.

Kakutani, Michiko. "Portrait of the Artist as a First Novelist." *New York Times Book Review,* 8 June 1980, 7ff. Kakutani discusses Gordon among others.

Levine, Paul. "Recent Women's Fiction and the Theme of Personality." In *The Origins and Originality of American Culture,* edited by Tibor Frank (Budapest: Akadémiai Kiadó, 1984), 333–43. Links women's liberation with death in the family; *Final Payments* is discussed on pages 340–1.

Mahon, Ellen Macleod. "The Displaced Balance: Mary Gordon's *Men and Angels.*" In *Mother Puzzles: Daughters and Mothers in Contemporary American Literature,* edited by Mickey Pearlman (Westport,CT: Greenwood Press, 1989), 91–9.

Mahon, John W. "Mary Gordon: The Struggle with Love." In *American Women Writing Fiction: Memory, Identity, Family, Space,* edited by Mickey Pearlman (Lexington: UP of Kentucky, 1989), 47–60.

Morey, Ann-Janine. "Beyond Updike: Incarnated Love in the Novels of Mary Gordon." *Christian Century,* 20 November 1985, 1059–63.

Neary, John M. "Mary Gordon's *Final Payments:* A Romance of the One True Language." *Essays in Literature* (Spring 1990): 94–110.

Newman, Judie. "Telling a Woman's Story: Fiction as Biography and Biography as Fiction in Mary Gordon's *Men and Angels* and Alison Lurie's *The Truth About Lorin Jones.*" In *Neo-Realism in Contemporary American Fiction* (Postmodern Studies 5), edited by Kristiaan Versluys (Amsterdam and Atlanta, GA: Rodopi, 1992), 171–92.

Payant, Katherine B. "Mary Gordon: Christianity and Feminism." In *Becoming and Bonding: Contemporary Feminism and Popular Fiction by American Women Writers* (Westport, CT: Greenwood Press, 1993). Payant's "Introduction" provides a very helpful context for Chapter Five on Gordon.

Perry, Ruth. "Mary Gordon's Mothers." In *Narrating Mothers: Theorizing Maternal Subjectivities,* edited by Brenda O. Daly and Maureen T. Reddy (Knoxville: University of Tennessee Press, 1991), 209–21.

Seabury, Marcia Bundy. "Of Belief and Unbelief: The Novels of Mary Gordon." *Christianity and Literature,* vol. 40, no. 1 (Autumn 1990): 37–55.

Sorel, Nancy. "A New Look at 'Noble Suffering.'" *New York Times Book Review,* 26 January 1986, 1, 30–1. Gordon mentioned on page 30.

Suleiman, Susan Rubin. "On Maternal Splitting: A Propos of Mary Gordon's *Men and Angels.*" *Signs* 14 (Autumn 1988): 25–41.

Usandizaga, Aranzazu. "Women's Quest Plot in Mary Gordon's Work." In *Neo-Realism in Contemporary American Fiction* (Postmodern Studies 5), edited by Kristiaan Versluys (Amsterdam and Atlanta, GA: Rodopi, 1992), 193–210.

Ward, Catherine. "Wake Homes: Four Modern Novels of the Irish-American Family." *Eire, Ireland; a Journal of Irish Studies,* vol. 26, no. 2 (Summer 1991): 78–91.

Ward, Susan. "In Search of 'Ordinary Human Happiness': Rebellion and Affirmation in Mary Gordon's Novels." In *Faith of a (Woman) Writer,* edited by Alice Kessler-Harris and William McBrien (Westport, CT: Greenwood Press, 1988), 303–8.

Wymward, Eleanor B. "Mary Gordon: Her Religious Sensibility." *Cross Currents* 37 (1987): 147–58.

Book Reviews

Final Payments (1978):

Ableman, Paul. "Last Things." *Spectator,* 13 January 1979, 23–4.

Allen, Bruce. "*Final Payments.*" *Sewanee Review* 86 (Fall 1978): 616.

Bell, Pearl K. "Family Affairs." *Commentary* 66 (September 1978): 70–3.

DeMott, Benjamin. "*Final Payments.*" *Atlantic* (May 1978): 94. See Chapter Two, note 13.

Duffy, Martha. "Irish Lib." *Time,* 24 April 1978, 92, 94–5.

Grumbach, Doris. "Two Catholic Firsts." *Saturday Review,* 4 March 1978, 32.

Howard, Maureen. "Salvation in Queens." *New York Times Book Review,* 16 August 1978, 1, 32–3.

Leonard, John. "The Saint as Kill-Joy." *New York Times,* 4 April 1978, 31.

Lodge, David. "The Arms of the Church." *Times Literary Supplement,* 1 September 1978, 965.

McKenzie, Madora. "Paying Your Dues, or Life Begins at 30." *Christian Science Monitor,* 25 May 1978, 23.

Pompea, Irene N. "*Final Payments.*" *Best Sellers* 38 (August 1978): 141.

Prescott, Peter S. "Living Sacrifice." *Newsweek,* 10 April 1978, 92, 94.

Rawley, James M. and Robert F. Moss. "The Pulp of the Matter." *Commonweal,* 27 October 1978, 685–9. Gordon reviewed on 685–7.

Robertson, Nan. "A Young Author Probes Old Themes." *New York Times,* 31 May 1978, C1, 8. See comments under interviews.

Sabolik, Mary. *"Final Payments." America,* 17 June 1978, 490–1.

Sheed, Wilfrid. "The Defector's Secrets." *New York Review of Books,* 1 June 1978, 14–5. Reprinted as "Mary Gordon: *Final Payments"* in *The Good Word and Other Words,* author and editor, Wilfrid Sheed (New York: Dutton, 1978), 259–65.

Stelzmann, Rainulf A. "Major Themes in Recent American Novels." *Thought,* vol. 55, no. 219 (December 1980): 476–86. Gordon review on pages 483–4.

Sullivan, Walter. "Model Citizens and Marginal Cases Heroes of the Day." *Sewanee Review* 87 (Spring 1979): 337–44. Gordon review on 339–40.

Taliaferro, Frances. *"Final Payments." Harper's* (April 1978): 84–5.

White, Edmund, "Sex, Death, and Duty." *Washington Post Book World,* 9 April 1978, E1, 4.

Wiehe, Janet. *"Final Payments." Library Journal,* 15 March 1978, 683.

The Company of Women (1980):

Armstrong, Marion. "Subcutaneous Probings." *Christian Century,* 22 April 1981, 454, 456.

Becker, Brenda L. "Virgin Martyrs: *The Company of Women." American Spectator* 14 (August 1981): 28–32.

Berret, Anthony J. "Religion and Comedy in Recent Fiction." *New Catholic World* (November/December 1982): 254–6.

Bras, Benvenuta. *"The Company of Women." Critic* 39 (May 1981): 4.

DeMott, Benjamin. "Women Without Men." *Atlantic* (March 1981): 86–90. Gordon review is on pages 89–90.

Fitzgerald, Sally. "Harsh Love and Human Happiness." *Commonweal* 108, 19 June 1981, 375–7.

Gray, Francine du Plessix. "A Religious Romance." *New York Times Book Review,* 15 February 1981, 1, 24, 26.

Greenwell, Bill. "Novels for Contortionists." *New Statesman* 102, 17 July 1981, 21–2. Gordon review is on page 22.

Griffin, Emilie. "Man, Woman, Catholic III." *America,* 11 July 1981, 8–9.

Harrison, Barbara Grizzuti. "Eccentrics in Love." *Saturday Review* (February 1981): 62–3.

Hulbert, Ann. *"The Company of Women." New Republic,* 28 February 1981, 33–4.

Hunt, George. "Man, Woman, Catholic II." *America,* 11 July 1981, 6–8.

Kolbenschlag, Madonna. "Man, Woman, Catholic I." *America,* 11 July 1981, 4–6. George Hunt's and Emilie Griffin's reviews of *The Company of Women* follow Kolbenschlag's.

Lardner, Susan. "No Medium." *New Yorker,* 6 April 1981, 177–80. Lardner also discusses *Final Payments.*

Lehmann-Haupt, Christopher. *"The Company of Women."* *New York Times,* 13 February 1981, C28.

―――. "Effects a Writer Gets, but Didn't Intend." *New York Times,* 4 June 1981, C17.

McNeil, Helen. "Miraculous Births." *Times Literary Supplement,* 3 July 1981, 747.

O'Rourke, William. "A Father Father Figure." *The Nation,* 28 February 1981, 245–6.

Prescott, Peter S. "Honor and Humiliation." *Newsweek,* 16 February 1981, 89.

Sandmaier, Marian. *"The Company of Women."* *New Directions for Women* 10, May–June 1981, 13.

Sheppard, R. Z. "A Prodigal Daughter Returns." *Time,* 16 February, 1981, 79.

Sipper, Ralph B. "Five women . . . and a priest." *Los Angeles Times Book Review,* 22 February 1981, 1, 11.

Towers, Robert. "Reconciliations." *New York Review of Books,* 19 March 1981, 7–8.

Weeks, Brigitte. "Group Portrait with Felicitas," *Washington Post Book World,* 22 February 1981, 3.

Wolcott, James. "More Catholic Than the Pope." *Esquire* (March 1981): 21, 23. Review also comments on *Final Payments.*

Men and Angels (1985):

Becker, Alida. "The Arts of Love." *Washington Post Book World,* 31 March 1985, 6.

Brown, Rosellen, "The Wages of Love." *New Republic,* 29 April 1985, 34–6.

Clemons, Walter. "Let Charity and Love Prevail." *Newsweek,* 1 April 1985, 75.

Costello, John. *"Men and Angels."* *America,* 13 July 1985, 19.

Craig, Patricia. "On the Wrong Side of Charity." *Times Literary Supplement,* 25 October 1985, 1202.

Drabble, Margaret. "The Limits of Mother Love." *New York Times Book Review,* 31 March 1985, 1, 32–3.

Eder, Richard. *"Men and Angels."* *Los Angeles Times Book Review,* 14 April 1985, 3, 7.

Gray, Paul. *"Men and Angels."* *Time,* 1 April 1985, 77.

Greenland, Colin. "Mother Care." *New Statesman* 110, 1 November 1985, 323.

Kakutani, Michiko. *"Men and Angels"* ["Books of the Times"]. *New York Times,* 20 March 1985, C21.

"Men and Angels." *New Yorker,* 29 April 1985, 132.

Phillips, Robert. "A Language for Compassion." *Commonweal,* 17 May 1985, 308, 312.

Simon, Linda. "Maternal love and its impact on moral life in Gordon's *Men and Angels." Christian Science Monitor,* 22 April 1985, 21, 23.

Yardley, Jonathan. "New in Paperback." *Washington Post Book World,* 30 March 1986, 12.

Temporary Shelter (1987):

Billington, Rachel. "Women at Bay." *New York Times Book Review,* 19 April 1987, 8.
Dooley, Susan. "Fictions of a Dutiful Daughter." *Washington Post Book World,* 6 April 1987, 8.
Gray, Paul. "*Temporary Shelter.*" *Time,* 20 April 1987, 74.
Lee, Hermione. "The Perils of Safety." *Times Literary Supplement,* 17 July 1987, 765.
Lehmann-Haupt, Christopher. "*Temporary Shelter*" ["Books of the Times"]. *New York Times,* 9 April 1987, C25.
See, Carolyn. "*Temporary Shelter.*" *Los Angeles Times Book Review,* 12 July 1987, 10.
"*Temporary Shelter.*" *Book World* 17, 26 April 1987, 8.
"*Temporary Shelter.*" *London Review of Books,* 23 July 1987, 24.
"*Temporary Shelter.*" *Village Voice,* 19 May 1987, 48.

The Other Side (1989):

Bell, Pearl K. "Last Exit to Queens." *New Republic,* 18 December 1989, 39–41. Bell first discusses Gordon's prior novels.
Bell, Madison Smartt. "'Terrible, the Way It Was in Families.'" *New York Times Book Review,* 15 October 1989, 9.
Bloom, Alice. "Why the Novel (Still) Matters." *Hudson Review* (Spring 1990): 155–64. Bloom deals specifically with Gordon on page 163.
Breslin, John B. "The blight in their baggage." *Commonweal,* 9 February 1990, 87–8.
Brookner, Anita. "The appeal of other people's awful families." *Spectator,* 27 January 1990, 37.
Donovan, Mary Ann. "Books for Christmas." *America,* 17 November 1990, 372.
Eder, Richard. "Harp Harpy and Her Brood." *Los Angeles Times Book Review,* 22 October 1989, 3, 12.
Flanagan, Mary. "Threnody for Marriage." *New Statesman,* 2 February 1990, 34.
Gable, Mona. "A Telling 'Other Side' of the Irish." *Los Angeles Times,* 17 December 1989, E20–1.
Macleish, Rod. [review of *The Other Side*]. "Morning Edition," National Public Radio, 12 October 1989 (2:30 minutes). Macleish describes this as Gordon's best novel.
Reed, Kit. "The Devlins and Their Discontents." *Washington Post Book World,* 8 October 1989, 4. Reed mistakenly names the Irish-American family "Devlin" when, in fact, "MacNamara" is appropriate.
Thurman, Judith. "Sad But True." *New Yorker,* 12 March 1990, 97–100. Good reviews also of Gordon's prior novels.
Toolan, David. "*The Other Side.*" *America,* 13 January 1990, 15–6.

Good Boys and Dead Girls and Other Essays (1991):

Baumann, Paul. "A Search for the 'Unfettered Self.'" *Commonweal,* 17 May 1991, 327–31.
Baumgaertner, Jill P. "Mary Gordon's Catholic Questions." *The Christian Century,* 20–27 November 1991, 1101–4.
Deleeuw, Patricia A. "Good Boys and Dead Girls." Book Reviews. *America,* 19 October 1991, 275.
Earnshaw, Doris. *"Good Boys and Dead Girls and Other Essays."* *World Literature Today* (Spring 1992): 349–50.
Martin, Wendy. *"Good Boys and Dead Girls and Other Essays."* *New York Times Book Review,* 28 April 1991, 9.
"Men and Angels." The Economist, 15 June 1991, 87–8. While the review briefly discusses several of Gordon's books, it also includes *Good Boys and Dead Girls and Other Essays* as well as several interesting comments by Gordon.

The Rest of Life (1993):

Ager, Susan. *"The Rest of Life." Detroit Free Press,* 1 August 1993, H7.
Ermelino, Louisa. *"The Rest of Life." People,* 30 August 1993, 30–1.
Grossman, Mary Ann. "Mary Gordon wants to be known as more than a 'Catholic' writer." *St. Paul Pioneer Press,* 27 October 1993, E10. Review picked up by Knight-Ridder.
Hospital, Janette Turner. "Body Maps." *London Review of Books,* 7 April 1994, 23–4.
Kakutani, Michiko. "After Faith and Family, Stories of Sexual Love." *New York Times,* 3 August 1993, C17.
Lurie, Alison. "Love Has Its Consequences." *New York Times Book Review,* 8 August 1993, 1, 25.
Mathews, Laura. "The Lover Who Changed Her Life." *Glamour* (August 1993): 152.
Messud, Claire. "Travelling hopefully." *Times Literary Supplement,* 4 February 1994, 21.
"The Rest of Life." New Yorker, 13 September 1993, 127.

The Shadow Man (1996):

My book was completed prior to reviews of *The Shadow Man.*

Matson, Peter, 11
McCarthy, Joe, 168
McCarthy, Mary, 2, 17, 24, 129, 134–35,
  138, 147
memoir-biography, 1, 103–5, 165–181
Mencken, H. L., 173
metaphor, 19, 21–22, 25, 28–34, 36, 40,
  77, 92
Metropolitan Museum of Art, 15
Midsummer Night's Dream, A
  (Shakespeare), 179
Milhaven, Annie Lally, 126
Minty's Magic Garden, 167
mirroring, 69–70, 86
Mitgang, Herbert, 109
Ms., 17, 89, 141
Modersohn-Becker, Paula, 73
monologues, 45–46, 59, 68, 69, 101, 111
Morisot, Berthe, 140
Moss, Robert F., 18, 21
motherhood, 71, 74–77, 82–84, 95–100

Naipaul, V. S., 2, 147
narrative voice, 69, 101, 113, 151
Nation, 168
Ndembu people, 32–33
New American Poetry, 10, 17
New Criticism, 192n.20
Newman, Judie, 70–71, 83, 84
New Republic, 168
Newsweek, 142
New York Public Library, 167–68, 170
New York Review of Books, 17
New Yorker, 12, 16–17, 139, 142
New York Times, 12, 16–17, 139, 142
New York Times Book Review, 12, 17, 48,
  66, 90, 128, 130, 136, 143, 153
New York Times Magazine, 14, 176
New York Newsday, 142
Nochlin, Linda, 73

oblation, 35–36, 38
obsessions, 70–72, 78, 179–80
O'Connor, Flannery, 2, 17
O'Connor, John (Cardinal), 142
opposites, 48–49
O'Rourke, William, 43, 44, 45

Orpheus and Eurydice myth, 152,
  154–55, 195n.9

"Pale Horse, Pale Rider" (Porter), 136
Percy, Walker, 2
Perelman, Bob, 146
permeability, 59–60, 153–54, 164
Plante, David, 132–34, 168
Polhemus, Robert M., 22
Porter, Katherine Anne, 131, 136–37,
  138
postmodernism, 71
Pound, Ezra, 6, 146, 173
Prescott, Anne, 9, 27
Prescott, Peter, 54–55

Rabbit (John Updike), 129
radical love, 51–69, 98
Random House Publishers, 11, 90, 165
Rawley, James M., 18, 21
reader, 132, 166
Redbook, 11, 42, 89
religious fiction, 2, 26, 60–67, 103,
  141–43
reviews, 17–19, 42–43, 68–69, 89–90,
  128–29, 144, 146, 147, 153–54
Rich, Arlene, 172
Rilke, Rainer Maria, 134
Robertson, Nan, 16
Room of One's Own, A (Woolf), 130, 132
"Roosevelt the Antichrist," 6
Rosenberg executions, 168
Roth, Henry, 173
Rushdie, Salman, 2, 61, 142, 147

sacrifice, 19, 30–31, 34–39, 51
Sartre, Jean-Paul, 2
Save Me The Waltz (Zelda Fitzgerald), 137
Schmidt, Jan Zlotnick, 92, 108
secrecy, 25–26, 122–23, 126–27
sexuality, 18, 36–40, 44, 46–47
Sheed, Wilfred, 17, 23–24, 63
Shelley, Percy Bysshe, 146
similes, 21
Sloane, David, 169
Snodgrass, W. D., 9
social drama, 32–34, 185–86n.28

social systems, 28, 38–40, 46–50, 57–58, 60, 77
State University of New York, New Paltz, 10, 12, 92
Stein, Gertrude, 28
structure, 19, 30–34, 36, 40, 44–46, 69–70, 77, 81, 86, 89–90, 101, 102, 105, 113, 114, 148, 151, 154–55. *see also* genre
Suleiman, Susan Rubin, 71, 75
syntax, 19–21, 116–118
Syracuse University, 9–10, 27

Taliaferro, Francis, 17, 66
Tempest, The (Shakespeare),179
Thackeray, William, 2, 147
Thaddeus, Janice Farrar, 9, 27
Thomas, Dylan, 127
Thurman, Judith, 113, 115, 120
Tillich, Paul, 60
Toolan, David, 112–13
Towers, Robert, 45
Turner, Edith, 32
Turner, Victor, 32–34
Twain, Mark, 147

Updike, John, 2, 67, 129
U. S. News and World Report, 22

Vatican Council II, 7–8, 26
Virginia Quarterly Review, 10, 17, 89–90
Vuillard, 15, 72–73, 139–140, 141, 188n.8

Wales, 9, 104
Ward, Catherine, 127
Warhol, Andy, 141
Wariner, Marina, 124
Washington Post, 17
Washington Post Book World, 42
"Water Lilies" (Claude Monet), 8
Waugh, Evelyn, 2
Weeks, Brig"tte, 42–43
Wharton, Edith, 134–35
White, Edmund, 17
Wills, Garry, 128
Wilson, Helen Miranda, 92
Wilson, Monica, 34
Wolcott, James, 18–19, 42
Wolf, Christa, 132–33, 138
"Woman in a Striped Dress" (Vuillard), 72–73
Woman's Day, 89
Woolf, Virginia, 9–10, 27, 130, 132
World War II, 62–63
Wouk, Herman, 16

You've Got to Read This: Contemporary American Writers Introduce Stories That Held Them in Awe, 135

Zelda Fitzgerald: The Collected Writings, 136
Zinsser, William, 2

The Author

Alma Bennett, assistant professor of humanities and English at Clemson University, received a PhD in humanities from the University of Texas at Dallas, an MS in English literature from Radford University, and a BM in piano from Belhaven College. She also studied musicology and piano at Indiana University, Manhattan School of Music, and Westminster Choir College. A former music librarian as well as head of Information and Publications, Copyright Office, at the Library of Congress in Washington, D.C., Bennett has performed multimedia lecture-recitals throughout the United States, North Africa, and Asia. In Tokyo, Japan, she also had acting roles in NHK National Broadcasting Corporation television series, in four operas with La Scala Opera Company of Milan, Italy, and in Broadway musicals presented by the Tokyo International Players.

At Clemson University, Bennett teaches interdisciplinary humanities, twentieth-century literature, and literary genres. In addition, she teaches medieval and Renaissance arts and culture at the summer Sessione Senese per la Musica e l'Arte in Siena, Italy. She has published articles on Ezra Pound, Mary Gordon, and interdisciplinary exchanges between the arts and sciences, as well as poems. Bennett is currently working on a book on Tennessee Williams.

The Editor

Frank Day is a professor of English and head of the English Department at Clemson University. He is the author of *Sir William Empson: An Annotated Bibliography* (1984) and *Arthur Koestler: A Guide to Research* (1985). He was a Fulbright lecturer in American literature in Romania (1980–81) and in Bangladesh (1986–87).